FRESHWATER EXOTIC FISHES
PROBLEMS AND PROSPECTS

FRESHWATER EXOTIC FISHES

PROBLEMS AND PROSPECTS

By

Dr. Vishwas Balasaheb Sakhare

Head
Department of Zoology
Yogeshwari Mahavidyalaya
Ambajogai - 431 517
Maharashtra (India)

&

Dr. B. Vasanthkumar

Head
Department of Zoology
Government Arts and Science College
Karwar - 581 301
(India)

DPH

DISCOVERY PUBLISHING HOUSE PVT. LTD.
NEW DELHI-110 002

Published by:
Namit Wasan
DISCOVERY PUBLISHING HOUSE PVT. LTD.
4383/4B, Ansari Road, Darya Ganj
New Delhi-110 002 (India)
Phone : +91-11-23279245, 43596064-65
Fax : +91-11-23253475
E-mail : discoverypublishinghouse@gmail.com
namitwasan9@gmail.com
sales@discoverypublishinggroup.com
web : www.discoverypublishinggroup.com

First Edition: **2016**

ISBN: 978-93-5056-780-7

Freshwater Exotic Fishes: *Problems and Prospects*

Printed at:
Infinity Imaging Systems
Delhi

Foreword

Dr. Yugraj Singh Yadava
Director, BOBP-IGO

The movement of plants and animals from their native homes to exotic locales is as old as the history of mankind's travels to different parts of the world. While many introductions have been unintentional, most others have been carried out with a purpose. In the fisheries sector of India, the introduction of exotic fish species could be traced back to the mid-1800s, with the stocking of trout species in the upland waters by the then British rulers. Since then a large number of exotic aquatic species have found their way to India for game, food and ornamental purposes. In this long history of introduction of exotics, there have been both good and bad lessons, making us more cautious now while considering introduction of exotic species into our waters.

Authored by Dr. Vishwas Balasaheb Sakhare and Dr. B Vasanthkumar, the book 'Freshwater Exotic Fishes – Problems and Prospects' provides an excellent analysis of the contributions of four exotic species namely, tilapia (*Oreochromis mossambicus*), common carp (*Cyprinus carpio*), grass carp (*Ctenopharyngodon idella*) and silver carp (*Hypophthalmichthys molitrix*) from six small reservoirs (Majalgaon, Wan, Harni or Katgaon, Gharni, Siddeshwar, Bhategaon) located in the Marathwada region of Maharashtra. Investigations carried out for a period of three years, from 2011 to 2014, showed that the exotic species stocked along with Indian Major Carps- IMC (Catla, rohu, mrigala), contributed between 7- 37 percent in the total fish production from these reservoirs. Following 'put and take' practice, these small water bodies were subjected to a near-total harvesting, thus providing sound data to draw conclusions on the contributions of the exotics *vis-à-vis* IMC species.

The book in its concluding chapter lists a set of six recommendations that suggest (i) training of officials of the Department of Fisheries (DoF) in identification of exotic species; (ii) provision of powers with the DoF to enforce existing guidelines on introduction of exotic species; (iii) creation of awareness amongst stakeholders on the dangers of unauthorised introduction of exotic species; (iv) investment in research to develop technology for propagation of indigenous fish species; (v) investigations to assess the impact of exotics introduced in various water bodies; and (vi) formulation of stringent regulations for import of exotic species. The authors have also suggested a review of the laws and procedures regulating the introduction of exotic species into the Indian waters.

Drs. Sakhare and Vasanthkumar and the two researchers (Ms Ashvini Chalak and Mr S G Rawate) deserve full compliments in enhancing our knowledge base on the role of exotic aquatic species in the Indian waters. The book will be of immense use to students/researchers, fisheries and aquaculture managers and policy makers in understanding the contributions of exotic species and help in formulating approaches in managing species that have already been introduced and in regulating introduction of new species.

(Y S Yadava)

Acknowledgements

We would like to express my deep sense of gratitude to University Grants Commission, New Delhi for the financial support extended for completing this work.

We are thankful to Dr. Balasaheb Chavan, Principal, Yogeshwari Mahavidyalaya, Ambajogai for necessary help rendered to me for the completion of this project. The assistance of government departments like Directorate of Fisheries and Irrigation Department are worthy to mention here. The most valuable help from the Secretaries and other employees of Fishermen Co-operative Societies from all the six reservoirs deserves special thanks. Only because of their whole hearted co-operation, I could able to finish this study.

Our research scholars helped us to analyse the survey report and also helped for the completion of this work. we use this occasion to express my deep sense of thanks to them.

We thank to my publisher Shri Tilak Wasan of Discovery Publishing House Private Limited, New Delhi for taking pains in bringing out the book.

We are also thankful to my colleagues and office staffs of my department for their valuable help to finish this report.

Finally, we will always remain a debtor to all my well-wishers for their blessings, without which this volume would not have come into existence.

Dr. Vishwas Balasaheb Sakhare

Dr. B.Vasanthkumar

Contents

CHAPTER - 1

Introduction of Exotic Fish Species *A Global Review*

There is a long history of introduction of non-native fishes in fresh waters. For researchers, managers, and policy makers interested in conserving freshwater diversity, understanding the magnitude and array of potential impacts of non-native fish species is of utmost importance. The freshwater aquatic biodiversity is depleting alarmingly due to the introduction of exotic species and other anthropogenic activities. The indiscriminate transfer of exotic fishes has brought about a wide array of problems including extirpation of indigenous species. The exotics compete with the indigenous species for food, habitat and may even prey upon them, introduce new parasites and diseases, result in the production of hybrids and cause genetic 'erosion' of indigenous species and degradation of the physico-chemical nature of aquatic ecosystems. The potential risks not only affect the biodiversity, but also the socio-economic aspects of the human community that depend on aquatic ecosystems for their sustenance (Bijukumar, 2000).

Shafland and Lewis (1984) defined an exotic as an organism whose entire range is outside the country to which it is introduced. Exotic species of fishes were introduced in many parts of the world for:

1. improving local fishery potential and for broadening species diversity in aquaculture programmes;
2. sport fishing;
3. for aquarium keeping; and
4. controlling of unwanted organisms. Further, there are accidental and/ or unauthorized introductions.

The first attempt to document fish introductions on a global scale was undertaken by FAO under the stewardship of Dr. Robin Welcome (Welcome, 1988). There are 1354 introductions of 237 species into 140 countries (Welcome,

1988). Out of 237 species recorded from 140 countries, it is interesting to note that only 9 species have gained entry to more than 30 countries. Among 9 species, it is the common carp (*Cyprinus carpio*), black tilapia (*Oreochromis mossambicus)* and raibow trout (*Salmo gairdneri*) that have become pan-global in distribution, with each species being introduced in more than 50 host countries.

Invasive alien species may affect livelihood and other economic opportunities in multiple ways. In addition to their impact on the supply of environmental goods, they also affect the integrity of ecosystems, undercutting essential environmental services.

Majority of species have been introduced into only a few countries. Eighty-six percent of the species introduced have been recorded from 10 countries or less.29 countries have only 1 species introduced, 6 countries have had only 2 species introduced and so on. Continental United States leads the list with a spectacular 70 species introductions followed by island state of Hawaii (44 introductions), Columbia (40), Mexico (33) and others (Ambekar *et al.*2008).

The ecological impact of exotic introductions resulted in the disappearance of native species in many countries. Out of 160 species of freshwater fishes introduced in 120 countries, hardly 10% were found satisfactory. During 1950s, Lake Victoria, the world's largest tropical lake was the home of more than 300 species of endemic fishes. Due to introduction of an exotic fish, Nile Perch (*Lates niloticus*) which is a predator and voracious feeder, the species composition of the lake changed drastically with a loss of 99% of the species diversity which came down to less than 1% of the total fish catch. The establishment of Nile Perch in Lake Victoria is not only on economic and ecological tragedy but a loss to the evolutionary biology (Barel *et al.* 1985). The introduction of carnivore *Clarias gariepinus* to the Eastern Cape in South Africa has similarly devastated some native fishes and crabs.

The introduction of sea lamprey (*Petromyzon marinus*), Raibow smelt (*Osmenus mordax*) and common carp (*Cyprinus carpio*) have affected the native species like mosquito fish (*Gambusia affinis*) and *Fundulus heterochitus* (Gracia Marian *et al.*1990).

Release of non-indigenous fishes in United States began as early as the 1600s with the introduction of the goldfish (*Carassius auratus*) (Crossman, 1991) and by the late 1800s, non-indigenous fish introductions were also accompanied by translocation of native fishes to new locations (Carlander, 1954, Courtenay 1979, Courtenay 1990, Crossman 1991). With reference to history, Crossman (1991) stated that there were two major periods of fish introductions in North America, the late 1800s and the time following the 1950s. This resulted in 35 exotic fishes established in North America by 1980 with an additional 68 species by 1991 (Crossman 1991). Nico and Fuller (1999) and Fuller *et al.* (1999) provided the most current information on distribution of non-indigenous fishes in the United States noting that 316 native fishes have been introduced outside their normal geographic range by humans, 185 species have been introduced from foreign countries, and 35 species are hybrids. The numbers of introduced species cited by Nico and Fuller (1999) and Fuller *et al.* (1999) are somewhat higher than those of past researchers because they included all fish introduced into the United States since the 1800s whether established or not, and they also count stocked fish as being introduced, even if it was moved within its normal geographic range (i.e., translocated) (Neil and John, 2001).

Tilapia was first introduced in China, in 1956 from Vietnam and Africa. The tilapia industry in China is maintaining an annual growth rate of about 15%. The China's ministry of Agriculture and the provincial governments are encouraging tilapia culture by providing subsidies to the farmers to the extent of US $ 300-500 per ha. The returns from tilapia culture are higher than that from other cultured fish. In view of this, many farmers, who were traditionally culturing carps, are now changing over to tilapia culture and tilapia culture is considered as a major means of raising income for rural population (Rao, 2008).

Brazil has imposed strict restrictions on introducing species into its river courses. Even trans-basin movements within the country are not allowed normally. But the small reservoirs in the nine states of the northeast are the exceptions where many Chinese and African species have been exceptionally well in the small water bodies of the northeast especially in the states of Ceara and Pernambuco (Gurgel, 1984; Sugunan, 1996).

Introduction of *Oreochromis mossambicus* in Parakrama Samudra reservoir of Sri Lanka resulted into increase of fish production from 10 kg/ha/yr (in 1953) to 450-500 kg/ha/yr (in 1978). Indigenous fishes have not been negatively affected and, on the contrary, it appears that they have benefited from the presence of tilapias. It seems likely that the high densities of tilapia speed up mineralization thus enhancing plant growth. Parakrama Samudra supports a very dense fish eating bird population and also indigenous piscivorous fish species. Tilapias probably reduce predation pressure on indigenous carps. Overall, the average fish yields in Srilankan reservoir fisheries is about 300 kg/ha/yr and *Oreochromis mossambicus*, introduced in 1952, accounts forever 70% of the total landings and do not compete with native species (Jerome and Lionel, 2002).

Pakistan has introduced several alien exotic fish species e.g. grass carp (*Ctenopharyngodon idella*), bighead carp, (*Aristichthys nobilis*), silver carp, (*Hypophthalmichthys molitrix*), common carp (*Cyprinus carpio*), gold fish (*Carassius auratus*), and three species of tilapia (*Oreochromis aureus, Oreochromis mossambicus, Oreochromis niloticus*) in warm waters along with rainbow trout (*Onchorynchus mykiss*) and brown trout (*Salmo trutta fario*). The exotic species are becoming invasive in the freshwater biomes of the Punjab and other provinces of Pakistan by reason of their potent reproductive potential and feeding competitions with the native freshwater fish fauna. Resultantly the native fish species viz; *Channa marulius, Wallago attu, Rita rita, Sperata sarwari, Gibelion catla, Cirrhinus mrigala* and *Labeo rohita*, which are of economic value are under threat (Khan *et al.*2011).

In Pakistan *Oreochromis mossambicus* was introduced from Malaya in 1951 (Naik, 1973). Whereas *Oreochromis aureus,* and *O. niloticus* were introduced from Egypt during the year 1985 under 1st aquaculture development programme sponsored by Asian Development Bank. Tilapia has escaped from aquaculture and has established on its own in many wetlands in Sindh, while grass carp, introduced in the 1970s into Haleji Lake for controlling weeds, has reportedly deprived the native 74 herbivorous fish of their food.*Oreochromis aureus* is the most commonly found alien species in the Trimmu and Balloki reservoirs.The economically important fishes of Pakistan (*Labeo rohita, Cirrhinus mrigala, Gibelion catla,*) are basically vegetarian or detritivorous, where as alien fish species *Oreochromis aurius, O. mossambicus, O.niloticus* are omnivorous that feed mainly on plankton and aquatic vegetation. *O. aureus* is a generalized feeder with a preference for detritus and decanted phytoplankton. It also eats small fish and fish larvae. Due to wide ecological range alien *Oreochromis aureus* has been established in the freshwater reservoirs of Pakistan. This species is in direct competition for food to native herbivore fishes.*O.aureus* may pose serious adverse impacts in future on native fishes of Pakistan such as *Labeo rohita, Cirrhinus mrigala, Gibelion catla, Sperata sarwari, Rita rita,Channa marulius* and *Wallago attu* due to its competition for food, breeding grounds, predation and habitat alteration.

A substantial proportion of Canada's freshwater fish and molluscs are at risk for a variety of reasons. Habitat alteration, pollution and alien invasive species are the dominant threat factors influencing species at risk in Canada.

The introduction and establishment of exotic freshwater fishes in Australia has been documented (McKay, 1989; Arthington and Mitchell, 1986; Polland *et al.* 1980). Brown trout feeding may have caused the decline of the Tasmania mountain shrimp, Anaspides tasmaniae, and has eliminated or reduced several Plecoptera and Trichoptera in Victorian streams (Fletcher, 1979). *P.latipinna, X.maculatus* and *P.caudimaculatus* are much more patchily distributed in Australia, but in sub-tropical and tropical areas of Australia, these species could spread and have an adverse effect on endemic fishes (McKay, 1978; Balla *et al.* 1985). *Gambusia affinis*, an introduced freshwater fish in Australian waters has become a very common species which is partly responsible for the decline of several endemic fishes, including species which play an important part in keeping mosquito populations under control (Arthington *et al.* 1983; Llyod 1984, 1986; Lloyd *et al.* 1986). Thus *G.affinis* is a pest species, or ecological 'weed' (Lloyd 1984; Lloyd *et al* 1986). It has had destructive effects on invertebrate populations in field situations (Stephanides 1964; Legner and Medved 1974). It attacks the eggs and fry of important sport fishes (Mayers, 1965) and also eats fish fry in aquaria (Johnson 1976; Lloyd 1987).

Since the late 19th century, a great number of exotic species of aquatic organisms have been introduced into Japan primarily with a view to enrich the fish resources of the country. While the introduction of some of these species have caused serious ecological problems in natural waters (Chiba *et al.*1989). More than 120 exotic species of aquatic animals have been brought to Japan up to 1986. Of these, only 36 species were introduced to Japan before 1945.Many of these species were introduced intentionally for stocking in the natural environment, commercial culture and/or sport fishing. Some species, such as the silver carp (*Hypophthalmichthys molitrix*) and the bitterling (*Rhodeous ocellatus*) came to Japan accidentally. These two species arrived in Japan mixed with fry of the grass carp (*Ctenopharyngodon idella*) (Nakamura, 1955). Of the 120 species brought into Japan, about 9 species accounting for 7.5% of the total number have acclimatized themselves to the natural environment as self-reproducing populations; about 32 or 26.7% have been successfully bred; about 26 or 24.6% have disappeared; the status of about 53 or 41.2% remains obscure (Chiba *et al.* 1989). In Japan, *Rhodeus ocellatus smithi* being replaced by *Rhodeus ocellatus*, colonization of northeastern Japan by native born species found in southwestern Japan, and the predation of largemouth bass *Micropterus salmoides* on many native fish species in certain places (Chiba *et al.*1989).

Fish introductions in Malaysia were started in the early 19th century along with the immigration of the Southern Chinese who brought along the techniques of fish farming (Ang *et al.* 1989). Shariff (1980) indicated that Lernaea was brought into the country probably through exotic ornamental fish.Intruduction of Chinese carps, Indian major carps, rainbow trout and black bass have very little visible ecological impact on the freshwater ecosystem (Ang *et al.* 1989). There is no negative impact of introduced species on human life-styles, customs or economic systems. In fact, some introduced food fishes such as Chinese carps and the snakeskin gouramy have positive economic impacts as well as nutritional contribution to rural communities (Ang *et al.*1989).

The first recorded introduction of an exotic fish species to the Philippines was in 1907.The Philippine freshwater catfish, *Clarias macrocephalus* became completely dominated by an exotic species, *Clarias batrachus*, imported from Thailand during the craze for catfish farming patterned after the success in Thailand. *Clarias batrachus* now dominates natural populations in lakes and rivers and the indigenous *Clarias macrocepahuls* can hardly be found in the markets (Juliano *et al.* 1989). Other introductions did not make much impact and these were not regarded by Filipinos as significant in terms of benefits and adverse effects.

The introduction of *Tilapia mossambica* was a real nightmare for brackishwater farming, competing for food in the farm with *Chanos chanos* (milkfish). *Tilapia mossambica* is now an established species in brackish water farms in the entire country (Juliano *et al.*1989).

There are 38 aquatic species known to have been introduced to Taiwan. History of introductions of exotic aquatic species into Taiwan has not been well recorded. Many of the exotic aquatic species introduced into Taiwan, such as the tilapias, have been greatly beneficial. A few, like the giant African snail, *Achatina fulica* and the apple snail, *Ampullarius insularum*, have caused serious damage to the local environment (Liao and Liu,1989).

The first record of an exotic aquatic species in Thailand can be traced back to Ayudhaya Period of about the year 1691-1692. At present there are about 15 species of fishes which were introduced for aquaculture purposes (Piyakarnchana, 1989). Among them only a few are confirmed as reproducing in the natural habitats. The exotic species in the aquarium trade on the contrary were reported to increase rapidly from 69 species in 1963 to about 92 in 1988. These fish carried parasites such as anchor worm (*Lernaea sp*), cotton wool disease (*Saprolegina sp*), and fish louse (*Argulus sp*). There are no reliable records on the degree of the destruction by these diseases to the native species. Records on the real impact to the natural ecosystem from the introduced species are scare.

Procambarus clarkia (Louisiana cryfish) has been introduced for aquaculture as well as a biological control agent for snails. It is escaped from aquaculture sites and is responsible for the disappearance of water lilies and submerged vegetation, as well as many species of snails, in the wetlands of Eastern and Southern Africa (Howard and Matindi, 2003). It threatens the existence of smaller fish, and its habit of burrowing can result in damage to dams.

Nile tilapia from Northern Africa has become an invasive alien species in Southern Africa. This species can hybridize with the Mozambique tilapia, threatening its very existence in its native habitat (Van der Waal, 2002).

Exotic and translocated fish species have become established in various parts of the inland waters of Turkey (Deniz Innal and Fu¨ sun Erk'akan). A total of 25 exotic species have been introduced.Some of these fish have been used only in closed systems while others have been released into open inland waters throughout the country. *Gambusia sp.* is possibly one of the earliest deliberate exotic introductions although there are no exact records. *Cyprinus carpio* was first cultured in Turkey at the beginning of 1960s. It successfully maintains populations from escapes and releases throughout Turkey. The mosquito fish was introduced into freshwater systems in Turkey for malaria control as an important alternative to pesticides. *Gambusia affinis*, introduced in various habitats for mosquito control, is known to be a threat to other fish. The species presence should be regarded as a serious threat to populations of *A. anatoliae* (Wildekamp and Valkenburg 1994).

CHAPTER - 2

Exotic Fish Introduction in India *A Review*

The introduction of exotic fishes in Indian waters can be traced as having more than a century old history. While the country was under British rule, such fishes were possibly introduced as a means for recreational fisheries. Sir Francis Day was probably the first person who tried to introduce the Brown trout (*Salmo trutta fario*) in the Nilgiri waters in the year 1863, but this attempt was unsuccessful. In the year 1874, McIvor has introduced the trench *Tinca tinca* and the gold fish (*Carassius carassius*) into the Ooty (Ootacmund) Lake of Nilgiris.In the year 1900, the sea trout (*Salmo trutta trutta*) was brought from U.K. Later, Wilson succeeded in introducing the rainbow trout (*Oncorhynchus mykiss*) in 1906 in Jammu and Kashmir, Himachal Pradesh, Western Himalaya and Nilgiris. Further, introduction of *Salmo lavenensis* and *Onchorhynchus nerka* ended up with unsuccessful results. The giant gouramy (*Osphronemus goramy*) was first introduced in Calcutta from Java unsuccessfully during the first half of nineteenth century. In 1916, Gouramy was further introduced in Tamil Nadu from Java and Mauritius and subsequently transplanted in other states.

The tilapia (*Oreochromis mossambicus*) was first introduced into pond ecosystems in 1952 and thereafter stocked in the reservoirs of south India. The three varieties of the Prussian (German) strain of common carp, viz., the scale carp (*Cyprinus carpio communis*), the mirror carp (*Cyprinus carpio specularis*) and the leather carp (*Cyprinus carpio nudus*) were introduced in India from Sri Lanka during 1939. They were stocked in several high altitude ponds and lakes during the 1950s. Later, in the 1957, the Chinese (Bangkok) strain of the common carp and silver carp was brought into the country with the objectives of broadening the species spectrum in aquaculture and increasing the yields through better utilization of trophic niches. The grass carp (*Ctenopharyngodon idella*) was introduced in 1959, mainly to control weeds in natural water bodies. The land-locked strain of the Atlantic salmon, *Salmo salar* was introduced into the trout hatcheries of Kashmir in 1960, but failed to establish. The big head carp (*Aristichthys nobilis*) and Nile tilapia (*Oreochromis niloticus*) have been reported from the culture systems of eastern India (Singh and Ponnia, 2001). Although their introduction is unauthorized, these two fishes are becoming popular among the Indian aquaculturists. The larvicidal fishes, such as *Poecilia reticulate* and *Gambusia affinis* were introduced in the year 1908 and 1928 respectively, to contain mosquito larvae in confined waters (Khan *et al.*, 2008).

Introduction of exotic fish species in various ecosystems have created tragic stories all over the country. Common carp (*Cyprinus carpio*) introduced into Kashmir valley has almost exterminated the indigenous schizothoracids. Similarly the *Osteobrama belangiri*, the endemic fish to Loktak Lake (Manipur) is disappearing fast due to the introduction of common carp (Lakra *et al.*, 2006).

In Gobindsagar reservoir (Himachal Pradesh) *Catla catla* has already been replaced by the silver carp (*Hypophthalmichthys molitrix*). The main fishery of Govindsagar reservoir consists of silver carp, which fetches low price with low keeping quality and low demand. The establishment of *Cyprinus carpio* and *Hypophthalmichthys molitrix* resulted in alarmingly decline of the Golden mahseer (*Tor putitora*) fishery in Gobindsagar. Common carp is also known to compete with indigenous species such as *Cirrhinus spp.* (Dehadrai, 2008).

When *Oreochromis mossambicus* was introduced in India in the year 1952, the country was in its early phase of inland fisheries development. The fish was thought to be an answer to our search of a species which adapted well, bred profusely, subsisted on a variety of food under diverse ecological situations, and contributed significantly to the country's fish production. Tilapia was first stocked in ponds and then in a number of reservoirs in South India. Although it was originally planned to stock them in selected reservoirs on an experimental basis.By the end of 1960s, most of the reservoirs in Tamil Nadu and those in the Palakkad and Trissur districts of Kerala were regularly stocked with tilapia with the hope of achieving quick hikes in yield rates. Somehow the fish failed to live up its promise. Its performance in ponds were discouraging from the very beginning due to early maturity, continuous breeding, overpopulation and dwarfing. In the worst cases, it was reported to mature at 6 cm length at an age of 75 days and breed at an interval of one month under tropical conditions. Performance of *O.mossmbicus* in different water bodies including the culture-based fisheries has been assessed by several authors. Menon and Chacko (1957), Menon and Krishnamoorthy (1956), and Menon *et al.* (1959) have tried to ascertain the performance of fish in respect of its feeding habits, growth and possibility of raising them as forage for the murrels under culture systems. Sreenivasan (1967) has summed up the utility of tilapia in Indian waters based on his elaborate analysis of its performance in Tamil Nadu waters. This seems to be the only serious and critical evaluation of the species in India till the 80s taking into consideration both its bio-ecology and production trends. Most other literature on the species is restricted to its yield prospects, studies on sex reversal and the physiological responses to environmental stresses. The second comprehensive review on tilapia in Indian waters was by Jhingran (1983) who analyzed in detail the pros and cons of tilapia's performance and expounding its role in the capture fishery systems of India. The committee for introduction of exotic aquatic species in India set up by the government of India has also gone into the details of the species and the possible impact of its wide –scale adoption in Indian waters for enhancing the production. Some commercial-houses have entered the field in the past by employing biotechnological approaches in tilapia farming, the most prominent among them was the venture of Vorion Chemicals, Madras which cultured the hybrid variety ,the golden tilapia (Rangaswami, 1988). M/S Vorion Chemicals is reported to have achieved a production rate of 65 t per hectare per year in its farm.

In Amaravathy reservoir tilapia forms about 90% of the catch (Das, 2008). In Krishnagiri reservoir, tilapia production increased and tilapia contributed 68.90% in the year 1989-90 with major carp fishing of 3.7 to 6.6%. In Vaigai reservoir, *Oreochromis mossambicus* is the single largest component of fishery. In Pambar reservoir percentage of fish yield obtained from tilapia production was the highest. Mahanta *et al.* (2003) observed that Chullair, Meenakara, Peechi and Malampuzha reservoirs in Kerala were stocked with tilapia in the early sixties and presently the fish contributes substantially in catch. In Malampuzha reservoir (2313 ha) tilapia forms 70% of the catch.Tilapia also found its way into Kolleru Lake in Andhra Pradesh and Sondur reservoir of Raipur district of Chattisgarh (Kurup and Radhakrishnan, 2008). Khan *et al.* (2008) noticed tilapia, *Oreochromis mossambicus* in the waters of the Chilka Lake (Orissa) where they were never introduced with a purpose. Such accidental or deliberate release of exotic fishes often takes place. In a number of Indian reservoirs, introduction of tilapia has resulted in poor growth rate or even elimination of the indigenous species and the transplanted Gangetic carps and it is certain that tilapia population is affecting the native fish fauna (Sugunan, 1995). The growth rate of *Catla catla, Labeo fimbriatus, Cirrhinus mrigala* and *Chanos chanos* were adversely affected due to their co-existence with tilapia (Sreenivasan, 1967). In Kabini reservoir of Karnataka, the catch of native carp species, *Cirrhinus reba* has decreased from 70% of total catch in 1980-81 to mere 20% in 1984-85 (Murthy *et al.* 1986).

Oreochromis mossambicus is now recorded from of the polluted rivers like Ganga and Yamuna. Invasion of *O.mossambicus* in the riverine fishery has been found to aggravate the threats to the indigenous fish diversity including environmental problems.

Invasion of *O.niloticus* has recently been reported in Yamuna river at Allahabad.The only demerit is that being a prolific breeder, it becomes a dominant species there by reducing the growth rate of the other species cultured along with it.

Tilapia caused the deaths of more than 100 gharials in Chambal waters (Awasthi, 2008). Circumstantial evidences suggest that the critically endangered reptiles could have consumed the fish abundantly found in the Yamuna which is polluted with heavy metals. The Yamuna meets the Chambal 40 km downstream of the affected area. A toxin in the fish could have entered the gharials' body and damaged their kidney, resulted in gout like symptoms and then death. Several studies have already shown that tilapia is a hardy fish and can withstand high pollution and toxins such as heavy metals tend to get accumulated in its body. The tilapia could have brought toxins from the Yamuna, where it is dominant. The tilapia link has surprised gharial experts who say gharials usually spare the invasive tilapia. They feed on local fish. But villagers in the region says illegal fishing has led to a sharp decline in local fish, forcing the gharials to target tilapia.Experts say tilapia could also harm human health and aquatic life. People in Chambal have been eating it, since few local varieties are available. Many now fear that tilapia, which is a predatory fish,may threaten fish in nearby rivers too.

The chances of survival of the common carp, which is sluggish in nature, are very poor in a predator-dominated reservoir. Sugunan (1995) observed that the presence of common carp has resulted in the decline of *Cirrhinus sp.* In Girna and Krishnarajsagar the mirror carp has threatened the survival of a number of native species.In Dal Lake, the fish propagated itself profusely causing serious damage to the populations of indigenous snow trouts like *Schizothoraichthys niger, S.esocinus* and *S.curvifrons*.The mirror carp has caused similar damage to the snow trouts in Gobindsagar reservoir and *Osteobrama belangiri* in Loktak Lake, Manipur. Vass and Gopakumar (2002) stated that introduction of *Cyprinus carpio* is an evidence for the decline of local snow-trout fishery in some of the upland lakes in India. Recent assessment survey revealed the infestation of Yamuna river by *Cyprinus carpio* resulting in the decline of precious Indian major carp fisheries at Allahabad (Singh *et al.*,2010). Common carp has now established itself in the Ganga river and the so colonized fishes contributed the bulk of the catch. Introduced common carp has been reported to implicate environmental changes principally eutrophication through an increase in turbidity and mobilization of nutrients to the water column from the benthos through its habit of rooting or digging in the bottom (Britton *et al.*, 2007, Khanna *et al.*, 2007, Rowe 2007). The declining trend of Indian major carps in the Ganga river and increasing appearance of common carp in the fishery is a warranting situation of biological invasion threatening ecological integrity. The problem of repopulating

Cyprinus carpio in degraded water of the river has come up to conserve rich fish genetic resources of the Ganga river before it faces a major alteration.

Africian catfish, *Clarias gariepinus* is native of rivers Niger and Nile and it extends to the Southern Africian rivers Limpopo, orange vaal, and Okavango and Cuene. It is now widely distributed in the world where it is native of the 40 countries while it has been introduced in more than 16 countries including India, Bangladesh and Nepal (Fish Base, 2004).

In India *Clarias gariepinus* has entered clandestinely in our culture system without any official sanction and rapidly adopted into culture practice in various parts of the country. It was first brought to West Bengal during 1993 possibly from Bangladesh from where it spread throughout the country (Thakur, 1998). In Assam it was introduced in 1994 by private fish seed traders (Baruah *et al.*, 1999). The fish has tremendous potentialities of hybridization with the local *Clarias batrachus* and *Heteropneustes fossilis*. It can also hybridize with another exotic fish *Pangasius sutchi*. The introduction of *Clarias gariepinus* has not been a success as several socio-economic aspects were neglected (Singh and Lakra, 2008). In India consumers refuse to buy *Clarias gariepinus* even at reasonable price because of its taste, relatively large head and also because of the fact that this fish consumes slaughter house waste. The fishermen of Kolleru Lake believe that Africian catfish weighing 100 kg each are now present in the lake, and that presently the common indigenous fish species have declined/disappeared due to the invasion of *Clarias gariepinus* into the Lake (Ravindranath, 2008). It was also reported that locally available catfishes and cultured carps were badly affected due to introduction of this species in ponds and nallahs at Middle, North and South Andamans. Consequent upon this report, the Directorate of Fisheries, Andaman and Nicobar Administration took serious note of it and put complete ban over import of this live species to islands by deploying field staff at airport and seaports followed by a massive drive for eradication of the species from the culture system during 2002-2003 (Sarangi, 2008).

Silver carp (*Hypophthalmichthys molitrix*) is known for its ability to efficiently consume phytoplankton, which is the most dominant fraction of plankton in Rihand reservoir of Uttar Pradesh (Haque *et al.* 2008). This may be just one reason of steady increase of silver carp in Rihand reservoir. But the trend may prove catastrophic for the catla fishery, which has now attained a declining status or more or less similar production over the last several years.

Big head carp (*Aristichthys nobilis*) was introduced by CARI during 1992 in the experimental ponds. The species registered good average growth but considerable impact on catla growth was observed. The species though accepted by the consumers, the same is not recommended for the culture system to safe-guard the growth of catla (Sarangi, 2008).

Minimol (2000) observed overlap of food items in case of *Hypselabarbus kurali* and exotic fishes which might have reduced the size of *H.kurali* in Periyar Lake.

Pacu (*Piaractus brachypomus*) is relished as food and is also popular as aquarium fish. It is native of Amazon and Orinoco river basins of South America. It was illegally brought to India for aquarium trade and culture purpose during 2003-2004 via Bangladesh. Pacu has been reported in natural waters of Maharashtra, Andhra Pradesh, Tamil Nadu, Kerala and West Bengal. The impact of Pacu on biodiversity on long term is not properly documented. Since Pacu has a higher longevity, high fecundity and is an opportunistic omnivore, it feeds on anything, and is able to tolerate harsh environment. It can also be a competitor to the native species (Ghatge *et al.*, 2014). They are known to be a traumatogenic species for humans as its strong teeth can cause serious bites (Frose and Pauly, 2011). Persons engaged in capturing the fish for test sampling reported bites on their legs, thighs and on palms. Pacu has bitten off the testicles of bathing men in rivers (Smith, 2007). In many countries Pacu are legally banned for aquarium trade and aquaculture. This species is not cleared by the exotic committee in India. In spite of official ban, Pacu was brought clandestinely. Introduction of such species in freshwater would cause long term damage to our systems besides eliminating the indigenous and already existing food and ornamental fishes.

CHAPTER - 3

Materials and Methods

Fishes for the purpose of study were collected with the help of local fishermen in spite of buying from the market. Three sampling sites were chosen for study; the outlet, the inlet and an approximate intermediate of the water body. The collected fishes were brought to the laboratory after noting their original colour and capturing photographs. The collected fishes were preserved in 5% formalin solution in to the laboratory for further study. The identification of fishes was done with the help of standard keys (Jhingran and Talwar 1991 and Day 1878).

A personal contact and interview method was used to gather data on fish seed stocking, fish catch, catch composition and environmental impact of exotic fishes on indigenous fish species.

For the analysis of physico-chemical parameters samples from three sampling stations were collected monthly in the morning hours in between 8-11am, for a period of three years from June 2011 to May 2014. The water samples were collected in plastic containers of one litre capacity and brought to laboratory for further analysis. Some physical parameters like atmospheric temperature, water temperature, pH, total dissolved solids and chemical parameters like dissolved oxygen, free carbon dioxide and alkalinity were analyzed at the sampling sites while remaining parameters like salinity, chlorinity are analyzed in the laboratory.

The analysis of physico-chemical parameters was done with the help of methodology by Kodarkar *et.al.*, (1998), Trivedy and Goel (1984) and APHA (1985).

Temperature (°C): The atmospheric temperature as well as surface water temperature was recorded with a mercury thermometer having 0.1°C division and a range of 00 to 50°C.

Transparency (cm): Transparency of water was measured at the respective sampling sites with the help of Secchi disc which is a weighted metallic disc of 20 cm diameter, devised by an Italian oceanographer in the 19th century. The transparency was calculated as the mean of the depths at which the disc disappears (X) when viewed from the shaded side of the boat and at which it reappears (Y) upon raising after it has been lowered beyond visibility.

$$\text{Secchi disc transparency (cm)} = \frac{X+Y}{2}$$

Potent Hydrogeni (pH): The hydrogen ion concentration values were measured with the help of Hanna made pH meter at the respective water sample collection sites.

Total Dissolved Solids (mg/l): The total dissolved solids were recorded with the help of digital TDS Meter No:CD:600 (Milwaukee) and the results were noted as mg/l.

Dissolved oxygen (mg/l): For the calculation of dissolved oxygen modified Winkler's method was used. The water samples were collected in glass Stoppard oxygen bottles from the respective sampling sites and analyzed immediately. One ml of manganese chloride and one ml of alkaline potassium iodide was added with the help of micropipette. The bottle was shake properly so as to mix the content thoroughly and then kept to settle down the brown precipitate. Then few drops of concentrated hydrochloric acid were added drop wise through the side of bottle and were well shake to dissolve the precipitate. 100 ml of this solution was taken in conical flask and used for titration after adding few drops of 1% starch as an indicator. After adding the indicator the solution turns to blue colour and finally titrated against N/80 sodium thiosulphate till the colour disappears.

$$\text{Dissolved oxygen (mg/l)} = \frac{X \times N \times 8 \times 1000}{Y}$$

Where,

X = Volume of sodium thiosulphate used (ml)

Y = Volume of sample taken for titration (ml)

N = Normality of sodium thiosulphate (N)

Free carbon dioxide (mg/l): 100 ml of sample was taken in conical flask and few drops of phenolphthalein were added. If the colour turns pink free carbon dioxide is absent. If it remained colourless then titrated against 0.05N NaOH till the colour appears.

$$\text{Free } CO_2 \text{ (mg/l)} = \frac{\text{(ml} \times \text{N) of NaOH} \times 1000 \times 44}{\text{ml of sample}}$$

Total Alkalinity (mg/l): 2-3 drops of methyl orange indicator were added to the solution used to determine phenolphthalein alkalinity and titrated with 0.1N HCl up to the end point, when the colour changes from yellow to pink.

$$\text{Total Alkalinity } CaCO_3 \text{ (mg/l)} = \frac{B \times \text{Normality of HCl} \times 1000 \times 50}{\text{ml of sample}}$$

Where, B = ml of HCl used with phenolphthalein and methyl orange.

Total hardness (mg/l): 50 ml of water sample was taken in conical flask in to which 1ml of ammonia buffer and a pinch of NaCN (inhibitor) was added. A pinch of erichrome black T indicator was added to develop wine red colour. The sample was then titrated against 0.01m EDTA solution to end point wine red to blue.

$$\text{Total hardness (mg/l) } (Caco_3) = \frac{T \times 1000}{v}$$

Where

T = Titrant (ml)

v = sample (ml)

Chlorides (mg/l): The chloride concentration was analyzed in the laboratory. 10 ml of water sample was taken in a conical flask and few drops of K_2CrO_4 were added in to it. The sample was titrated with 0.02 $AgNO_3$ to the end point from yellow to brick red.

$$\text{Chlorides (mg/l)} = \frac{V \times Nx\ 35.45 \times 1000}{v}$$

Where

V = Volume of titrant (ml)

N = Normality of $AgNO_3$ (0.02)

v = Volume of sample in ml.

The reservoirs under present investigation possesses varied fishery resources which depend mainly on the primary and secondary production. No serious attempts have so far been made to assess the abundance of plankton population in relation with the fishery potential of the reservoirs. An understanding of their seasonal abundance will help in the proper assessment of population structure, abundance, growth and spawning of many food fishes. With these views in mind, a study regarding the species composition, abundance and seasonal variation of population communities of the reservoirs was attempted.

Phytoplankton collection was made towing a net made-up of bolting silk Net No. 25 for five minutes. Sedimentation of phytoplankton was made in 5% formaldehyde. Algal monographs of Tripathi and Pandey (1990) were followed to identify the phytoplankton. Drop count method of Trivedy and Goel (1984) was followed for enumeration of phytoplankton and expressed as organisms per liter.

The studies on the zooplankton diversity and density were carried out for a period of three years (2011-12 to 2013-14) in six reservoirs from

Marathwada region of Maharashtra. Qualitative zooplankton samples were collected with the help of plankton net made of bolting cloth No. 25 (mesh size approximately 56μ) from three different zones of the reservoir. For the collections from littoral zones, sweeps were made in all directions with the help of a long pole. For the collection from pond waters, net was thrown to maximum possible distance from the shore and towed gradually avoiding littoral macrophytes. Net was also towed from the boat for some distance in open water as and when feasible. Similarly, vertical hauls were made from open water by dropping the net with anchor from the boat to the bottom and pulling rapidly.

For the quantitative samples, 50 litres of water was filtered through the net, both from littoral and open water zones. Samples were transferred to a small enamel tray. The inside of the net was washed so as to collect any sticking plankter. Few drops of formalin were put to nacrotize the animals and when they became motionless and settled down, the supernatant water was discarded slowly and concentrated samples were collected. All samples were preserved in 5% formaldehyde solution. Preserved zooplankton samples were examined under a binocular microscope with different magnifications. Detailed taxonomic identification was carried out following Needham and Needham (1962), Edmondson (1959), Mellan by (1963), Pennak (1978), Tonapi (1980), Sehgal (1983), Michael and Sharma (1988), Battish (1992), Ahmad (1996), Shiel (1995), Murugan *et.al.* (1998), Roy (1999), Sharma (1999), Dhanapathi (2000), Khan (2003), Lynne (2004).

CHAPTER - 4

Majalgaon Reservoir

The Majalgaon dam is part of the Jaikwadi Scheme (2400 km^2), one of the largest irrigation areas in Maharashtra. The salient features of reservoir are given in Table 4.1. The first phase of this scheme was financed by World Bank and began in 1970s. It is located at 19°8′59″ North and 76°13′48″ East on river Sindphana, which is the tributary of the river Godavari. The river Godavari originates at Trimbakeshwar (hill) in Nashik district of Maharashtra and travels about 1500 km to join the Bay of Bengal. It has a catchment area of 312.812 sq. km of which 63.3% lies in Maharashtra. Its main tributaries are Pravara, Purna, Penganga, Wainganga, Manjara, and Sindphana. There are many pilgrim centers on the bank of Godavari out of which Trimbakeshwar, Nashik, Paithan and Nanded are major one where millions of peoples gather on festivals. Many cities and villages are situated on the bank of this river which utilises the river water. Hence Godavari river in considered as the 'Ganga of Deccan'.

River Sindphana is the main tributary of the Godavari River. On the right bank, its origin is in the Balaghat range about 50 km away from Majalgaon city. It merges in Godavari River near Manjarath village.

The climate of this region is dry except in south west monsoon season (June to September). There are wide seasonal variations in temperature of the region. December is the coldest month of the year. Sometimes the region is affected by cold waves, which are associated with the westward passage of the western disturbances across north India. In the period from March to May there is continuous rise in both day and night temperatures. May is the hottest month of the year. With the one set of monsoon by the second week of June, the temperature goes down and the weather is very pleasant throughout the southwest monsoon. The relative humidity is high during the southwest monsoon season. The summer season is the driest period of the year.

Table 4.1: **Salient Features of Majalgaon Reservoir**

Location	Majalgaon
Year of completion	1987
River	Sindhphana
Basin	Godavari
Type of dam	Earthfill
Catchment Area (Th ha)	384
Length of dam (meters)	6488
Maximum height above foundation (meter)	31.19
Maximum water level (meters)	434.8
Full Reservoir Level (meter)	431.8
Gross storage capacity (MCM)	453.64
Live storage capacity (MCM)	311.3
Type of spillway	Ogee
Type of spillway gates	Radial
Length of spillway (meters)	239
Number of spillway gates	16
Size of spillway gates (mxm)	12 × 8
Total land affected (Th ha)	7.48
Number of villages affected	20
Purpose of dam	Irrigation and hydelpower generation

Surveys were conducted in all the major fishing sites of Majalgaon reservoir and semi-structured interviews were carried out with fishermen to study the fish yield and the overall status of fisheries of the reservoir. The fish catches and species composition were studied for a period of three years from June 2011 to May 2014. A total of 29 fish species belonging to 6 orders have been encountered in Majalgaon reservoir (Table 4.2). During the present investigation 13 species of Cypriniformes (including 1 exotic), 6 species of Siluriformes, 3 species of Channiformes, 3 species of Perciformes, 2 species of Mastacembeliformes and 2 species of Cluepeiformes were recorded.

The year wise monthly variations in the fish catches for the period of 2011-12, 2012-13 and 2013-14 are depicted in Table 4.3, 4.4 and 4.5 respectively.

In the first year, the fish catch from reservoir ranged from 3292.25 kg (January 2012) to 12489.25 kg (July 2011) with monthly average of 5659.31 kg (Table 4.3). The catch of exotics (*Cyprinus carpio* and *Oreochromis mossambicus*) contributed to about 30.42% of the total catch, while Indian major carps and local fishes contributed to about 69.58% (Fig. 4.1). The species which commonly occurred in the catches include *Cyprinus carpio,Oreochromis mossambicus, Catla catla, Mastacembelus spp, Chanda ranga* and *Channa spp.*

Table 4.2: Fish Diversity in Majalgaon Reservoir of Beed district

Order: Clupeiformes **Suborder: Notopteroidei** **Family: Notopteridae**	
1.	*Notopterus notopterus (Pallas)*
2.	*Notopterus chitala (Ham.)*
Order: Cypriniformes **Suborder: Cyprinoidei** **Family: Cyprinidae**	
3.	*Chela phulo (Ham.)*
4.	*Catla catla (Ham.)*
5.	*Labeo rohita (Ham.)*
6.	*Labeo fimbriatus (Bloch)*
7.	*Cirrhinus mrigala (Ham.)*
8.	*Cyprinus carpio (Linn)*
9.	*Amblypharyngodon mola (Ham.)*
10.	*Discognathus modestus (Ham.)*
11.	*Osteobrama cotio (Ham.)*
12.	*Puntius sarana sarana (Ham.)*
13.	*Puntius ticto ticto (Ham.)*
14.	*Puntius chola (Ham.)*
Family: Cobitidae	
15.	*Nemacheilus botia (Ham.)*
Order: Siluriformes **Family: Bagridae**	
16.	*Mystus cavasius (Ham.)*
17.	*Mystus seenghala (Sykes)*
18.	*Mystus vittatus (Bloch)*
Family: Heterpneustidae	
19.	*Heteropnesutes fossilis (Bloch)*
Family: Siluridae	
20.	*Wallago attu (Bloch and Schneider)*
21.	*Ompak bimaculatus (Bloch)*
Order: Channiformes **Family: Channidae**	
22.	*Channa gachua (Haml.)*
23.	*Channa striatus (Bloch)*
24.	*Channa marulius (Ham.)*
Order: Mastacembeliformes	
25.	*Mastacembelus pancalus (Ham.)*
26.	*Mastacembelus armatus (Lacepede)*
Order: Perciformes **Family: Anabantidae**	
27.	*Anabas testudineus (Bloch)*
Family: Cichlidae	
28.	*Oreochromis mossambicus (Peters)*
Family: Ambassidae	
29.	*Chanda ranga (Ham.)*

Table 4.3: Fish Catches from Majalgoan Reservoir of Beed District (Year 2011-12)

	Carps and Local Fish	Exotics	Total
July 2011	9104.75	3384.5	12489.25
August 2011	5419.5	1323	6742.5
September 2011	2699.5	961.5	3661
October 2011	2551	1227.5	3778.5
November 2011	3229	1264.5	4493.5
December 2011	2651.75	1476	4127.75
January 2012	3112.25	180	3292.25
February 2012	4649.5	150	4799.5
March 2012	2250	1230.5	3480.5
April 2012	2894.5	1627	4521.5
May 2012	4209	1258.5	5467.5
June 2012	4483	6575	11058
Total	47253.75	20658	67911.75

Table 4.4: Fish Catches from Majalgoan Reservoir of Beed District (Year 2012-13)

	Carps and Local Fishes	Exotics	Total
July 2012	4721.5	427	5148.5
August 2012	2764.5	912.5	3677
September 2012	2769.5	1170	3939.5
October 2012	3057.5	2609	5666.50
November 2012	3173.5	1802	4975.5
Decemebr 2012	2651.75	450	3101.75
January 2013	1149	835	1984
February 2013	979	464	1443
March 2013	975	458	1433
April 2013	1140	3760	4900
May 2013	150	780	930
June 2013	519.28	620.5	1139.78
Total	24050.53	14288	38338.53

Table 4.5: **Fish Catches from Majalgoan Reservoir of Beed District (Year 2013-14)**

	Carps and Local Fishes	Exotics	Total
July 2013	346.5	1924.25	2270.75
August 2013	654.25	4765	5419.25
September 2013	696	938	1634
October 2013	1312.5	1410	2722.5
November 2013	3625	2837.5	6462.5
December 2013	4350	1215	5565
January 2014	2462	1009.5	3471.5
February 2014	2011.5	835.5	2847
March 2014	1291	723.5	2014.5
April 2014	896	524.5	1420.5
May 2014	2170	591	2761
June 2014	1493	912	2405
Total	21307.75	17685.75	38993.5

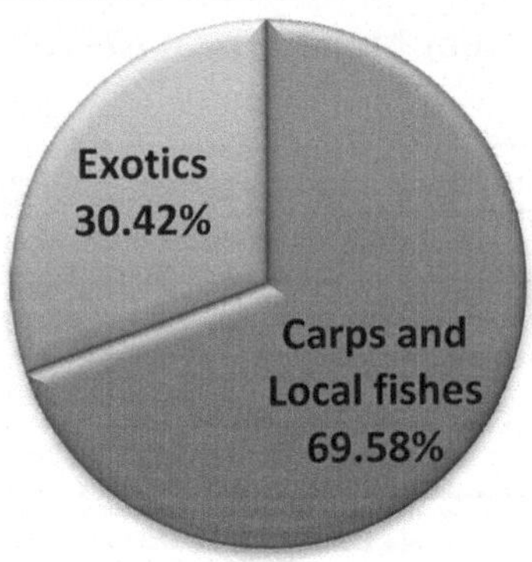

Fig.4.1: **Fish Landing Contribution in Majalagaon Reservoir (Year 2011-12**

In second year of investigation (2012-13) the fish catch fluctuated from 930 kg (May 2013) to 5666.50 kg (October 2012) with monthly average of 3195 kg (Table 4.4). During the period exotics' contribution was 37.27%,while Indian major carps and local fish species together contributed to about 62.73% (Fig. 4.2).

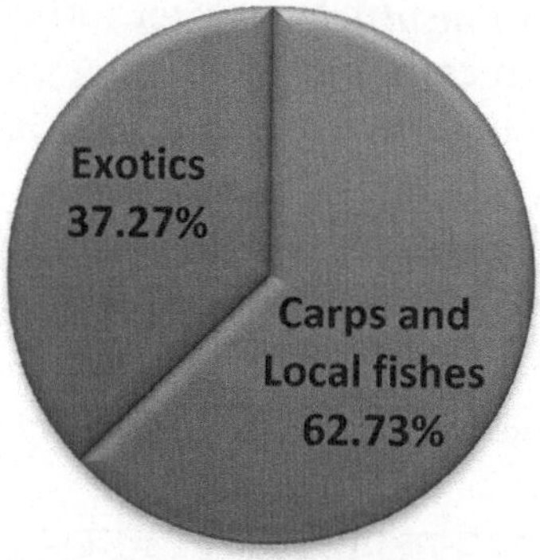

Fig.4.2: **Fish Landing Contibution in Majalgaon Reservoir (Year 2012-13)**

In third year (2013-14) the exotics viz., *Cyprinus carpio* and *Oreochromis mossambicus* accounted 45.36% of the total catches while Indian major carps and local fishes accounted for 54.64% of the total catch (Fig. 4.3). The month wise fish catch ranged from 1420.5 kg (April 2014) to 6462.50 kg (November 2013) with monthly average of 3249.46 kg (Table 4.5).

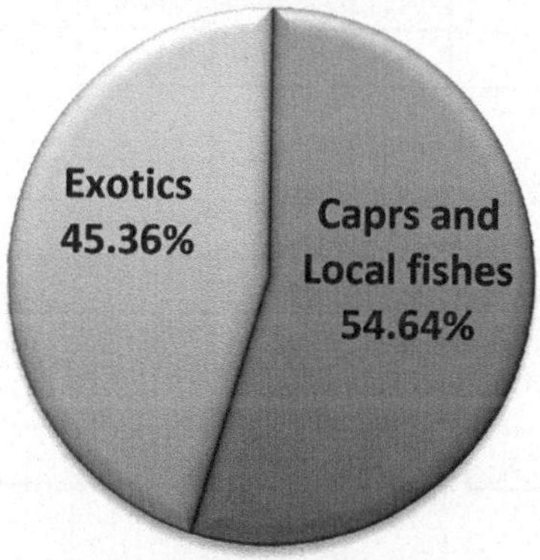

Fig.4.3: **Fish Landing Contrubtion in Majalgaon Reservoir (Year 2013-14)**

In Majalgaon reservoir two exotic species viz., *Cyprinus carpio* and *Oreochromis mossambicus* contributed more than 37% of the total fish catch. Continuous stocking of *Cyprinus carpio* resulted in decline of *Cirrhinus mrigala* from the reservoir.These findings corroborate with Sugunan (1995) who reported the decline in *Cirrhinus sp* due to entry of *Cyprinus carpio*.

The society generally purchased fish seed from the private fish seed farm, about 10 kms from the reservoir site. During 2011-12 society stocked

36,00,000 fish seed. Recently during 2012-13 and 2013-14 the reservoir was not stocked. It was due to insufficient water in reservoir. The seed of catla, rohu, mrigal and common carp is stocked.

The fishery is exploited by fishermen who have been organized from different villages into co-operative society.

Physico-chemical environment: The year wise seasonal averages of various physico-chemical parameters of Majalgaon reservoir are depicted in Table 4.6.

Table 4.6: Seasonal Fluctuation in Water Quality Parameters of Majalgaon Reservoir

Season/ Year	Water Temp. (°C)	Transpar- encey (cm)	pH	TDS (mg/l)	DO (mg/l)	CO_2 (mg/)	TA (mg/l)	Cl^- (mg/l)	TH (mg/l)
2011-12									
Monsoon	26.5	30	7.8	245	11.5	10.4	270	38.1	132.5
Winter	20.5	59	8.7	215	8.9	Nil	160	36.2	114.5
Summer	28	87	8.2	190	6.4	3.7	172.5	62.2	153
Mean	25	58.66	8.23	216.6	8.93	4.7	200.8	45.50	133.33
2012-13									
Monsoon	24.8	58	7.9	230	10.9	7.3	280	39.3	127
Winter	20	82	8.9	150.3	9.2	Nil	180.2	42.2	119
Summer	26.5	110	8.4	210	7.8	4.9	222	68.3	138
Mean	23.76	83.33	8.4	196.7	9.3	4.06	227.4	49.93	128
2013-14									
Monsoon	26	60	8.2	210.5	9.8	8.2	267.3	32.1	129.2
Winter	23	62	8.6	140	9.3	Nil	172.5	36.3	123
Summer	28.5	77	8.3	190.4	8.2	6.2	201.8	60	136
Mean	25.83	66.33	8.36	180.3	9.1	4.8	213.8	42.80	129.4
Grand Mean	24.86	69.44	8.33	197.9	9.11	4.52	214	46.07	130.24

Water temperature is the most important variable affecting the natural productivity of aquatic ecosystems and directly or indirectly affects all the other water quality variables. The surface water temperature varies throughout the year with seasonal changes in atmospheric temperature, day length, and solar radiation (Boyd and Tucker, 2009).

The surface temperature values ranged from 20.5 to 28 °C during 2011-12, 20 to 26.5°C during 2012-13 and 23 to 28.5°C during 2013-14 with overall mean of 24.86 °C. The surface water temperature was minimum in winter and maximum in summer season. Such type of observations were made by Sakhare (2007) and Jetithor (2010).

Reservoirs having water temperature more than 22°C are the highly productive reservoirs (Sugunan 1995). The average surface water temperature was recorded at 25°C, 23.7° C and 25.83°C during first, second and third year of study, which reveals that Majalgaon reservoir is highly productive.

Water transparency is a physical measurable variable and is quite significant for production. Transparency is inversely proportional to turbidity created by suspended inorganic and organic matter. Results of the present study reveals that the transparency in Majalgaon reservoir was recorded in the range of 30 to 87 cms,58 to 110 cms and 60 to 77 cms during first, second and third year respectively. The minimum transparency values found in monsoon months and maximum in summer months.

pH of most surface water varies diurnally as photosynthesis and respiration cause changes in dissolved carbon dioxide concentrations. During daylight, aquatic plants remove carbon dioxide from water for use in photosynthesis. Both plants and animals continually release carbon dioxide into the water by respiration. However during daylight, aquatic plants usually remove carbon dioxide from the water faster than it can be replaced by respiration, and pH increases. During the night, carbon dioxide accumulates and pH declines. The magnitude of the daily fluctuation in pH depends on the buffering capacity of the water and the rates of photosynthesis and respiration.

The seasonal mean pH values were 8.23, 8.4 and 8.36 in first, second and third year with grand mean of 8.33. The minimum pH value has been noted in monsoon months while the maximum in winter. pH was alkaline throughout the study period. The optimum pH for growth and health of most freshwater aquatic animals is in the range of 6.5 to 9.0 (Boyd and Tucker, 2009).Thus, the pH range indicate that Majalgaon reservoir which is having a pH range 7.8 to 8.9 is suitable for fish growth.

Total dissolved solids gives indication about total concentration of constituents in water. The value of total dissolved solid affect taste of water and water from different areas are characterized as tasteless, sweet, brackish, saline, bitter etc. Water with high total dissolved solids is generally not suitable and may not quench thrusts and may have laxative effect on people. During first year (2011-12), total dissolved solids ranged between 190 to 245 mg/l, during second year (2012-13) 150.3 to 230 mg/l and during third year (2013-14) 140 to 210.5 mg/l with grand mean of 197.90 mg/l. The total dissolved solids were recorded more during rainy season. This Observation is similar to the investigation made by Pentewar (2013) in Dhanora dam of Nanded district. High values of total dissolved solids in rainy season may be due to addition of solids from runoff water.

Dissolved oxygen in water is of great importance to all aquatic organisms and is considered to be an important factor which reflects physical and biological process taking place in water body. It is important in the production and support of life and also necessary for the decomposition and decay of organic matter. Dissolved oxygen concentration in water is mainly dependent upon temperature, dissolved salts, wind velocity, pollution load, photosynthetic activity and respiration rate

In the present investigation dissolved oxygen values ranged between 6.4 to 11.5 mg/l, 7.8 to 10.9 mg/l and 8.2 to 9.8 mg/l in first, second and third year respectively. The maximum values were recorded in monsoon and minimum in summer. The present findings are in accordance with the findings of workers like Sakhare (2007) and Mudgal *et al* (2013).Oxygen content was maximum at the surface and decreased gradually with depth. Such type of depth distribution of oxygen is a characteristics of a productive reservoir (Sreenivasan, 1970).

Total alkalinity is the sum of titratable bases in water. In most waters, bicarbonate and carbonate are the predominant bases that contribute to alkalinity. The range of total alkalinity values in inland surface waters is similar to that for groundwaters, but surface waters usually have a lower total alkalinity than groundwaters in the same vicinity because surface waters usually have lower carbon dioxide level than groundwaters. The total alkalinity of water will be higher in areas with outcrops of limestone or in areas with considerable inflow of groundwater from limestone aquifers (Boyd and Tucker, 2009).

Aquatic animals do not have significance physiological requirement for water borne bicarbonate or carbonate, but total alkalinity is an important environmental variable in fisheries because it interacts with other variables that affect the health of aquatic animals or the fertility of aquatic ecosystem.

During present investigation total alkalinity ranged from 160 to 270 mg/l, 180.2 to 280 mg/l and 172.5 to 267 mg/l during 2011-12, 2012-13 and 2013-14 respectively.

Free carbon dioxide was absent in winter, considerably higher values were recorded during monsoon and summer. The present findings corroborate with findings by Siddiqui and Khan (2002).The high rate of decomposition during summer due to rapidly receding water level and higher temperature followed by scanty rains during monsoon, were probably responsible for higher values of carbon dioxide.

Lendhe and Yeragi (2004) encountered higher concentration of carbon dioxide in May and minimum in December in Phirange Kharbv Lake of Thane. The free carbon dioxide range of reservoir was from 1.76 to 4.84 mg/l.

Sakhare (2007) studied some aspects of fisheries and limnology of Yeldari reservoir in Maharashtra and reported presence of carbon dioxide in March and April 2000 and it was totally absent in second year (2000-2001).

Chlorides in the form of cl ions is one of the major inorganic anions in water. In potable water, the salty taste produced by chloride concentration is variable and dependent on the chemical composition of water. Some water containing 250 mg/l chloride may have a desirable salty taste if the cation is sodium.

Chloride contents of the reservoir water varied between 32.1 to 68.3 mg/l. The peak was observed during summer. The chloride values during winter and rainy season were almost similar.

Traditionally hardness is a measure of the capacity of water to react with soap. It is often desired as carbonate (temporary) and non carbonate (permanent) types of hardness. During present investigation, the total hardness values ranged from 114.5 to 153 mg/l, 119 to 138 mg/l and 123 to 136 mg/l in first, second and third year respectively. The overall mean of hardness was 130.24.Highest concentrations of total hardness have been observed during summer while lowest during winter. A similar observation was also made by Jayabhaye (2013).

Zooplankton Diversity: During first year of investigation five groups of zooplankton were obtained from Majalgaon reservoir i.e; Protozoa, Rotifera, Cladocera, Copepoda and Ostracoda (Table 4.7). Monthly variations of the zooplankton at Majalgaon reservoir showed the minimum and maximum density in June (159 org/liter) and in February (544 org/liter) respectively.

Temperature directly affects plankton. During summer the temperature is high and the plankton population is also reach to maximum and when the temperature is low during winter the plankton population is also reach to the minimum (Shukla *et al.*2013). During present investigation zooplankton was most abundant during summer and least during monsoon season. Among the five zooplankton groups, rotifer constituted the major portion (34.36%), Cladocera was the second dominant group which contributed to 25.93% of the total zooplankton (Fig. 4.4).

Density of protozoa varied from 12 org/L to 57 org/L. Minimum density was recorded in monsoon and maximum density in summer. This group was represented by three species. *Diffugia sp* showed their presence round the first year of investigation. *Paramecium caudatum* and *Opercularia sp.* were absent in July and August respectively.

Rotifers were represented by eight species.*Brachionus calyciflorus* was absent in two months (September and May) and *B. falcatus* in three months (August, October and January). *Keratella tropica* was absent in October and *Lecane (Monostyla) bulla* in July and October. Other species were present round the first year of investigation. The rotifer density fluctuated from 44 org/l (October) to 183 org/l (March) with annual average of 105 org/l. This group showed maximum species among zooplanktons.

Table 4.7: Monthly Analysis of Zooplankton Diversity in Majalgaon Reservoir (Year 2011-12)

Species/Month	June	July	August	September	October	November	December	January	February	March	April	May
Protozoa												
Paramecium caudatum	15	00	05	15	18	05	14	08	15	08	20	05
Diffugia spp.	04	07	10	05	06	05	10	10	20	15	10	10
Opercularia spp.	05	05	00	04	08	10	10	12	22	05	03	05
Total	**24**	**12**	**15**	**24**	**32**	**20**	**34**	**30**	**57**	**28**	**33**	**20**
Rotifera												
Brachionus calyciflorus	05	05	02	00	12	22	14	12	25	30	25	00
Brachionus falcatus	05	10	00	07	00	14	20	00	15	20	20	20
Brachionus diversicornis	10	12	10	05	10	15	07	18	28	30	30	35
Keratella tropica	10	05	15	12	00	20	15	16	20	15	35	32
Keratella quadrata	08	08	05	15	05	05	10	10	05	20	30	25
Lecane (monostyla) bulla	15	00	05	10	00	05	04	05	35	28	18	15
Trichocera porcellus	05	05	15	05	12	10	10	10	05	15	04	10
Filina longiseta	09	10	08	20	05	10	15	18	15	25	20	25
Total	**67**	**55**	**60**	**74**	**44**	**101**	**95**	**89**	**148**	**183**	**182**	**162**
Cladocera												
Indialona ganapati	05	10	04	12	11	20	05	20	20	15	08	30
Moina micrura	10	15	10	00	11	00	15	11	35	15	15	17
Diaphanosoma sarsi	05	07	10	14	20	14	11	15	40	25	25	28
Diaphanosoma excisum	07	12	05	15	00	00	15	15	25	22	17	12
Alona rectangular	00	00	00	10	05	11	08	05	30	38	18	09
Ceriodaphnia cornuta	05	05	00	05	05	10	05	10	35	20	13	31
Total	**32**	**49**	**29**	**56**	**52**	**55**	**59**	**76**	**185**	**135**	**96**	**127**

(Contd...)

Species/Month	June	July	August	September	October	November	December	January	February	March	April	May
Copepoda												
Diaptomus marshianus	10	10	10	14	08	20	14	05	15	18	09	25
Phylladiaptomus lindbergi	05	00	00	10	16	12	20	00	27	10	22	29
Mescyclops leukarti	10	15	12	05	05	12	20	15	20	25	05	30
Mesocyclops hyalinus	07	08	15	00	05	14	05	06	32	26	35	19
Cyclops viridis	04	10	10	10	15	00	12	18	25	11	26	20
Total	**20**	**43**	**47**	**39**	**49**	**58**	**71**	**44**	**119**	**90**	**97**	**122**
Ostracoda												
Cypris obensa	00	05	05	05	02	10	10	14	20	22	15	19
Cyclocypris globosa	10	05	00	08	08	20	15	16	15	18	16	12
Candocypria osborni	00	02	00	05	05	05	10	05	00	05	05	10
Total	**10**	**12**	**05**	**18**	**15**	**35**	**35**	**35**	**35**	**45**	**36**	**41**

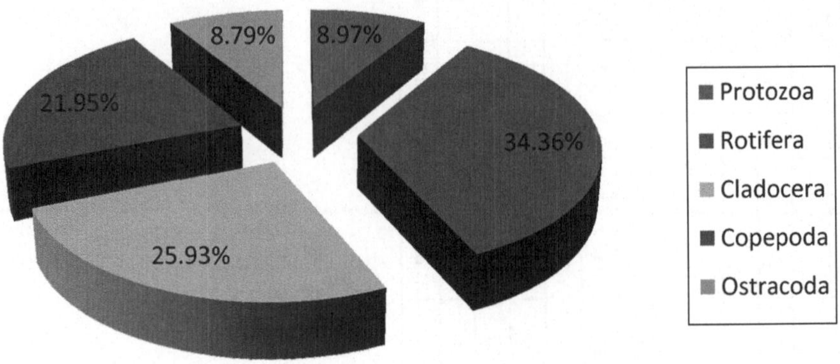

Fig. 4.4: **Quantitative Occurance of Zooplankton in Majalgaon Reservoir (Year 2011-12)**

Cladocera was represented by 6 species, with maximum density in summer and minimum in monsoon. Its density ranged from 32 org/l to 185 org/l with annual average of 79 org/l. *Indialona ganapati* and *Diaphanosoma sarsi* were present throughout the first year of investigation, while *Moina micrura* was absent in two months (September and November), *Diaphanosoma excisum* in two months (October and November), *Alona rectangular* in three months (June, July and August).

The group copepoda was represented by five species. Its density ranged from 36 org/L (June) to 122 org/l (May) with annual average of 67 org/l. *Phylladiaptomus lindbergi* was absent in July, August and January. *Mesocyclops hyalinus* in September and *Cyclops viridis* in November. Other species were observed round the first year of investigation.

The population density of ostracoda ranged from 5 org/l (August) to 45 org/l (March) with annual average of 27 org/l. *Candocypria osborni* was not seen in three months (June, August and February). *Cypris obensa* in one month (June) and *Cyclocypris globosa* in one month (August).

The seasonal variations of various zooplanktonic forms observed in second year of investigation is shown in Table 4.8. Five groups of zooplankton viz, Protozoa, Rotifera, Cladocera, Copepoda and Ostracoda constituted zooplankton population of the Majalgaon reservoir. The annual average percentage composition of different groups of zooplankton is presented in Fig. 4.5.

Among protozoans *Opercularia spp.* were absent in four months (June, July, August and October). *Paramecium caudatum* and *Diffugia sp* were absent in June and November respectively.The density of this group ranged from 05 org/l (June) to 40 org/L (May) with annual average of 19 organism/liter.

Table 4.8: Monthly Analysis of Zooplankton Diversity in Majalgaon Reservoir (Year 2012-13)

Species/Month	June	July	August	September	October	November	December	January	February	March	April	May
Protozoa												
Paramecium caudatum	00	05	05	04	05	05	05	07	05	10	12	15
Diffugia spp.	05	02	02	02	06	00	08	05	08	12	15	15
Opercularia spp.	00	00	00	02	00	05	04	08	10	15	10	10
Total	**05**	**07**	**07**	**08**	**11**	**10**	**17**	**20**	**23**	**37**	**37**	**40**
Rotifera												
Brachionus calyciflorus	10	11	14	05	10	14	14	17	20	13	11	18
Brachionus falcatus	10	05	00	10	09	10	12	10	16	20	20	24
Brachionus diversicornis	12	05	05	15	09	00	15	08	18	18	11	25
Keratella tropica	10	00	04	10	11	12	12	10	22	17	18	20
Keratella quadrata	10	04	00	05	12	10	14	15	11	25	27	19
Lecane (monostyla) bulla	00	05	00	15	14	05	10	15	16	17	22	30
Trichocera porcellus	00	05	10	10	12	17	10	10	18	28	15	20
Filina longiseta	05	05	15	00	12	10	11	15	20	20	25	20
Total	**57**	**40**	**48**	**70**	**89**	**78**	**98**	**100**	**141**	**158**	**149**	**166**
Cladocera												
Indialona ganapati	05	11	05	08	11	15	19	19	22	18	22	27
Moina micrura	05	10	12	06	04	15	10	14	18	20	24	30
Diaphanosoma sarsi	10	07	05	10	10	18	14	16	20	20	24	19
Diaphanosoma excisum	12	10	04	02	05	12	16	14	22	18	20	28
Alona rectangular	10	02	05	00	10	14	12	18	19	22	30	15
Ceriodaphnia cornuta	02	05	08	00	10	15	15	18	20	22	26	28
Total	**44**	**45**	**39**	**26**	**50**	**89**	**86**	**99**	**121**	**120**	**146**	**147**

(Contd…)

Species/Month	June	July	August	September	October	November	December	January	February	March	April	May
Copepoda												
Diaptomus marshianus	02	05	05	12	07	15	18	20	18	30	30	15
Phylladiaptomus lindbergi	05	10	05	12	03	10	20	22	17	19	22	20
Mescyclops leukarti	05	10	04	10	05	14	10	16	20	22	30	30
Mesocyclops hyalinus	10	08	10	04	10	10	15	24	28	30	28	32
Cyclops viridis	05	05	05	05	12	15	12	10	12	15	15	15
Total	**27**	**38**	**29**	**43**	**37**	**64**	**75**	**92**	**95**	**116**	**125**	**152**
Ostracoda												
Cypris obensa	05	05	03	02	10	10	07	05	05	12	07	12
Cyclocypris globosa	04	10	03	00	02	05	05	05	08	10	12	10
Candocypria osborni	00	00	00	00	00	00	00	00	00	00	00	00
Total	**09**	**15**	**06**	**02**	**12**	**15**	**22**	**10**	**13**	**22**	**19**	**22**

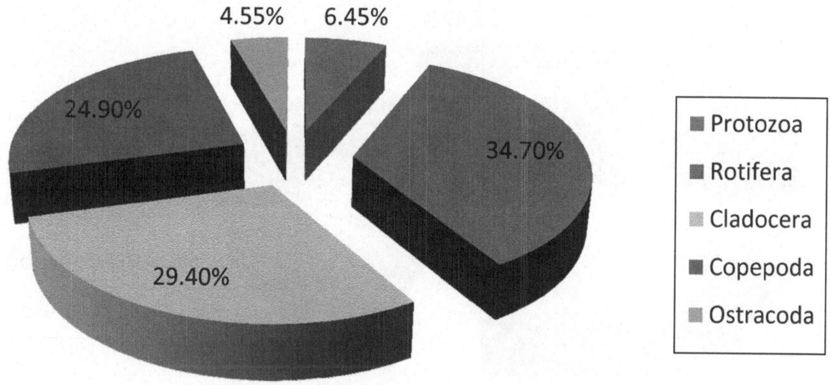

***Fig. 4.5:* Quantitative Occurance of Zooplankton in Majalgaon Reservoir (Year 2012-13)**

Rotifers showed superiority over other groups (34.70%) both in terms of number of species and population density. They were found in maximum numbers in summer and minimum in numbers in monsoon season.

Cladocerans ranked second in the order of dominance (29.40%). They constituted the peak in summer. The average annual density was estimated at 84 organisms/liter. *Alona rectangular* and *Ceriodaphnia cornuta* were absent in September. Other 4 species were present round the second year of investigation.

Copepods ranked third in the order of dominance (24.90%) among the zooplanktonic fauna (Fig. 4.5). the density of copepods ranged from 27org/liter (June) to 152 (May) org/liter with annual average of 71 org/liter.

During second year of investigation, among ostracods, *Candocypria osborni* was totally absent. *Cyclocypris globosa* was not recorded in September, while *Cypris obensa* was present throughout the second year of investigation. The density of this group ranged from 02 org/liter (September) to 22 org/liter (December, March and May) with an annual average of 13 org/liter. Ostracods contributed to about 4.55% of the total zooplankton (Fig. 4.5).

In third year of investigation, zooplankton diversity of Majalgaon reservoir consisted of 7.42% of Protozoa, 38.10% of Rotifer, 28.77% of Cladocera, 17.58% of Copepoda and 8.13% of Ostracoda (Fig. 4.6).

Among protozoans *Paramecium caudatum* was seen in all seasons, while *Diffugia spp* were absent in August and *Opercularia spp* in June and July. Annual average of this group was 23 org/liter with minimum density of 7 org/liter in July and maximum density of 47org/liter in May (Table 4.9).

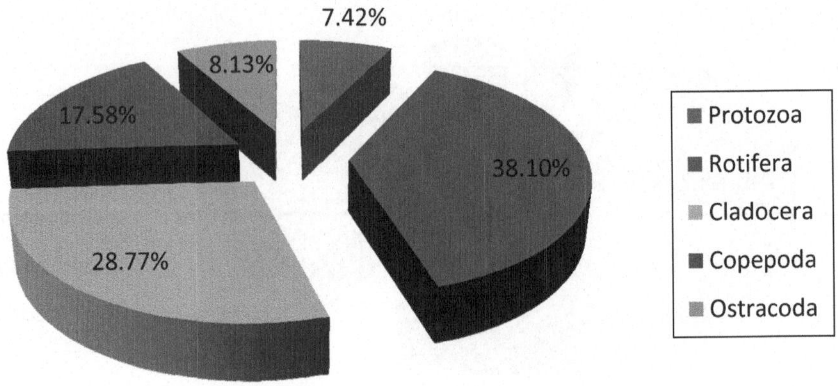

Fig. 4.6: **Quantitative occurance of zooplankton in Majalgaon Reservoir (Year 2013-14)**

Rotifers were represented by eight species, out of which *Brachionus calyciflorus, B. diversicornis, Keratella tropica, K. quadrata, Trichocera porcellus* and *Filinia longiseta* were observed round the year. *B. falcatus* and *Lecane (Monostyla) bulla* were not observed in August and June respectively. The density of rotifers ranged from 49 org/liter to 209 org/liter with annual average of 120 org/liter. This group dominated over the other zooplanktonic groups (38.10%).

Among cladocera, *Moina micrura, Alona rectangular* and *Ceriodaphnia cornuta* were present in all months. *Indialana ganapati* was not seen in July, *Diaphanosoma sarsi* in June and July and *D. excisum* in June. The density of this group ranged from 27org/liter (June) to 151 org/liter (March) with an average of 91 org/liter (Table 4.9).

Copepods were represented by five species, out of which *Diaptomus marshianus* and *Cyclops viridis* were recorded throughout the third year of investigation, while *Phylladiaptomus lindbergi* was absent in one month (July), *Mesocyclops leukarti* n three months of rainy season (June, August and September), and *Mesocyclops hyalinus* in one month (July). The average density of the group was 56 org/liter.

Ostracods were represented by three species with average density of 2 org/liter. *Cypris obensa* was not seen in two months of rainy season (June and August) and *Cyclocypris globosa* in August. *Candocypria osborni* was found in all the months. The density of ostracods ranged from 7 org/liter (June) to 42 org/liter (March).

The seasonal trends in total zooplankton density was reported as summer>winter>monsoon.

Table 4.9: Monthly Analysis of Zooplankton Diversity in Majalgaon Reservoir (Year 2013-14)

Species/Month	June	July	August	September	October	November	December	January	February	March	April	May
Protozoa												
Paramecium caudatum	06	05	13	02	04	06	10	13	13	15	15	20
Diffugia spp.	05	02	00	05	05	08	05	08	10	12	10	15
Opercularia spp.	00	00	02	02	05	10	08	05	05	15	10	12
Total	**11**	**07**	**15**	**09**	**14**	**24**	**23**	**26**	**28**	**42**	**35**	**47**
Rotifera												
Brachionus calyciflorus	10	15	14	13	10	14	15	22	19	16	20	30
Brachionus falcatus	12	12	00	05	10	10	12	16	24	32	27	25
Brachionus diversicornis	08	05	15	05	10	15	12	16	20	21	22	35
Keratella tropica	05	05	07	18	10	11	18	24	25	28	20	30
Keratella quadrata	10	05	10	05	12	14	15	20	30	24	26	22
Lecane (monostyla) bulla	00	05	05	17	04	18	11	16	17	18	20	22
Trichocera porcellus	02	02	02	05	08	15	20	18	25	22	27	30
Filina longiseta	02	05	02	05	10	12	12	20	25	24	22	25
Total	**49**	**54**	**55**	**73**	**74**	**109**	**115**	**152**	**185**	**185**	**184**	**209**
Cladocera												
Indialona ganapati	10	00	05	05	15	18	14	20	20	20	18	30
Moina micrura	10	02	05	10	12	22	15	18	24	24	22	22
Diaphanosoma sarsi	00	00	04	02	10	15	20	20	20	28	27	25
Diaphanosoma excisum	00	02	08	04	14	20	16	22	30	35	30	19
Alona rectangular	02	15	05	05	12	16	18	28	18	24	24	20
Ceriodaphnia cornuta	05	10	02	05	16	18	15	15	20	20	20	25
Total	**27**	**29**	**29**	**31**	**79**	**109**	**98**	**123**	**132**	**151**	**141**	**141**

(Contd...)

Species/Month	June	July	August	September	October	November	December	January	February	March	April	May
Copepoda												
Diaptomus marshianus	02	05	02	02	05	05	10	12	18	20	18	30
Phylladiaptomus lindbergi	04	00	05	05	05	10	08	12	15	22	15	24
Mescyclops leukarti	00	05	00	00	08	15	10	10	20	18	30	32
Mesocyclops hyalinus	02	00	10	05	10	05	08	10	25	08	15	20
Cyclops viridis	05	04	05	05	12	12	05	10	20	28	20	20
Total	**13**	**14**	**22**	**17**	**40**	**47**	**41**	**54**	**98**	**96**	**98**	**126**
Ostracoda												
Cypris obensa	00	10	00	04	05	08	10	12	12	14	14	10
Cyclocypris globosa	05	08	00	04	08	05	08	08	18	16	15	15
Candocypria osborni	02	05	05	10	05	08	10	10	10	12	12	10
Total	**07**	**23**	**05**	**18**	**18**	**21**	**28**	**40**	**40**	**42**	**41**	**35**

Phytoplankton diversity: The study of the phytoplankton sampled in Majalgaon reservoir showed 17 species (Table 4.10, 4.11 and 4.12). The phytoplankton assemblage was represented by three classes viz. Bacillariophyceae, Cyanophyceae Chlorophyceae and Euglenophyceae.

The class Bacillariophyceae was was reported by 5 species. The class was represented by species such as *Navicula gracilis, Navicula viridula, Nitzschia subtilis, Bacillaria paradoxa* and *Synedra affinis*

The class Cyanophyceae was represented by 4 species. It was represented by *Oscillatoria limnosa, Anabaena constricta, Microcystis aerugenose* and *Merismopedia punctata.*

The class Chlorophyceae was represented by 6 genera i.e; *Zygnema sp., Pediastrum duplex, Pediastrum simplex, Scendesmus armatus, Ankistrodesmus falcatus* and *Chlorella vulgaris.*

The class Euglenophyceae was represented by two species i.e., *Euglena stellata* and *Euglena pisciformis.*

During first year of study (2011-2012), the phytoplankton consisted of 28.12% of Bacillariophyceae, 25.62% of Cyanophyceae, 35.18% of Chlorophyceae and 11.08% of Eugelnophyceae (Fig. 4.7).Mishra *et al.*(2010) also reported chlorophyceae as the dominant grouop from Dhaura and Baigul reservoirs of Uttarakhand.It was revealed that the class Chlorophyceae was dominant with annual average of 105.83 units/liter, followed by Bacillariophyceae (84.58 units/liter), Cyanophyceae (77.08 units/liter) and Euglenophyceae (33.33 units/liter).

In case of Bacillariophyceae, *Navicula viridula* and *Bacillaria paradoxa* were the dominant species which were recorded throughout the year. Their number was high in summer season. *Navicula gracilis* and *Nitzschia subtilis* were seen during ten months with peak in summer. *Synedra affinis* was absent in one month i.e., July 2011.

Among blue-green algae, *Oscillatoria limnosa, Anabaena constricta, Merismopedia punctata* and *Microcystis aerugenose* were recorded. *Anabaena constricta* and *Microcystis aerugenose* were observed throughout the first year of investigation with maximum and minimum density in summer and monsoon season respectively. The variation in the population density of blue-green algae ranged from 25 to 120 units/liter and contributed to 25.62% of the total phytoplankton population. *Merismopedia punctata* was recorded in ten months only. It was absent in two months of monsoon season (Table 4.10). *Oscillatoria limnosa* was absent in June. The density of *Oscillatoria limnosa* ranged from nil to 30 units/liter. *Anabaena constricta* 5 to 30 units/liter, *Merismopedia punctata* nil to 30 units/liter and *Microcystis aerugenose* 5 to 35 units/liter.

Table 4.10: Monthly Analysis of Phytoplankton Diversity in Majalgaon Reservoir (Year 2011-12)

Species/Month	June	July	August	September	October	November	December	January	February	March	April	May
Chlorophyceae												
Zygnema sp	15	15	20	25	20	25	20	20	25	25	20	25
Pediastrum duplex	05	10	10	15	20	20	15	15	20	20	25	30
Pediastrum simplex	10	05	00	15	20	25	25	25	30	35	30	30
Scendesmus armatus	05	05	10	15	15	25	20	25	25	25	35	25
Ankistrodesmus falcatus	10	05	10	00	15	15	20	20	20	25	25	25
Chlorella vulgaris	00	00	10	10	05	10	10	15	15	25	20	20
Total	**45**	**40**	**60**	**80**	**95**	**120**	**110**	**120**	**135**	**155**	**155**	**155**
Cyanophyceae												
Oscillatoria limnosoa	00	15	20	20	25	20	25	25	30	25	30	30
Anabaena constricta	10	05	15	15	10	15	20	15	25	30	25	20
Merismopedia punctata	10	00	15	00	20	20	20	25	20	25	30	25
Microcystis aerugenose	05	15	20	15	15	20	25	20	25	25	35	25
Total	**25**	**35**	**70**	**50**	**70**	**75**	**90**	**85**	**100**	**105**	**120**	**100**
Bacillariophyceae												
Navicula gracilis	00	00	10	10	10	05	15	15	25	25	20	20
Navicula viridula	05	10	15	10	15	20	20	25	25	35	30	35
Nitzschia subtilis	10	05	00	00	15	15	15	20	25	30	35	30
Bacillaria paradoxa	15	10	10	05	10	15	20	10	20	25	20	25
Synedra affinis	15	00	15	10	15	15	25	20	25	30	25	35
Total	**45**	**25**	**50**	**35**	**65**	**70**	**95**	**90**	**120**	**145**	**130**	**145**
Euglenophyceae												
Euglena stellata	00	00	05	10	15	15	10	20	20	20	25	25
Euglena pisciformis	05	15	10	10	20	20	25	20	25	30	30	25
Total	**05**	**15**	**15**	**20**	**35**	**35**	**35**	**40**	**45**	**50**	**55**	**50**

Table 4.11: Monthly Analysis of Phytoplankton Diversity in Majalgaon Reservoir (Year 2012-13)

Species/Month	June	July	August	September	October	November	December	January	February	March	April	May
Chlorophyceae												
Zygnema sp	10	15	15	10	15	15	20	15	25	30	30	20
Pediastrum duplex	15	15	15	05	15	20	20	20	20	25	25	25
Pediastrum simplex	10	15	15	10	15	15	10	20	25	25	30	30
Scendesmus armatus	05	10	05	00	05	10	10	15	15	20	15	15
Ankistrodesmus falcatus	05	10	00	10	00	15	15	25	25	25	25	30
Chlorella vulgaris	10	05	10	00	10	15	15	20	20	30	30	25
Closterium limneticum	05	10	10	15	15	25	25	30	30	45	40	40
Total	**60**	**80**	**70**	**50**	**75**	**115**	**115**	**145**	**160**	**200**	**195**	**185**
Cyanophyceae												
Oscillatoria limnosoa	00	10	15	05	15	15	25	25	30	35	35	35
Anabaena constricta	05	05	00	15	15	20	20	25	35	40	35	45
Merismopedia punctata	10	15	15	00	15	20	30	35	35	40	35	35
Microcystis aerugenose	15	15	20	15	20	25	25	30	30	35	40	45
Total	**30**	**45**	**50**	**35**	**65**	**80**	**100**	**115**	**130**	**150**	**145**	**160**
Bacillariophyceae												
Navicula gracilis	10	10	10	05	10	20	25	25	35	35	40	40
Navicula viridula	00	15	15	10	15	25	20	25	30	40	45	35
Nitzschia subtilis	10	10	05	00	10	15	25	20	25	30	25	30
Bacillaria paradoxa	10	15	05	15	20	25	30	30	30	25	35	30
Synedra affinis	15	15	10	05	20	20	20	25	35	35	35	25
Total	**45**	**65**	**45**	**35**	**75**	**105**	**120**	**125**	**155**	**165**	**180**	**160**
Euglenophyceae												
Euglena stellata	15	15	10	10	15	15	25	25	35	40	35	40
Euglena pisciformis	20	20	25	25	30	30	30	25	35	40	35	30
Total	**35**	**35**	**35**	**35**	**45**	**45**	**55**	**50**	**70**	**80**	**70**	**70**

Table 4.12: Monthly Analysis of Phytoplankton Diversity in Majalgaon Reservoir (Year 2013-14)

Species/Month	June	July	August	September	October	November	December	January	February	March	April	May
Chlorophyceae												
Zygnema sp	15	15	10	05	10	20	20	25	25	40	45	35
Pediastrum duplex	10	10	15	10	15	15	25	35	30	45	40	40
Pediastrum simplex	10	10	15	15	20	25	25	25	30	35	40	45
Scendesmus armatus	15	10	15	00	15	30	30	35	45	35	40	45
Ankistrodesmus falcatus	00	15	15	15	15	25	30	25	40	35	40	40
Chlorella vulgaris	15	15	20	10	20	30	30	40	50	55	40	45
Total	**65**	**75**	**90**	**55**	**95**	**145**	**160**	**185**	**220**	**245**	**245**	**250**
Cyanophyceae												
Oscillatoria limnosoa	20	20	25	30	30	35	35	45	40	45	45	40
Anabaena constricta	10	15	10	25	25	35	35	40	40	45	45	40
Merismopedia punctata	20	15	20	25	05	25	25	25	35	30	25	45
Microcystis aerugenose	20	25	15	15	20	20	20	25	30	25	25	20
Total	**70**	**75**	**70**	**95**	**80**	**115**	**115**	**135**	**145**	**145**	**140**	**145**
Bacillariophyceae												
Navicula gracilis	10	15	15	00	00	20	25	40	45	40	35	35
Navicula viridula	20	15	20	15	05	20	30	35	40	45	45	40
Nitzschia subtilis	20	25	20	10	25	25	25	25	35	30	35	40
Bacillaria paradoxa	15	20	20	00	25	30	30	25	35	45	45	40
Synedra affinis	05	15	20	15	15	20	25	30	30	35	35	35
Total	**70**	**90**	**95**	**40**	**70**	**115**	**135**	**155**	**185**	**195**	**195**	**190**
Euglenophyceae												
Euglena stellata	10	10	10	10	05	20	30	30	55	50	45	45
Euglena pisciformis	15	15	10	05	15	30	35	35	45	50	40	40
Total	**25**	**25**	**20**	**15**	**20**	**50**	**65**	**65**	**100**	**100**	**85**	**85**

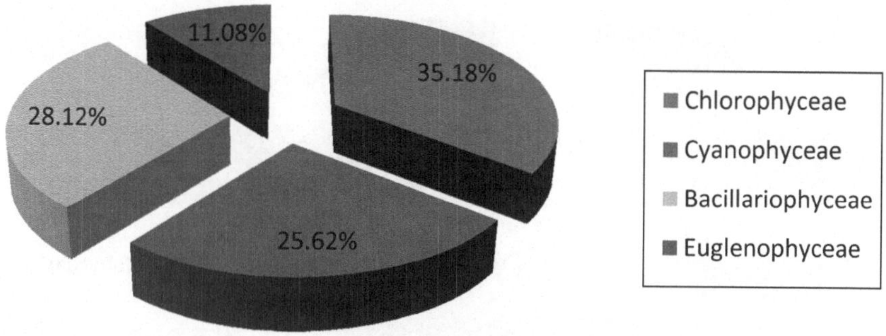

Fig.4.7: **Quantitative Occurance of Phytoplankton in Majalgaon Reservoir (Year 2011-12)**

The green algae were represented by *Zygnema sp, Pedistrum duplex, Pediastrum simplex, Scendesmus armatus, Ankistrodesmus falcatus* and *Chlorella vulgaris.*The population density of green algae was between 40 to 155 units/ liter and contributed to 35.18 % of the phytoplankton (Fig. 4.7). It was recorded maximum in summer and minimum in monsoon. Among the green algae, *Zygnema sp, Pediastrum duplex* and *Scendesmus armatus* were observed throughout the study period, while *Pediastrum simplex* and *Ankistrodesmus falcatus* were recorded in eleven months and *Chlorella vulgaris* in ten months (Table 4.10). Higher population density of *Zygnema sp* was recorded in summer and minimum in monsoon season. The population density of this species varied from 15 to 25 units/liter. Similarly, population density of *Pediastrum duplex* and *Pediastrum simplex* was in the range of 5 to 30 units/liter and nil to 35. units/liter respectively. The population density of *Scendesmus armatus, Ankistrodesmus falcatus* and *Chlorella vulgaris* varied from 5 to 35 units/liter, nil to 25 units/liter and nil to 25 units/liter respectively.

In case of Euglenophyceae, *Euglena pisciformis* was dominant. It was recorded throughout the year. Its number was high in the month of March and April (30 units/liter). *Euglena stellata* was seen during ten months with peak in summer. It was absent in two months i.e., June and July.

During second year (2012-2013) of investigation, a total number of 18 species (5 species of Bacillariophyceae, 4 species of Cyanophyceae, 2 species of Euglenophyceae and 7 species of Chlorophyceae) of phytoplanktons were recorded in Majalgaon reservoir. The phytoplankton consisted of 28.62% of Bacillariophyceae, 24.80% of Cyanophyceae, 32.55% of Chlorophyceae and 14.03% of Euglenophyceae (Fig. 4.8).The class Chlorophyceae was dominant with annual average of 121 units/liter, followed by Bacillariophyceae (106 units/liter), Cyanophyceae (92 units/liter) and Euglenophyceae (52 units/ liter).

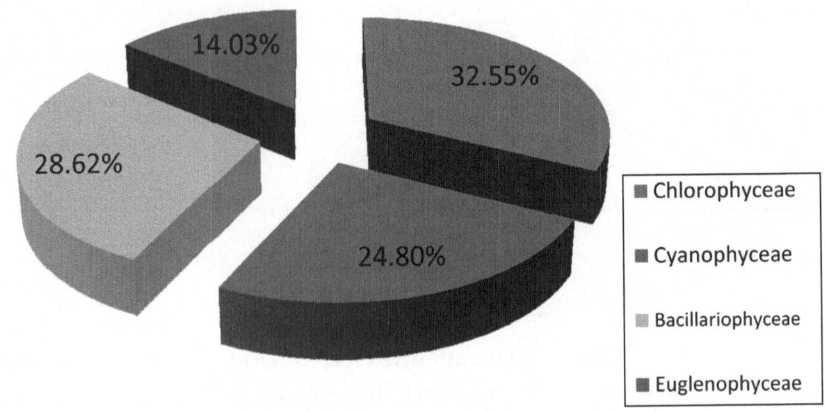

Fig.4.8: **Quantitative Occurance of Phytoplankton in Majalgaon Reservoir (2012-13)**

In case of diatoms, *Navicula gracilis, Bacillaria paradoxa* and *Synedra affinis* were recorded throughout the second year of investigation (Table 4.11). *Navicula viridula* and *Nitzschia subtilis* were recorded in eleven months. These species showed their absence in one month.The density of diatoms ranged from 35 units/liter to 180 units/liter. It was maximum in month of April and minimum in September. On an average, diatoms contributed 28.62% of the total phytoplanktonic population (Fig. 4.8).

The blue green algae were represented by four species. *Microcystis aerugenose* was observed throughout the year.*Oscillatoria limnosoa, Anabaena constricta* and *Merismopedia punctata* appeared only in eleven months. The variation in the population density of blue green algae ranged from 30 to 160 units/liter and contributed to about 24.80% of the total phytoplankton population. The density of *Oscillatoria limnosoa* ranged from nil to 35 units/liter, *Anabaena constricta* from nil to 45 units/liter, *Merismopedia punctata* from nil to 40 units/liter and *Microcystis aerugenose* from 15 to 45 units/liter (Table 4.11).

The green algae were represented by seven species. Maximum green algae were recorded in summer and minimum number in rainy season. The percentage contribution of green algae was 32.55% of the total phytoplankton population. The population density of green algae ranged from 50 to 200 units/liter. *Zygnema sp, Pediastrum duplex, Pediastrum simplex* and *Closterium limneticum* were recorded throughout the study period. Their number was high in summer and minimum in rainy season.*Scendesmus armatus* and *Chlorella vulgaris* were absent in September and *Ankistrodesmus falcatus* was absent in two months i.e., August and October (Table 4.11).

In case of Euglenophyceae, both species (*Euglena stellata* and *Euglena pisciformis*) were recorded throughout the second year of investigation. Their number was high in summer and minimum in rainy season.

During third year of study (2013-2014), the phytoplankton consisted of 28.69% of Bacillariophyceae, 24.86% of Cyanophyceae, 34.21% of Chlorophyceae and 12.24% Eugelnophyceae (Fig. 4.9). It was revealed that the class Chlorophyceae was dominant with annual average of 152 units/liter, followed by Bacillariophyceae (128 units/liter), Cyanophyceae (111 units/liter) and Euglenophyceae (55 units/liter).

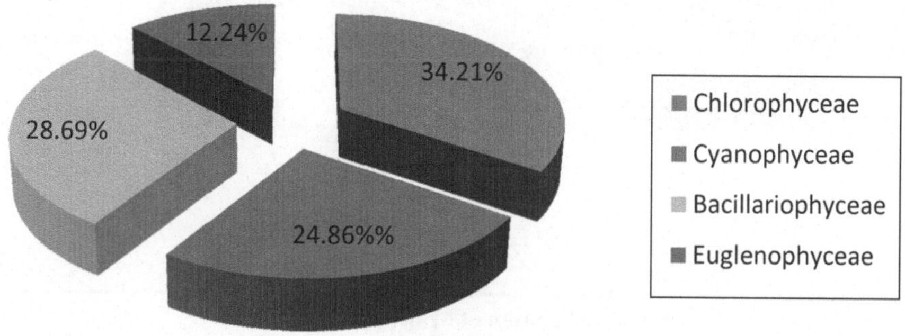

Fig.4.9: **Quantitative Occurance of Phytoplankton in Majalgaon Reservoir (2013-14)**

Sluice Gates of Majalgaon Reservoir

Active Fishermen of Majalgaon Reservoir

In case of Bacillariophyceae, *Navicula viridula, Nitzschia subtilis* and *Synedra affinis* were recorded throughout the year. Their number was high in summer and low in rainy season. *Navicula gracilis* was seen during ten months with peak in February.*Bacillaria paradoxa* was seen in eleven months and absent in September (Table 4.12).

Among blue-green algae, *Oscillatoria limnosa, Anabaena constricta, Merismopedia punctata* and *Microcystis aerugenose* were recorded. All (seven) species were observed throughout the third year of investigation with maximum and minimum density in summer and monsoon season respectively. The variation in the population density of blue-green algae ranged from 70 to 145 units/liter and contributed to 24.86% of the total phytoplankton population (Fig. 4.9). The density of *Oscillatoria limnosoa* ranged from 20 to 45 units/liter, *Anabaena constricta* from 10 to 45 units/liter, *Merismopedia punctata* from 5 to 45 units/liter and *Microcystis aerugenose* from 15 to 30 units/ liter (Table 4.12).

The green algae were represented by *Zygnema sp, Pediastrum duplex, Pediastrum simplex, Scendesmus armatus, Aknistrodesmus falcatus* and *Chlorella vulgaris.*The population density of green algae was between 55 to 250 units/ liter and contributed to 34.21% of the phytoplankton (Fig. 4.9). It was recorded maximum (250 units/liter) in May and minimum (55 units/liter) in September.Among the green algae, *Zygnema sp, Pediastrum duplex, Pediastrum simplex* and *Chlorella vulgaris* were observed throughout the study period, while *Scendesmus armatus* and *Ankistrodesmus falcatus* were present in eleven months (Table 4.12). Higher population density of *Zygnema sp* was recorded in April (45 units/Liter) and minimum in September (5 units/Liter). The population density of *Pediastrum duplex* varied from 10 to 45 units/liter. Similarly, population density of *Pediastrum simplex* and *Scendesmus armatus* was in the range of 10 to 45 units/liter and nil to 45 units/liter respectively. The population density of *Ankistrodesmus falcatus* varied from nil to 40 units/liter and *Chlorella vulgaris* from 10 to 55 units/Liter.

Euglenophyceae was represented by two species i.e., *Euglena stellata* and *Euglena pisciformis*.Both the species were recorded throughout the year.Density of group varied from 15 units/Liter (September) to 100 units/Liter (February and March). *Euglena stellata* was recorded maximum (55 units/Liter) in February and minimum (5 units/Liter) in October.Similarly *Euglena pisciformis* showed minima (5 units/Liter) in September and maxima (50 units/Liter) in March (Table 4.12).

CHAPTER - 5

Wan Reservoir

The Wan reservoir (Fig. 5.1) is a medium sized reservoir near Parli (Vaijyanath) city in Marathwada region. The reservoir was constructed in year 1963 across the river Wan. The reservoir is bounded by latitude 18°53'N and Longitude 76°27'. It is the oldest reservoir in district with water spread area of 347 ha.The reservoir has an opportunity to irrigate 7567 ha of agricultural land. Besides supply of water for irrigation, the reservoir also supplies drinking water to Parli Vaijnath town and Vaijnath Co-operative Sugar Factory. The area around reservoir comprises forest-covered hills.The reservoir has two small canals through which water supply goes to agricultural lands of the villages like Nagapur, Pangri, Deshmukhtakli, Talegaon, Limbota, Kowthali,Sangam, Gopalpur, Mandekhel, Bhilegaon, Tandoli, Selu, Parchondi, Sirsala, Kanadi and Pimpalgaon. The salient features of the reservoir are depicted in Table 5.1.

Fish fauna: In the present study 26 fish species have been identified (Table 5.2). They include carps, feather backs, catfishes and other. Out of 26 species *Labeo rohita, Channa spp., Cyprinus carpio and Oreochromis mossambicus* were noted to be predominant and occurred throught the year. The fishery of *Catla catla* was badly affected by the accidental entry of *O. mossambicus.* The exotics such as *Cyprinus carpio* and *O. mossambicus* together contribute to about 14.79% of the total fish catch.

The details of the fish production in Wan reservoir are depicted in Table 5.3. The study of the data revealed that the maximum fish production was recorded at 82.88 kg/ha/yr in year 2013-14. The minimum fish production was during 2012-13 at 66.92 kg/ha/yr. During the present investigation the catch of local fishes showed the higher catches than those of carps (Table 5.3).

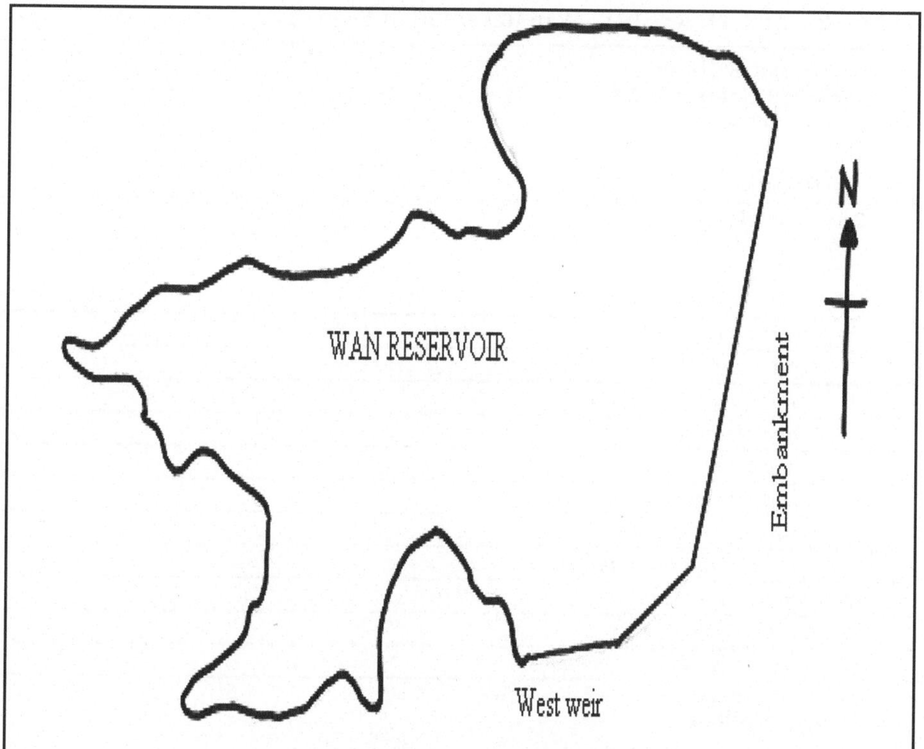

Fig.5.1: **Map of Wan Reservoir**

Table 5.1: Salient Features of Wan Reservoir, Maharashtra

River	Wan
Year of construction	1963
Nearest city	Parli (Vaijyanath)
Water spread area (ha)	347
Height of dam (m)	19.81
Length of dam (m)	2188
Gross storage capacity (mcm)	25.181
Catchment area (km^2)	379.92
Full tank level	454.87
High flood level (m)	456.40
Irrigation potential (ha)	7567
Length of canal • Right canal (m) • Left canal (m)	 12.03 9.65
Rainfall at catchment area (mm)	535

Table 5.2: Fish Diversity in Wan Reservoir of Beed district

Order: Clupeiformes **Suborder: Notopteroidei** **Family: Notopteridae** 1. *Notopterus notopterus (Pallas)*
2. *Notopterus chitala (Ham.)*
Order: Cypriniformes **Suborder: Cyprinoidei** **Family: Cyprinidae** 3. *Chela phulo (Ham.)*
4. *Catla catla (Ham.)*
5. *Labeo rohita (Ham.)*
6. *Labeo fimbriatus (Bloch)*
7. *Cirrhinus mrigala (Ham.)*
8. *Cyprinus carpio (Linn)*
9. *Amblypharyngodon mola (Ham.)*
10. *Osteobrama cotio (Ham.)*
11. *Puntius sarana sarana (Ham.)*
12. *Puntius ticto ticto (Ham.)*
13. *Puntius chola (Ham.)*
14. *Rasbora daniconius (Ham.)*
Order: Siluriformes **Family: Bagridae** 15. *Mystus cavasius (Ham.)*
16. *Mystus seenghala (Sykes)*
17. *Mystus vittatus (Bloch)*
Family: Claridae 18. *Clarias batrachus (Linn.)*
Family: Siluridae 19. *Wallago attu (Bloch and Schneider)*
Order: Mugiliformes **Family: Mugilidae** 20. *Mugil cephalus (Linn.)*
Order: Channiformes **Family: Channidae** 21. *Channa striatus (Bloch)*
22. *Channa marulius (Ham.)*
Order: Perciformes **Family: Anabantidae** 23. *Anabas testudineus (Bloch)*
Family: Cichlidae 24. *Oreochromis mossambicus (Peters)*
Family: Gobiidae 25. *Glassogobius giuris (Ham.)*
Family: Ambassidae 26. *Chanda ranga (Ham.)*

Table 5.3: Year wise Fish Catch in Wan Reservoir (kg)

Year	Indian Major Carps	Common Carp	Tilapia	Local Fishes	Total	Fish Yield (kg/ha/yr)
2011-12	7895	3250	3355	13340	27840	80.23
%	28.36%	11.67%	12.05%	47.92%		
2012-13	4600	3027	4815	10780	23222	66.92
%	19.80%	13.04%	20.74%	46.42%		
2013-14	8400	5200	3780	11380	28760	82.88
%	29.21%	18.08%	13.14%	39.57%		

During first year of investigation (2011-12), Indian major carps, common carp, tilapia and local fishes contributed to 28.36%, 11.67%, 12.05% and 47.92% of the total catch respectively.

During second year of investigation (2012-13), local fishes formed 46.42% of the total catch, while Indian major carps, common carp and tilapia contributed to about 19.80%, 13.04% and 20.74% of the total fish catch. Exotic species (common carp and tilapia) togetherly contributed to about 33.78% of the total fish catch.

During third year (2013-14) of the investigation, local fishes dominated over the carps and contributed to about 39.57% of the total catch. Indian major carps, common carp and tilapia contributed to 29.21%, 18.08% and 13.14% of the total catch. The contribution from two exotics (common carp and tilapia) was more than 31% of the total catch.

In Wan reservoir tilapia (*Oreochromis mossambicus*) affected the phenomenal growth of *Catla catla.* The growth of *Catla catla* never exceeded 850 gms after entry of tilapia. From the interview with fishermen it is learned that tilapia accidentally entered in reservoir in last five years. It may be due to other predatory fishes present in the reservoir, tilapia population could not proliferate much. Tilapia is a non-predatory fish, comes to maturity early and starts breeding, almost continuously, from the age of three months. The new recruits also multiply, compete for food and space, not only among themselves, but also with fish fauna present in the water body, which results in an over population of small sized fishes of very low/no market value. Hence, many regard tilapias as a pest and it affect adversely indigenous fish population, mainly *Catla catla.* Though this fish became a favorite of fish culturists through the world it has certain undesirable traits such as early maturity, prolific breeding and stunted growth. Being a prolific breeder, it over-populates, and very small sized tilapia are obtained due to its precocious breeding. It is therefore difficult to culture all the progeny to a marketable size and hence there is market decline, in its culture operations and is now braded as a 'trash fish'. It is not suitable for stocking with carps as it is competed with carps for space, food and oxygen besides predating on the carp fry. The accidental entry of tilapia in wan reservoir posed a great challenge for its effective control.

Physico-chemical Environment: The year wise seasonal averages of various physico-chemical parameters are presented in Table 5.4. The surface temperature values ranged from 20 °C to 28 °C during 2011-12,23 to 29 °C during 2012-13 and 19 to 30 °C during 2013-14. The overall mean recorded as 24.77. The surface temperature vales were maximum during summer and minimum in winter season.

Transparency was found to be 30 to 40 cms during 2011-12, 15 to 35 cm during 2012-13 and 34 to 43 cm during 2013-14. The overall mean transparency was 33.44. The minimum transparency values found during rainy months and maximum in summer months. The rainwater brought in a lot of dissolved and undissolved inorganic and organic materials that made water turbid and caused low transparency in rainy months. These observations are in agreement with the findings of Timms and Midgley (1970) and Sawant *et al* (2011).

pH is considered as an important ecological factor and is of the result of the interaction of various substances in solution in water and is also of numerous biological phenomenos. During present investigation, the pH values ranged from 8.2 to 8.5 during 2011-12, 8.1 to 8.5 during 2012-13 and 8.3 to 8.6 during 2013-14. The overall mean of pH of the reservoir water was 8.36. During present investigation minimum pH was recorded in summer and maximum in monsoon months.

pH is indicative of hydrogen ion concentration and it express the intensity of acidity or alkalinity of water. Any change in pH of water is accompanied by changes in other physic-chemical aspects of the medium. The functional stability of aquatic ecosystem depends upon the buffering capacity of water. This was reflected in the range of fluctuation of the hydrogen ion concentration brought about by the operational dynamics of carbon dioxide, bicarbonates and carbonates. Most of the freshwater bodies are alkaline due to the above components.

Optimum growth and survival of aquatic plants and animals require that their environment pH should be confined with a very short range below or above which they will be subjected to various kinds of stresses, and the diurnal fluctuation of pH of water body should remain in the range of 6.4 to 8.5 in order to support the optimum growth of fish (Das, 1996). The average pH value (8.36) of Wan reservoir is suitable for optimum fish growth.

Rajasekhar *et al.* (2012) recorded the range of pH between 7.9 to 8.5 in Nizamsagar reservoir of Andhra Pradesh. High pH values were recorded in pre-monsoon season and low values in monsoon.

Table 5.4: Seasonal Fluctuation in Water Quality Parameters of Wan Reservoir

Season/Year	Water Temp. (°C)	Transpar-encey (cm)	pH	TDS (mg/l)	DO (mg/l)	CO_2 (mg/)	TA (mg/l)	Cl^- (mg/l)	TH (mg/l)
2011-12									
Monsoon	23	30	8.5	142	7.9	0.7	112.2	35.18	48
Winter	20	35	8.3	190.2	8.7	1.6	132.4	30.2	48.5
Summer	28	40	8.2	257	8.5	4.1	220	59.2	93.2
Mean	23.66	35	8.3	196.4	8.36	2.13	154.8	41.52	63.23
2012-13									
Monsoon	29	15	8.5	167.2	6.2	0.7	128	24.7	114
Winter	23	30	8.4	200.4	8.3	3.8	170	14.3	138
Summer	26	35	8.1	244.7	8.0	10.7	188.4	55.2	168
Mean	26	26.66	8.3	204.1	7.5	5.06	162.1	31.4	140
2013-14									
Monsoon	25	34	8.6	160.2	3.7	0.9	160	37.8	123
Winter	19	39	8.4	210.6	9.4	4.1	174.2	25.80	157
Summer	30	43	8.3	280.4	7.8	12	190.3	48.4	180
Mean	24.66	38.66	8.4	217	6.96	5.66	174.8	37.33	153.33
Grand Mean	24.77	33.44	8.3	205.8	7.6	4.28	163.9	36.75	118.85

Results of present study reveals that the total dissolved solids were found to be in the range of 142 to 257 mg/l in first year (2011-12), 167.2 to 244.7 mg/l in second year (2012-13) and 160.2 to 280.4 mg/l in third year (2013-14) with grand mean of 205.85.

During present study the total dissolved solids were high in summer followed by winter and monsoon. Devi (1997) also reported the maximum total dissolved solids during pre-monsoon season and lowest during monsoon in Shathamraj and Ibrahimbagh reservoirs of Andhra Pradesh. Tripathi and Pandey (1990) reported the seasonal fluctuations in total dissolved solids from two ponds of Uttar Pradesh where the maximum concentration of total dissolved solids was recorded during summer which decreased during rainy season due to dilution of pond water. A similar observation was also made by Sakhare (2007).

In the present study, the dissolved oxygen value ranged between 3.7 to 8.7 mg/l with mean of 7.60. Dissolved oxygen is one of the important parameters in water quality assessment and reflects the physical and biological processes prevailing in waters. Dissolved oxygen was found to be high in winter season when the water temperature was low. Thus, it has an inverse relationship did not affect the dissolved oxygen much. However, Sreenivasan (1974) reported that the water temperature did not affect the dissolved oxygen much. Relatively higher values of dissolved oxygen might be due to increased solubility of oxygen at low temperature (Chatterjee and Raziuddin, 2002). It was found that there exists an inverse relation between dissolved oxygen and temperature. In summer with the increase in water temperature there was reduction in dissolved oxygen, whereas in winter months due to decrease in temperature, the level of dissolved oxygen increased. These results are in conformity with Srivastava *et al.* (2003) and Solanki *et al.* (2007).

The alkalinity in water is usually interpreted as the quantity and kinds of compounds such as bicarbonates, carbonates and hydroxides present which collectively shift the pH to the alkaline side of neutrality.

During first year (2011-12), the total alkalinity ranged between 112.2 to 220 mg/l, during 2012-13 128 to 188.4 mg/l and during 2013-14 160 to 190.3 mg/l with grand mean of 163.94. The ideal value of total alkalinity for fish culture is 50 to 300 mg/l (Santosh and Singh, 2007). The grand mean value (163.94) of total alkalinity is suitable for fish culture.

Free carbon dioxide in water is the by-product of metabolism. More than a particular level, carbon dioxide in water is toxic to the life in water. Fishes surfacing in the early morning is an indication of carbon dioxide stress (Santosh and Singh, 2007). Lagler (1978) mentioned that the amount of free carbon dioxide in water is important in fish management because it is perhaps the best single criterion of environmental suitability for fishes. High concentrations of free carbon dioxide which are in themselves toxic to fish are usually accompanied by low values for dissolved oxygen. Free carbon dioxide in excess of 20 ppm may be regarded as harmful to fishes, although lower values may be equally harmful in waters of low oxygen content (less than 3 to 5 ppm).

During the present study carbon dioxide in Wan reservoir water ranged between 0.7 to 12 mg/l with average value of 4.28 mg/l. Water supporting good fish population should contain less than 5 mg/l free carbon dioxide. The water of Wan reservoir was with less than 5 mg/l of carbon dioxide and is suitable for fish. Free carbon dioxide was maximum during the summer months and minimum in rainy months. Free carbon dioxide was observed throughout the investigation period.

Chloride values ranged from 30.2 to 59.2, 14.3 to55.2 and 25.80 to 48.4 mg/l with an average values of 41.52, 31.4 and 37.33 mg/l in first, second and third year respectively. The maximum concentration of chloride was recorded during summer and minimum during winter. Gonzalves and Joshi (1946) and Tripathi and Pandey (1990) also observed an increase of chloride during summer. The increase in chloride during summer months might be due to low level of water in reservoir.

Although chlorides are not harmful, concentrations beyond 250 mg/l impart a peculiar taste to water rendering it unacceptable from aesthetic point of view for drinking purpose. Presence of chlorides above the usual background concentration in a water source is also used as an indicator of pollution by domestic sewage (NEERI, 1979).

During present investigation values of total hardness ranged from 48 to 93.2 mg/l during 2011-12,114-168 mg/l during 2012-13 and 123 to 180 mg/l during 2013-14 with a grand mean of 118.85. Higher values of total hardness was recorded during summer and lowe values during monsoon. The present findings are in accordance with the findings of workers like Rajasekhar *et al.* (2012) and Koliyar and Rokade (2008). Many authors (Devi 1985; Devi 1997; Sakhare 2007; Pawar and Shembekar 2012) have discussed the fluctuation in total hardness values of various waterbodies and have recorded maximum hardness in summer season.

Sawyer (1960) classified water on the basis of hardness into three categories i.e., soft (0-75 mg/l), moderately hard (75-150 mg/l) and hard (151-300 mg/l). According to this classification, Wan reservoir falls in the category of moderately hardwater body with average mean of total hardness at 118.85.

Zooplankton diversity: During present investigation, altogether 25 species were recorded which comprised 35 species of protozoa, 8 of rotifer, 6 of cladocera, 5 of copepoda and 3 of ostracoda.

The protozoans were represented by *Paramecium caudatum, Diffugia sp.* and *Opercularia sp.*

The rotifers were represented by *Brachionus calyciflorus, B. falcatus, B. diversicornis, Keratella tropica, Keratella quadrata, Lecane (Monostyla) bulla, Trichocera porcellus* and *Filinia longiseta.*

The cladocerans, which were represented by *Indialana ganapati, Moina micrura, Diaphanosoma sarsi, Diaphanosoma excisum, Alona rectangular* and *Ceriodaphnia cornuta.*

The copepods were represented by *Diaptomus marshianus, Phylladiaptomous lindbergi, Mesocyclops leukarti, Mesocyclops hyalinus* and *Cyclops viridis.* The ostracods were represented by lowest number of species i.e; *Cypris obensa, Cyclocypris globosa* and *Candocypria osborni.*

During first year of investigation (2011-2012), the zooplankton consisted of 7.70% of Protozoa, 35.45% of Rotifer, 26.43% of Cladocera, 25.57% of Copepoda and 4.85% of Ostracoda (Fig. 5.2). It is revealed that the rotifers were dominant with annual average of 140 org/liter, followed by Cladocera (164 org/liter), Copepoda (101 org/liter), Protozoa (30 org/liter) and Ostracoda (19 units/liter) (Table 5.5).

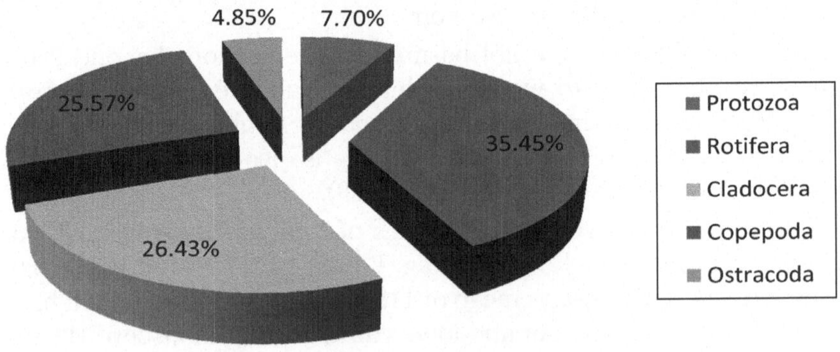

Fig. 5.2: **Quantitavtive Occurance of Zooplankton in Wan Reservoir (Year 2011-12)**

Among Protozoans, *Paramecium caudatum* was absent in August and September and *Diffugia spp* were not observed in June. Maximum density of Protozoa was recorded in summer, followed by winter and monsoon season.

Among Rotifers, *Keratella tropica* was absent in June, while other rotifer species were present throughout the year, with minimum density in monsoon. The maximum density of rotifers was recorded in summer season. The average annual rotifer density was calculated at 140 org/liter.

Among Cladocera, *Moina micrura* and *Diphanosoma sarsi* were not recorded in July and August respectively. The other species showed their presence throughout the year. The annual average of cladocera was recorded at 104 org/liter. The maximum density was observed in summer, followed by winter and monsoon season.

Table 5.5: Monthly Analysis of Zooplankton Diversity in Wan Reservoir (Year 2011-12)

Species/Month	June	July	August	September	October	November	December	January	February	March	April	May
Protozoa												
Paramecium caudatum	02	02	00	00	04	05	05	14	14	18	18	20
Diffugia spp.	00	05	02	04	05	08	12	15	18	16	20	20
Opercularia spp.	04	04	02	04	05	10	13	12	16	18	22	27
Total	**06**	**11**	**04**	**08**	**14**	**23**	**30**	**41**	**48**	**52**	**60**	**67**
Rotifera												
Brachionus calyciflorus	10	05	05	10	14	12	15	24	30	28	28	30
Brachionus falcatus	05	05	05	10	15	18	18	17	26	30	24	32
Brachionus diversicornis	08	12	12	15	18	18	15	18	29	28	22	32
Keratella tropica	00	10	10	10	19	15	20	20	20	25	30	29
Keratella quadrata	12	05	10	15	18	08	15	18	22	30	30	30
Lecane (monostyla) bulla	10	04	04	04	20	20	15	20	22	32	28	25
Trichocera porcellus	05	04	04	10	15	18	15	22	24	32	28	28
Filina longiseta	04	04	02	02	15	20	22	20	28	25	25	25
Total	**54**	**49**	**52**	**76**	**134**	**129**	**135**	**169**	**201**	**230**	**215**	**231**
Cladocera												
Indialona ganapati	04	02	02	05	08	15	20	15	15	25	35	35
Moina micrura	05	00	02	08	10	15	22	18	18	28	32	40
Diaphanosoma sarsi	04	02	00	08	15	18	15	24	28	26	32	35
Diaphanosoma excisum	02	04	04	12	15	20	20	20	28	35	35	32
Alona rectangular	02	05	05	10	12	18	22	20	28	30	38	33
Ceriodaphnia cornuta	05	05	04	08	10	20	15	18	32	30	33	33
Total	**22**	**18**	**17**	**51**	**70**	**106**	**114**	**115**	**149**	**174**	**205**	**208**

(Contd…)

Species/Month	June	July	August	September	October	November	December	January	February	March	April	May
Copepoda												
Diaptomus marshianus	10	14	12	15	12	12	20	24	25	32	29	30
Phylladiaptomus lindbergi	00	11	11	05	18	25	25	25	24	28	30	32
Mescyclops leukarti	11	12	11	10	15	20	28	28	25	35	32	30
Mesocyclops hyalinus	15	10	10	02	10	18	25	26	25	35	30	38
Cyclops viridis	12	05	05	02	25	20	24	26	32	30	29	28
Total	**48**	**52**	**49**	**34**	**80**	**95**	**122**	**129**	**131**	**160**	**150**	**158**
Ostracoda												
Cypris obensa	00	02	02	02	02	04	05	05	10	14	15	11
Cyclocypris globosa	00	00	04	02	04	05	05	08	12	12	15	11
Candocypria osborni	00	02	02	02	04	05	05	05	14	10	12	18
Total	**00**	**04**	**08**	**06**	**10**	**14**	**15**	**18**	**36**	**36**	**42**	**40**

Among Copepods, *Phylladiaptomus lindbergi* was absent in June. Except this species, all other four species were observed throughout the first year of investigation. The maximum and minimum density of copepods was observed in summer and monsoon season only. Copepods contributed 25.57% of the total zooplankton with annual average density of 101 org/liter.

Ostracods were represented by three species and contributed to 4.85% with an annual average of 19 org/liter. Ostracods were absent in June. *Cyclocypris globosa* was not seen in July. The maximum density of ostracods was recorded in summer followed by winter and monsoon. This group contributed to about 4.85% of the zooplankton with annual average of 19 org/liter.

During the second year (2012-2013) of investigation, zooplankton consisted of 7.66% Protozoa, 33.69% of Rotifera, 29.09% of Cladocera, 20.90% of Copepoda and 8.66% of Ostracoda (Fig. 5.3).

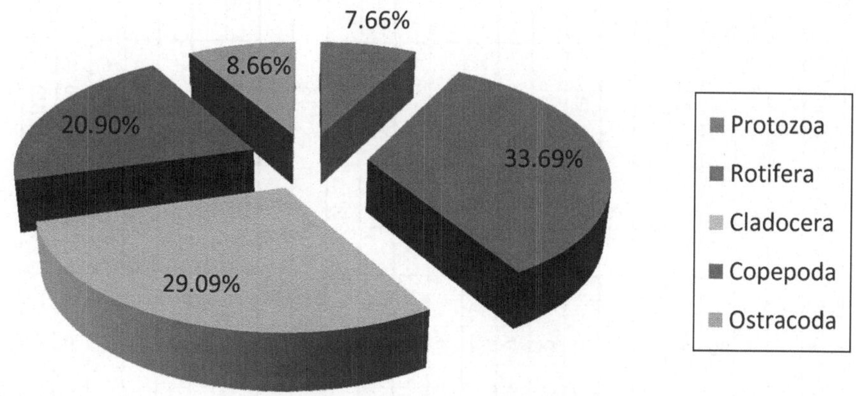

Fig. 5.3: **Quantitative Occurance of Zooplankton in Wan Reservoir (Year 2012-13)**

The density of protozoa ranged from 8 to 67 org/liter with maximum density in summer, followed by winter and monsoon season. The annual average of Protozoa, Rotifera, Cladocera, Copepoda and Ostracoda was recorded at 31, 146, 126, 91 and 38 org/liter respectively (Table 5.6).

In case of rotifers *Lecane (Monostyla) bulla* was absent in August. The other members of rotifers such as *Brachionus calyciflorus, B. falcatus, B. diversicornis, Keratella tropica, Keratella quadrata, Trichocera porcellus* and *Filinia longiseta* were recorded throughout the second year of investigation. The density of rotifers ranged from 46 org/liter to 244 org/liter with annual average of 146 org/liter. On average rotifers contributed to 33.69% of the total zooplankton.

Table 5.6: Monthly Analysis of Zooplankton Diversity in Wan Reservoir (Year 2012-13)

Species/Month	June	July	August	September	October	November	December	January	February	March	April	May
Protozoa												
Paramecium caudatum	04	02	05	08	08	10	12	10	14	15	20	20
Diffugia spp.	02	04	05	05	08	10	10	12	15	20	22	25
Opercularia spp.	02	04	02	05	10	08	08	15	18	18	20	22
Total	**08**	**10**	**12**	**18**	**26**	**28**	**30**	**37**	**47**	**53**	**62**	**67**
Rotifera												
Brachionus calyciflorus	05	10	05	10	15	20	22	16	26	32	25	30
Brachionus falcatus	05	08	04	12	10	18	18	22	28	33	30	33
Brachionus diversicornis	10	08	08	10	15	15	18	24	32	32	33	35
Keratella tropica	05	05	10	12	12	14	15	18	18	24	27	30
Keratella quadrata	10	00	05	15	20	18	20	20	28	30	28	24
Lecane (monostyla) bulla	10	05	00	15	18	16	18	18	26	32	30	25
Trichocera porcellus	04	00	08	18	18	17	24	20	25	29	25	30
Filina longiseta	04	10	10	20	20	18	20	24	25	32	26	32
Total	**53**	**46**	**50**	**112**	**122**	**136**	**155**	**162**	**208**	**244**	**224**	**239**
Cladocera												
Indialona ganapati	05	10	12	10	15	15	22	28	29	34	35	30
Moina micrura	05	05	00	05	22	22	25	26	30	34	34	30
Diaphanosoma sarsi	05	10	05	00	24	28	26	30	33	30	32	35
Diaphanosoma excisum	00	10	15	10	28	23	27	30	32	29	32	28
Alona rectangular	05	10	05	05	26	23	20	25	28	30	35	30
Ceriodaphnia cornuta	10	05	05	05	25	18	25	26	34	37	30	35
Total	**30**	**50**	**42**	**35**	**140**	**129**	**145**	**165**	**186**	**204**	**198**	**188**

(Contd...)

Species/Month	June	July	August	September	October	November	December	January	February	March	April	May
Copepoda												
Diaptomus marshianus	10	08	08	04	08	12	15	24	28	27	27	32
Phylladiaptomus lindbergi	10	02	05	10	10	15	15	24	22	24	26	35
Mescyclops leukarti	10	05	08	06	15	15	18	22	24	25	28	32
Mesocyclops hyalinus	02	12	05	10	18	15	22	24	28	30	30	33
Cyclops viridis	10	10	12	15	15	20	24	20	30	30	35	33
Total	**42**	**32**	**38**	**45**	**66**	**77**	**94**	**114**	**132**	**136**	**146**	**165**
Ostracoda												
Cypris obensa	05	00	10	00	04	05	15	15	20	22	24	24
Cyclocypris globosa	05	05	05	02	02	05	05	20	18	25	22	26
Candocypria osborni	05	05	02	02	15	10	15	18	22	24	20	28
Total	**15**	**10**	**17**	**04**	**21**	**20**	**35**	**53**	**60**	**71**	**66**	**78**

Cladocerans were represented by 6 species. Maximum Cladocerans were recorded in summer and minimum in monsoon season with an annual average of 126 org/liter. This group contributed to about 29.09% of the zooplankton. *Moina micrura, Diaphanosoma sarsi* and *Diaphanosoma excisum* were absent in August, September and June respectively.

Copepods were represented by five species which were present throughout the year with maximum density in summer followed by winter and monsoon season. Copepods showed annual average of 91 org/liter with 20.09% contribution of the total zooplankton.

Ostracods contributed to 8.66% of the total zooplankton with an annual average of 38 org/liter. Maximum ostracods were recorded in summer and minimum in monsoon season. *Cypris obensa* was absent in July and September. *Cyclocypris globosa* and *Candocypria osborni* were observed throughout the second year of investigation.

In third year (2013-2014) of investigation there were five groups consisting 25 species of zooplankton belonging to five groups i.e; Protozoa (3 species), Rotifera (8 species), Cladocera (6 species), Copepoda (5 species) and Ostracoda (3 species) (Table 5.7). The total density of zooplankton was found maximum during summer while it was minimal during rainy months.Increase in temperature and high evaporation during summer season enhances the rate of decomposition due to which the water becomes nutrient rich resulting in increase in population density of zooplankton. Low population density during monsoon may be due to the dilution effect by rain water and high water level (Akbulut, 2004 and Mulani *et.al.* 2009).

The Protozoans were represented by three species. *Diffugia sp.* were absent in August and September and *Opercularia spp* in August. *Paramecium caudatum* appeared round the year with maximum density in summer. This group contributed to 6.31% of the total zooplankton with annual average of 24 org/liter. During the third year of investigation the rotifer group showed high abundance in the months of May (252 org/liter), while low abundance was recorded in the months of June (31 org/liter) (Table 5.7). The annual average of this group was 126 org/liter with contribution of 33.18% of the total zooplankton (Fig. 5.4). Among the rotifer group, *Brachionus falcatus* was absent in June, while other 7 species were recorded round the year.

Cladocera showed high abundance in the month of April (206 org/liter), while low abundance was recorded in the month of August (24 org/liter). Among cladocerans, *Alona rectangular* was not observed in August and *Ceriodaphnia cornuta* in July, other four species were recorded round the third year of investigation. Cladocerans contributed to 26.48% of the total zooplankton with annual average of 100 org/liter.

Table 5.7: Monthly Analysis of Zooplankton Diversity in Wan Reservoir (Year 2013-14)

Species/Month	June	July	August	September	October	November	December	January	February	March	April	May
Protozoa												
Paramecium caudatum	02	06	02	02	02	04	04	10	06	10	15	20
Diffugia spp.	02	06	00	00	04	04	05	08	12	12	20	20
Opercularia spp.	04	02	00	10	04	04	08	08	10	18	18	25
Total	**08**	**14**	**02**	**12**	**10**	**12**	**17**	**26**	**28**	**40**	**53**	**65**
Rotifera												
Brachionus calyciflorus	10	15	15	10	10	12	15	20	22	28	25	30
Brachionus falcatus	00	04	10	10	12	10	18	18	22	25	20	35
Brachionus diversicornis	04	05	05	10	10	14	20	22	20	20	22	30
Keratella tropica	02	12	10	10	10	14	22	22	24	27	20	35
Keratella quadrata	02	05	10	05	10	12	19	24	18	27	25	24
Lecane (monostyla) bulla	04	04	05	05	10	10	16	18	26	20	28	28
Trichocera porcellus	04	02	05	05	08	15	15	16	22	24	30	35
Filina longiseta	05	02	05	05	10	15	18	18	25	26	32	35
Total	**31**	**49**	**55**	**60**	**80**	**102**	**143**	**158**	**179**	**197**	**202**	**252**
Cladocera												
Indialona ganapati	10	05	05	10	10	12	14	15	20	28	38	30
Moina micrura	02	05	05	10	08	10	15	19	25	35	30	36
Diaphanosoma sarsi	02	10	05	05	08	10	21	18	19	26	34	35
Diaphanosoma excisum	04	12	05	02	05	08	18	22	25	32	34	34
Alona rectangular	04	10	00	10	10	09	16	21	28	32	35	30
Ceriodaphnia cornuta	05	00	04	05	10	14	19	20	30	30	35	35
Total	**27**	**42**	**24**	**42**	**51**	**63**	**103**	**115**	**147**	**183**	**206**	**200**

(Contd...)

Species/Month	June	July	August	September	October	November	December	January	February	March	April	May
Copepoda												
Diaptomus marshianus	04	12	05	05	08	15	18	15	18	20	18	30
Phylladiaptomus lindbergi	02	10	10	10	10	15	20	18	15	20	25	22
Mescyclops leukarti	20	04	04	04	10	15	18	15	22	24	26	28
Mesocyclops hyalinus	00	05	04	00	12	15	15	22	25	27	28	25
Cyclops viridis	05	02	05	10	18	18	20	19	26	25	30	33
Total	**13**	**33**	**28**	**29**	**68**	**78**	**91**	**89**	**106**	**116**	**127**	**138**
Ostracoda												
Cypris obensa	05	10	05	00	10	10	15	22	26	29	32	34
Cyclocypris globosa	10	05	05	00	15	10	20	22	25	30	35	32
Candocypria osborni	10	10	05	00	15	10	25	25	28	28	30	38
Total	**25**	**25**	**15**	**00**	**40**	**30**	**60**	**69**	**79**	**87**	**97**	**104**

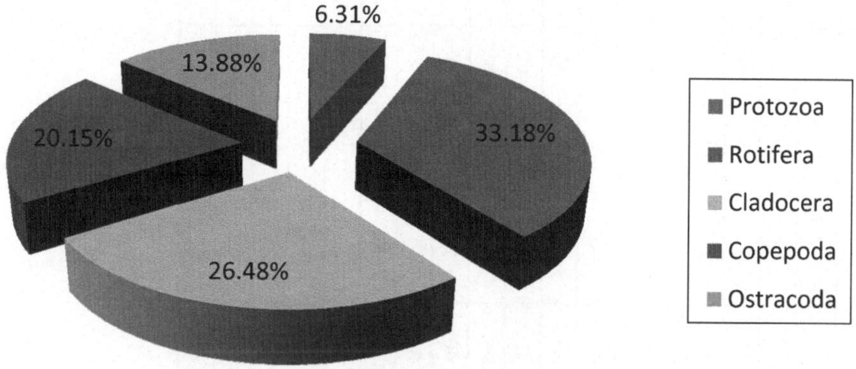

***Fig: 5.4:* Quantitative Occurance of Zooplankton in Wan Reservoir (Year 2013-14)**

During the study period, copepoda showed high abundance in the month of May (138 org/liter), while low abundance was recorded in the month of June (13 org/liter). Among the copepoda group *Mesocyclops hyalinus* was absent in June and September. The percentage contribution of this group was 20.15% of the total zooplankton with an annual average of 76 org/liter.

Ostracoda group was represented by *Cypris obensa, Cyclocypris globosa* and *Candocypria osborni.* High individuals were noticed during the summer season and low abundance was recorded during the monsoon season. All species of Ostracods were absent in September. This group contributed to 13.88% of the zooplankton with an annual average of 53 org/liter.

Phytoplankton diversity: The study of the phytoplankton sampled in Wan reservoir showed 21 species (Table 5.8, Table 5.9 and Table 5.10).The phytoplankton assemblage was represented by four classes viz. Chlorophyceae, Cyanophyceae, Bacillariophyceae and Euglenophyceae.The class Cyanophyceae was represented by 3 species, Chlorophyceae by 10 species, Bacillariophyceae by 6 species and Euglenophyceae by 2 species.

During first year of investigation (2011-12) the phytoplankton consisted of 55.38% of Chlorophyceae, 12.32% of Cyanophyceae, 23.25% of Bacillariophyceae and 9.05% of Euglenophyceae (Fig. 5.5).

During first year of investigation, the class Chlorophyceae being the most dominant. It was represented by *Zygnema sp, Ulothrix zonata, Pedistrum duplex, Pediastrum simplex,Scendesmus armaus, Oedogonium patulum, Ankistrodesmus falcatus, Chlorella vulgaris, Closterium limneticum* and *Cosmarium contractum. Zygnema sp, Ankistrodesmus falcatus* and *Cosmarium contractum* were appeared round the year. *Scendesmus armatus, Oedogonium patulum* and *Closterium limneticum* were absent in September, and *Ulothrix zonata* in October.

Table 5.8: Monthly Analysis of Phytoplankton Diversity in Wan Reservoir (Year 2011-12)

Species/Month	June	July	August	September	October	November	December	January	February	March	April	May
Chlorophyceae												
Zygnema sp	20	20	15	10	15	25	30	35	40	45	40	35
Ulothrix zonata	15	20	15	10		25	35	40	35	40	45	40
Pediastrum duplex	25	20	00	15	25	30	30	35	35	35	35	30
Pediastrum simplex	10	05	00	20	20	25	25	35	35	45	40	40
Scendesmus armatus	15	20	15	00	35	30	35	45	40	45	45	45
Oedogonium patulum	25	15	10	00	25	35	30	35	40	50	45	40
Ankistrodesmus falcatus	20	15	10	25	30	35	40	45	45	55	50	45
Chlorella vulgaris	30	25	15	00	00	20	25	25	35	30	35	45
Closterium limneticum	35	30	20	00	30	35	35	40	40	35	40	30
Cosmarium contractum	30	20	20	05	05	30	35	35	45	40	40	35
Total	**225**	**190**	**120**	**85**	**185**	**290**	**320**	**370**	**390**	**420**	**415**	**385**
Cyanophyceae												
Oscillatoria chlorime	20	20	15	10	10	20	25	30	30	35	35	30
Anabaena constricta	10	00	05	00	00	15	25	20	20	25	25	25
Merismopedia punctata	20	00	15	00	25	25	35	30	35	35	45	40
Total	**50**	**20**	**35**	**10**	**35**	**60**	**85**	**80**	**85**	**95**	**105**	**95**

(Contd…)

Species/Month	June	July	August	September	October	November	December	January	February	March	April	May
Bacillariophyceae												
Navicula gracilis	10	10	10	05	10	10	15	15	20	20	25	25
Navicula viridula	15	05	10	10	05	15	15	20	25	35	35	30
Nitzschia subtilis	25	15	00	00	25	20	35	35	40	45	45	25
Synedra affinis	10	15	20	10	30	25	35	35	35	40	55	35
Diatoms vuloare	05	05	00	00	10	10	15	15	15	20	20	20
Bacillria paradoxa	10	15	00	00	15	15	20	25	35	35	35	35
Total	**75**	**65**	**40**	**25**	**95**	**95**	**135**	**145**	**170**	**195**	**215**	**170**
Euglenophyceae												
Euglena stellata	15	15	10	10	15	20	25	25	30	40	40	45
Euglena viridis	10	10	05	10	15	20	30	30	30	35	35	35
Total	**25**	**25**	**15**	**20**	**30**	**40**	**55**	**55**	**60**	**75**	**75**	**80**

Table 5.9: Monthly Analysis of Phytoplankton Diversity in Wan Reservoir (Year 2012-13)

Species/Month	June	July	August	September	October	November	December	January	February	March	April	May
Chlorophyceae												
Zygnema sp	15	15	10	15	20	20	35	25	35	35	45	35
Ulotrix zonata	20	15	15	05	15	25	25	25	35	35	35	30
Pediastrum duplex	10	00	00	10	15	15	20	25	35	35	45	40
Pediastrum simplex	15	20	15	15	25	35	35	30	45	45	40	35
Scendesmus armatus	10	05	00	00	15	15	10	15	25	30	35	20
Oedogonium patulum	05	05	00	00	10	05	10	10	15	15	15	10
Ankistrodesmus falcatus	05	00	05	05	10	15	15	15	20	15	25	20
Chlorella vulgaris	10	05	05	05	05	10	15	15	20	20	15	15
Closterium limneticum	00	05	05	00	10	15	15	20	25	30	35	30
Cosmarium contractum	00	00	00	00	00	00	00	00	00	15	10	05
Total	**90**	**70**	**55**	**55**	**125**	**145**	**180**	**180**	**255**	**275**	**300**	**240**
Cyanophyceae												
Oscillatoria chlorime	10	15	10	15	15	20	25	30	00	35	35	55
Anabaena constricta	05	10	00	05	15	15	10	20	20	25	30	35
Merismopedia punctata	25	20	00	00	35	35	40	35	00	35	40	30
Total	**40**	**45**	**10**	**20**	**65**	**70**	**75**	**85**	**20**	**95**	**105**	**120**

(Contd...)

Species/Month	June	July	August	September	October	November	December	January	February	March	April	May
Bacillariophyceae												
Navicula gracilis	05	05	00	15	15	20	35	35	45	40	45	40
Navicula viridula	10	15	10	10	25	20	35	35	35	55	35	15
Nitzschia subtilis	15	10	10	00	10	15	20	20	35	25	35	35
Synedra affinis	00	10	00	05	15	15	10	40	45	00	45	30
Diatoms vuloare	00	00	00	00	00	00	10	15	15	15	15	10
Bacillaria paradoxa	15	10	10	00	05	10	15	15	25	25	20	10
Total	**45**	**50**	**30**	**30**	**70**	**80**	**125**	**160**	**200**	**160**	**195**	**140**
Euglenophyceae												
Euglena stellata	05	05	00	00	05	10	10	15	15	20	20	25
Euglena viridis	10	05	00	10	15	15	15	10	15	15	15	15
Total	**15**	**10**	**00**	**10**	**20**	**25**	**25**	**25**	**30**	**35**	**35**	**40**

Table 5.10: Monthly Analysis of Phytoplankton Diversity in Wan Reservoir (Year 2013-14)

Species/Month	June	July	August	September	October	November	December	January	February	March	April	May
Chlorophyceae												
Zygnema sp	10	15	00	10	15	15	15	20	25	25	25	20
Ulotrix zonata	15	15	00	05	10	15	25	20	25	35	35	30
Pediastrum duplex	10	20	00	00	10	15	20	30	35	35	30	30
Pediastrum simplex	20	20	10	10	15	20	20	25	25	45	40	35
Scendesmus armatus	20	15	10	15	15	20	20	35	35	40	40	35
Oedogonium patulum	25	20	15	15	15	20	15	25	35	45	35	35
Ankistrodesmus falcatus	25	20	10	10	20	20	20	25	35	30	35	30
Chlorella vulgaris	10	25	05	05	10	10	15	30	35	35	35	35
Closterium limneticum	05	10	00	10	15	15	25	20	25	35	30	30
Cosmarium contractum	05	15	00	00	20	20	25	25	30	35	35	30
Total	**145**	**175**	**50**	**80**	**145**	**170**	**200**	**255**	**305**	**360**	**340**	**310**
Cyanophyceae												
Oscillatoria chlorime	10	05	10	00	10	10	15	15	10	15	15	15
Anabaena constricta	15	10	10	10	20	15	20	20	25	25	30	25
Merismopedia punctata	15	10	10	05	10	20	20	25	25	25	35	20
Total	**40**	**25**	**30**	**15**	**40**	**45**	**55**	**60**	**60**	**65**	**80**	**60**

(Contd…)

Species/Month	June	July	August	September	October	November	December	January	February	March	April	May
Bacillariophyceae												
Navicula gracilis	15	10	15	15	20	25	25	25	35	45	35	35
Navicula viridula	20	15	15	00	15	15	25	35	35	40	30	30
Nitzschia subtilis	05	05	05	10	10	15	10	15	15	20	15	15
Synedra affinis	10	05	15	10	15	25	20	25	35	35	35	35
Diatoms vuloare	00	00	00	10	15	10	15	15	25	20	20	20
Bacillria paradoxa	15	05	00	00	05	15	15	20	20	35	25	25
Total	**65**	**40**	**50**	**45**	**80**	**105**	**110**	**135**	**165**	**195**	**160**	**160**
Euglenophyceae												
Euglena stellata	15	15	10	15	15	15	20	20	20	15	20	20
Euglena viridis	00	00	00	00	00	00	00	00	05	05	05	10
Total	**15**	**15**	**10**	**15**	**15**	**15**	**20**	**20**	**25**	**20**	**25**	**30**

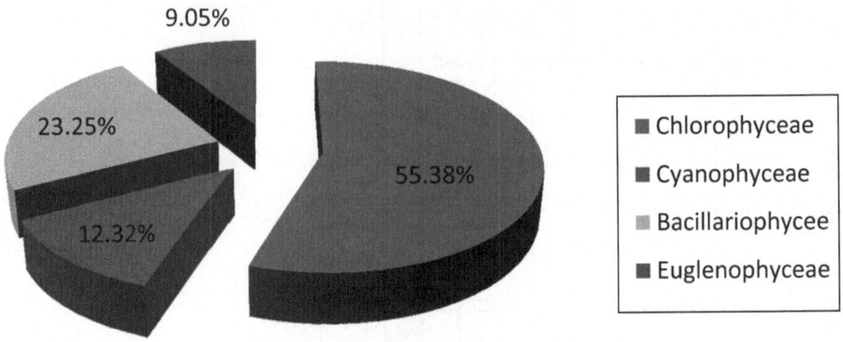

Fig. 5.5: **Quantitative Occurance of Phytoplankton in Wan Reservoir (2011-12)**

Pediastrum duplex and *Pediastrum simplex* were not seen in August and *Chlorella vulgaris* in two months i.e., September and October.The density of the group varied from 85 units/Liter (September) to 420 units/liter (March) with annual average of 283 units/Liter (Table 5.8).

In case of Cyanophyceae, *Anabaena constricta* was seen only in nine months and absent in three months i.e., July, September and October. *Merismopedia punctata* was absent in two months of rainy season i.e., July and September. The density of this group fluctuated from 10 to 105 units/Liter with annual average of 63 units/Liter. *Oscillatoria chlorine* was seen throughout the first year of investigation.

Among Bacillariophyceae, *Navicula gracilis, Navicula viridula* and *Synedra affinis* were recorded in all months. *Nitzschia subtilis, Diatoms vuloare* and *Bacillaria paradoxa* were not seen in August and September.The density of this group ranged from 25 to 215 units/Liter with annual average of 119 units/Liter.

The class Euglenophyceae was represented by two species i.e., *Euglena stellata* and *Euglena viridis*. Both species were observed throughout the first year of investigation with minima in rainy season and maxima in suumer. The density of this group ranged from 15 units/Liter (August) to 80 units/ Liter (May) with annual average of 46 units/Liter.

During second year (2012-13) of investigation, a total of 10 species of Chlorophyceae, 3 species of Cyanophyceae, 6 species of Bacillariophyceae and 2 species of Euglenophyceae were recorded (Table 5.9).

The phytoplankton consisted of 46.09% of Chlorophyceae, 17.54% of Cyanophyceae, 30.06% of Bacillariophyceae and 6.31% of Euglenophyceae (Fig. 5.6). The class Chlorophyceae was dominant with annual average of 164 units/Liter,followed by Bacillariophyceae (107 units/liter), Cyanophyceae (62 units/Liter) and Euglenophyceae (22 units/Liter).

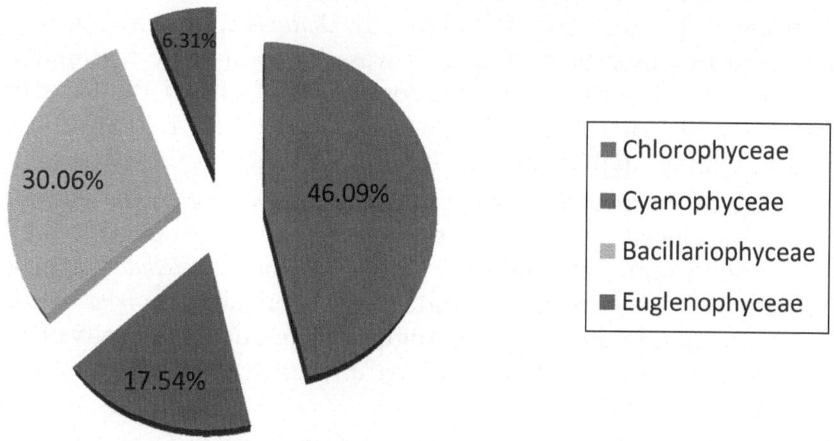

Fig.5.6: **Quantitative Occurance of Phytoplankton in Wan Reservoir (2012-13)**

In case of Chlorophyceae, *Zygnema sp, Ulothrix zonata, Pediastrum simplex* and *Chlorella vulgaris* were recorded throughout the second year of investigation. *Scendesmus armatus* and *Oedogonium patulum* were recorded in ten months and were absent in two months i.e., August and September.Similarly *Pediastrum duplex* was absent in July and August.*Closterium limneticum* was absent inJune and September. *Cosmarium contractum* was observed in only three months of summer season i.e., March, April and May. The density of Chlorophyceae ranged from 55 units/Liter (August and September) to 300 units/Liter (April) with annual average of 164 units/Liter.

The class Cyanophyceae was represented by three species viz., *Oscillatoria chlorine, Anabaena constricta and Merismopedia punctata. Oscillatoria chlorine* and *Anabaena constricta* were observed in eleven months. *Merismopedia punctata* was observed in nine months. It was absent in August, September and February. The density of *Oscillatoria chlorine* was high in the month of May (55 units/Liter). *Anabaena constricta* showed maximum density in May (35 units/Liter) and maximum density of *Merismopedia punctata* was observed in the month of December and April (40 units/Liter).

The variation in the population density of Cyanophyceae ranged from 10 to 120 units/Liter wuth annual average of 62 units/Liter.

Among Bacillariophyceae, *Navicula gracilis, Navicula viridula, Nitzschia subtilis, Synedra affinis, Diatoms vuloare* and *Bacillaria paradoxa* were recorded. *Navicula viridula* was seen throughout the second year of investigation with maximum density in summer and minimum density in rainy season. *Navicula gracilis* was observed in eleven months. It was absent in August. *Nitzschia subtilis* and *Bacillaria paradoxa* were recorded in eleven months. These species were absent in month of September. *Syndera affinis* was seen in nine months and was absent in June, August and March. *Diatoms vuloare* was seen only in summer and two months of winter. It was absent in rainy season and two months of winter. The variation in the population density of Bacillariophyceae ranged from 30 Units/Liter (August and September) to 200 units/Liter (February) with annual average of 107 units/Liter.

In case of Euglenophyceae, *Euglena stellata* and *Euglena viridis* were recorded. The density of this group ranged from nil (August) to 40 (May) units/Liter with annual average of 22 units/Liter.*Euglena stellata* was observed in ten months.It was absent in August and September.*Euglena viridis* was seen in eleven months and absent in August.The population density of *Euglena stellata* varied from nil to 25 units/Liter and *Euglena viridis* from nil to 15 units/Liter.

The study of phytoplankton sampled in third year of investigation showed 21 species (Table 5.10). The phytoplankton assemblage was represented by four classes viz., Chlorophyceae, Cyanophyceae, Bacillariophyceae and Euglenophyceae. 10 species of Chlorophyceae, 3 species of Cyanophyceae, 6 species of Bacillariophyceae and 2 species of Euglenophyceae were recorded. The phytoplankton consisted of 54.57% of Chlorophyceae,12.38% of Cyanophyceae, 28.20% of Bacillariophyceae and 4.85% of Euglenophyceae (Fig. 5.7).

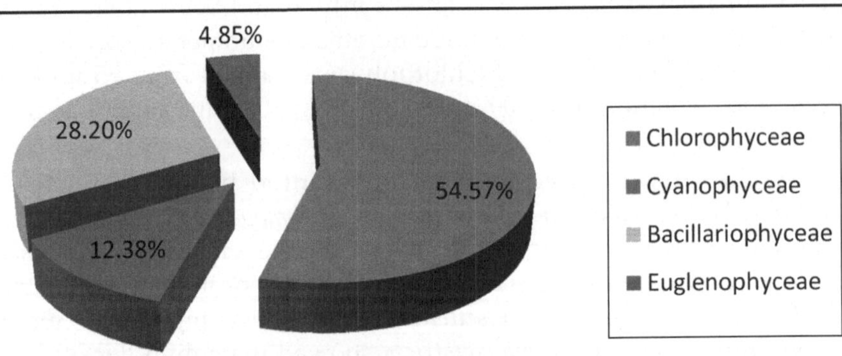

***Table 5.7:* Quantitative Occurance of Phytoplankton in Wan Reservoir (2013-14)**

The class Chlorophyceae was represented by *Zygnema sp*, *Ulothrix zonata*, *Pediastrum duplex*, *Pediastrum simplex*, *Scnedesmus armatus*, *Oedogonium patulum*, *Ankistrodesmus falcatus*, *Chlorella vulgaris*, *Closterium limneticum* and *Cosmarium contractum*. The population density of Chlorophyceae was between 50 to 360 units/Liter with annual average of 211 units/Liter. *Pediastrum simplex*, *Scendesmus armatus*, *Oedogonium patulum*, *Ankistrodesmus falcatus* and *Chlorella vulgaris* were observed through out the third year of investigation, while

Pediastrum duplex and *Cosmarium contractum* were present only in ten months (Table 5.10). *Zygnema sp, Ulothrix zonata* and *Closterium limneticum* were observed in eleven months.These species were absent in month of August.

Fishing in Progress

Oreochromis mossambicus from Wan Reservoir

A Haul of *Oreochromis mossambicus* from Wan Reservoir

In case of Cyanophyceae, *Oscillatoria chlorine, Anabaena constricta* and *Merismopedia punctata* were recorded. *Anabaena constricta* and *Merismopedia punctata* were observed throughout the third year of investigation with minima in rainy season and maxima in summer. *Oscillatoria chlorine* was recorded in eleven months. It was absent in September. The population density of this species varied from nil to 15 units/Liter. The population density of Cyanophyceae was between 15 (September) to 80 units/Liter (April) with annual average of 48 units/Liter.

The class Bacillariophyceae was represented by *Navicula gracilis, Navicula viridula, Nitzschia subtilis, Syndera affinis, Diatoms vuloare* and *Bacillaria paradoxa.* The population density of this group varied from 40 units/Liter (July) to 195 units/Liter (March) with annual average of 109 units/liter. *Navicula gracilis, Nitzschia subtilis* and *Synedra affinis* were seen in all months with maxima in summer and minima in rainy season. *Navicula viridula* was present in eleven months and absent in month of September. *Diatoms vuloare* and *Bacillaria paradoxa* were observed in nine and ten mnonths respectively.

The class Euglenophyceae was represented by two species i.e., *Euglena stellata* and *Euglena viridis. Euglena stellata* was observed in all months with density variation between 10 units/Liter to 20 units/Liter. *Euglena viridis* was present only in summer season. The population density of this species varied from nil to 10 units/liter. The population density of Euglenophyceae was between 10 to 30 units/Liter with annual average of 19 units/Liter.

CHAPTER - 6

Harni (Katgaon) Reservoir

It is situated near Katgaon village in Tuljapur tehsil of Osmanabad district and is connected by an approach road of the length of 6.5 km from Solapur-Hyderabad National Highway No. 9. This approach road takes off near the Khanapur stage on the National High-way. The project is constructed across Harni river, a tributary of river Bori, having catchment area of 190.624 km^2 (73.60 sq. miles) at the project site. The head works of the project were started in June 1961 and completed in June 1964. This project envisages construction of an earthen dam and includes other works such as ogee spillway with its appurtenant works, head regulator on right flank and canals on left and right flanks taking off from the same head sluice. The water spread area of reservoir is 239 hectares.The details of morphometry of reservoir are depicted in Table 6.1.

The fishing rights of the reservoir are given on lease to the co-operative society named 'The Jay Ambika Matsya Vyvsaik Sahakari Sanstha Limited'. The society was established on 22/03/1978 under Maharashtra Co-operative Act with registration number of OSM/RSR-552 Date 22/03/1978. The initial capital was Rs. 480/- only. At the time of registration there were a total of 49 members. The number of member has increased by about 2 times during the last 23 years. In the year 1987-88, the total number of members were 49. In 2001-2002 it increased to 51, further and in subsequent years finally the total number of members become 57. The members of the co-operative society belong to different castes and religions. These are the nontraditional fishermen like muslim (Islam), dhangar (bandi) and lingayat. All 57 members are not full time fishermen. All of them are part time fishermen. The study area is socio-economically backward.

Seed of major carps (*Catla catla, Labeo rohita, Cirrhinus mrigala*) and Common carp (*Cyprinus carpio)* were stocked in the reservoir. The details of stocking of seed are depicted in Table 6.2. On an average seed was stcoked @8,66,666 number/year.

Table 6.1: The Salient Features of Harni (Katgaon) Reservoir

1.	Name of River	Harni
2.	Location	Katgaon village
3.	Sub basin number	19
4.	Water Spread Area (ha)	239
5.	Year of Construction	1964
6.	Length of earthen dam	2,163.975 meters
7.	Length of ogee spillway	276.025 meters
8.	Maximum flood discharge	58,490 cusecs
9.	Maximum height of dam in river bed	17.080 meters
10.	Gross storage capacity(Mcum)	12.580
11.	Live storage capacity (Mcum)	11.170
12.	Carry Over capacity (Mcum)	1.410
13.	Catchment Area (km^2)	190.624
14.	Length of irrigation channel Left flank canal (km) Right flank canal (km)	 27.355 14.481
15.	Irrigation potential (ha)	1,660

Table 6.2: Details of Seed Stocking in Harni (Katgaon) Reservoir

Year	Catla	Rohu	Mrigal	Common carp	Total
2011-12	3 Lac	2 Lac	1 Lac	1 Lac	7 Lac
2012-13	4 Lac	2 Lac	3 Lac	2 Lac	11 Lac
2013-14	2 Lac	1 Lac	2 Lac	3 Lac	8 Lac

A check list of fishes recorded in Harni (Katgaon) reservoir is depicted in Table 6.3. During present investigation a totoal of 27 species of fishes belonging to 7 orders and 11 families have been recorded from reservoir. Order Cypriniformes was dominted by 11 species which was followed by Siluriformes with 6 species, perciformes with 3 species, Clupeiformes, Mastacembelifomes and Channiformes with 2 species each, and Mugiliformes was represented by 1 species only.

The fishery is exploited by fishermen who have been organized from village Katgaon into a co-operative society. The average fish production from the reservoir is 19.52 kg/ha/yr. During the study period the catch of carps showed the higher catches than those of local fishes. The details of fish production for the period of three years (2011-12 to 2013-14) are furnished in Table 6.4. The average fish production from the reservoir was 19.52 kg/ha/yr. It was 25.10 kg/ha/yr in 2011-12,12.55 kg/ha/yr in 2012-13 and 20.92 kg/ha/yr in 2013-14. The Indian major carps dominated with 11.46 kg/ha/yr (45.66%) and 5.96 kg/ha/yr (47.50%) during 2011-12 and 2012-13 respectively. During 2013-14 the local fishes (catfishes, murrels and others) dominated the catch with 10.67 kg/ha/yr (51%).

Table 6.3: Fish Fauna of Harni (Katgaon) Reservoir

Fish Fauna
Order: Clupeiformes **Suborder: Notopteroidei** **Family: Notopteridae** 1. *Notopterus notopterus (Pallas)*
2. *Notopterus chitala (Ham.)*
Order: Cypriniformes **Suborder: Cyprinoidei** **Family: Cyprinidae** 3. *Chela phulo (Ham.)*
4. *Catla catla (Ham.)*
5. *Labeo rohita (Ham.)*
6. *Labeo boggut (Sykes)*
7. *Cirrhinus mrigala (Ham.)*
8. *Cyprinus carpio (Linn)*
9. *Osteobrama cotio (Ham.)*
10. *Puntius sarana sarana (Ham.)*
11. *Puntius ticto ticto (Ham.)*
12. *Puntius sophore (Ham.)*
Family: Cobitidae 13. *Nemacheilus botia (Ham.)*
Order: Siluriformes **Family: Bagridae**
14. *Mystus cavasius (Ham.)*
15. *Mystus seenghala (Sykes)*
16. *Mystus vittatus (Bloch)*
Family: Heterpneustidae 17. *Heteropnesutes fossilis (Bloch)*
Family: Siluridae 18. *Wallago attu (Bloch and Schneider)*
19. *Ompak bimaculatus (Bloch)*
Order: Mugiliformes **Family: Mugilidae** 20. *Mugil cephalus (Linn.)*
Order: Channiformes **Family: Channidae** 21. *Channa gachua (Haml.)*
22. *Channa marulius (Ham.)*
Order: Mastacembeliformes 23. *Mastacembelus pancalus (Ham.)*
24. *Mastacembelus armatus (Lacepede)*
Order: Perciformes **Family: Anabantidae** 25. *Anabas testudineus (Bloch)*
Family: Gobiidae 26. *Glassogobius giuris (Ham.)*
Family: Ambassidae 27. *Chanda ranga (Ham.)*

Optimal growth and survival of aquatic plants and animals require that their environment pH should be confined with a very short range below or above which they will be subjected to various kinds of stresses, and the diurnal fluctuation of pH of a water body should remain in the range of 6.4 to 8.5 in order to support the optimum fish growth (Das, 1996). The average pH value (8.04) of Harni (Katgaon) reservoir is suitable for optimum fish growth.

Water transparency has a significant role in light attenuation with depth, affecting productivity. Reservoirs with rocky and gravel catchment such as those in Jammu and Kashmir, Himachal Pradesh and Jharkhand have deeper euphotic zones of more than 2 m (Vass and Sugunan, 2009). In these reservoirs the temporal variation in transparency is very wide unlike Madhya Pradesh reservoirs (Unni, 1985). As the reduced transparency in these reservoirs is due to suspended inorganic particles and phytoplankton production is much less, unlike reservoirs with high phytoplankton growth limiting light penetration. Normally the transparency of water decreases during the monsoon due to inflow being loaded with dissolved and suspended organic and inorganic particles, subsequently stabilising in the post-monsoon period (Vass and Sugunan, 2009). In Harni (Katgaon) reservoir maximum transparency was recorded in summer and minimum in rainy season.

Dissolved oxygen is probably the most critical water quality variable in fish culture, so the fish culturist should be familiar with dynamics of dissolved oxygen concentration in ponds. Dissolved oxygen enters a water body from the atmosphere and from oxygen producing plant life living in the water. The atmosphere is made of approximately 20 percent oxygen or 200,000 ppm; typical oxygen levels in surface waters are below 10 ppm (Department of Wildlife and Fisheries Sciences, 2005). The solubility of O_2 in water decreases with the increase of temperature (Pandey and Shukla, 2005). Dissolved oxygen concentration appear to be lowest in the early morning just after sunrise, increase during daylight hours to a maximum in later afternnon, and decrease again during the night. The magnitude of fluctuation is greatest in water bodies with heavy plankton blooms and least in water bodies with low plankton abundance. Dissolved oxygen concentrations are particularly low during periods of cloudy weather. The production of carbon dioxide on a cloudy day is less than a clear or partly cloudy day, so dissolved oxygen concentration do not increase to usual afternoon levels. This results in lower than usual dissolved oxygen concentrations the following morning. Extended periods of cloudy weather may result in dangerously low dissolved oxygen concentrations even in ponds with moderately heavy plankton blooms.

There are many factors that influence the amount of dissolved oxygen in a surface water. Oxygen is transferred from the atmosphere into moving waters (streams and rivers) at a higher rate than still waters, such as lakes.

Water at a colder temperature also has a higher saturation level of dissolved oxygen than water at a warmer temperature. In addition, water at a lower altitude has a higher saturation level than water at a higher altitude. The turbidity of surface water can also affect dissolved oxygen levels. High turbidity in surface water can reduce the level of dissolved oxygen by raising the water temperature and lowering photosynthesis due to the absorption of sunlight by suspended solids. Dissolved oxygen levels can provide information on the concentration of oxygen demanding pollutants that may be entering surface water via point and non-point sources. Oxygen is consumed by microorganisms as they degrade organic matter in water, which reduces the concentration of dissolved oxygen. These oxygen demanding substances may arise from farmland runoff, urban runoff and septic systems. In particular, fertilizers, animal waste (livestock or wildlife), and human waste contribute to the oxygen demand.

In the present investigation the dissolved oxygen was found to range between 6.3 to 10.2 mg/l and found highest during monsoon. The minimum concentration of dissolved oxygen recorded in summer months. The average values of dissolved oxygen were 8.4, 8.3 and 8.7mg/l during 2011-2012, 212-13 and 2013-2014 respectively.

The oxygen content of water bodies is one of the important parameters in water quality assessment. Its presence is essential in aquatic ecosystems to keep the organisms in balance. It also affects the solubility and availability of many nutrients, hence the productivity of an aquatic ecosystem. Oxygen content is poor during periods of high temperature such as summer season (Bhowmik 1968 and Chakrabarti 1980), while it is high in winter due to low water temperature (Moitra and Bhattacharya 1965 and Chakrabarti 1980).

The higher values of dissolved oxygen in monsoon season may be due to the surficial water of the reservoir was subjected to wind generated turbulence and resultant mixing of surface and subsurface water layers. Thus during monsoon months these establishes an oxygen equilibrium between the water and air. This is not disturbed by the vertical gradient of phytoplankton or bacterial populations. Devi (1997) also gave similar explanation for the fluctuations of dissolved oxygen.

Highly productive water should have a dissolved oxygen concentration of more than 5 mg/l (Vass and Sugunan, 2009). However, a very high concentration of dissolved oxygen leading to super saturation may become lethal to fish fry, as has been seen in some reservoirs predominantly infested with Microcystis blooms.

Many workers (Khabade and Mule 2010, Patil and Kulkarni 2010, Fokmare and Musaddiq 2005, Jetithor 2010 and Shastri 2005) have discussed the seasonal fluctuations in the dissolved oxygen content of various water bodies in Maharashtra.

Kiran and Puttaiah (2010) recorded 1.40 to 9.52 mg/l of dissolved oxygen in Bhadra reservoir of Karnataka. A reduction in the content of dissolved oxygen during summer months in all the stations could be attributed to higher temperature and increased process of microbial decomposition.

Total alkalinity is the sum of titratable bases in water. In most waters, bicarbonate and carbonate are the predominant bases that contribute to alkalinity. Aquatic animals thrive in waters over a wide range of total alkalinities and do not have a specific requirement for 'alkalinity'. Nevertheless, certain physiological and environmental benefits accure from the presence of ample alkalinity in waters used to raise aquatic animals. These benefits include buffering of water against changes in pH, enhanced natural fertility of waters, and decreased potential for metal toxicity.

The total alkalinity of waters ranges from less than 5 to over 500 mg/l as $CaCO_3$ and is determined by the geology of the aquifer or watershed.Bicarbonate and carbonate are derived primarily from the dissolution of basic minerals. Rivers and lakes in geological regions dominated by silicate rocks and acidic topsoils will have poorly mineralized waters with low alkalinities.

Total alkalinity is an important environmental variable in aquaculture because it interacts with other variables that affect the health of aquatic animals or the fertility of the ecosystem (Boyd and Tucker, 2009).

During the three years study period higher total alkalinity values were observed in winter followed by summer and monsoon.

Chloride is one of the important indicators of pollution. Chlorides are generally present in natural water. The presence of chloride in natural water can be attributed to dissolution of salt deposits, discharges of effluents from chemical industries; oil well operation and sewage discharge. High chlorides content recorded in summer and relatively low values recorded in post monsoon.

In the present investigation values of chlorides ranged between 42.3 to 76.3 mg/l.Similar range of chlorides was recorded by Piska *et al.* (2000), Sakhare (2007) and Jetithor (2010).In the first year of the study the higher values were recorded in summer and lower in monsoon. High values of chlorides in summer could be due to their correlation as a result of evaporative water loss. Lower values in monsoon could be attributed to dilution effect and renewal of water mass after summer stagnation.

Total hardness is the sum of the concentrations of calcium and magnesium in water. Total hardness is an aggregate property and cannot be precisely interpreted in relation to aquatic animal health or culture system management unless the concentrations of substances contributing to total hardness are known. The total hardness of natural waters ranges from less than 5 to over 10,000 mg/l as $CaCo_3$. The geology of the aquifer or watershed determines the total hardness and the relative concentrations of calcium and magnesium in fresh waters. Most inland surface waters have total hardness values ranging from less than 5 to 200 mg/l as $CaCo_3$.

Most freshwater animals grow well over a wide range of total hardness values but they may be more susceptible to adverse water quality conditions when hardness values (particularly calcium concentrations) are low. Total hardness values are also generally correlated with native fertility of freshwater systems.

During present investigation the higher values of total hardness were recorded during summer and lower values during the winter season.

Zooplankton diversity: In first year of investigation (2011-12), a total of 24 species of zooplankton were identified, among them two species were represented by 2 species of Protozoa, 8 species by Rotifera, 6 species of Cladocera, 5 species of Copepoda and 3 species of Ostracoda (Table 6.6). Among the five groups, Rotifera appeared to be a dominant group (36.45%), followed by Copepoda (22.91%), Cladocera (20.33%), Ostracoda (12.96%) and Protozoa (7.35%) (Fig. 6.1). On the seasonal basis, maximum zooplankton density was observed in summer. Zooplankton density was least in the monsoon season. The lower density of zooplankton during rainy season might be due to flood and fast water current. Normally, the monsoon is associated with lower population densities due to its dilution effect and decrease in photosynthetic activity by primary producers. Similar results have been shown by Baker (1979) and Ude *et.al.*, (2011).

Protozoans were represented by two species, i.e., *Diffugia spp* and *Opercularia spp. Diffugia spp* were present in eleven months and *Opercularia spp* were recorded in all the months. The group density ranged from 2 organisms/liter (July) to 53 organisms/liter (February) with annual average of 23 organisms/Liter.

Rotifers were represented by *Brachionus calyciflorus, B.falcatus, B.diversicornis, Keratella tropica, K.quadrata, Lecane (Monostyla) bulla, Trichocera porcellus* and *Filinia longiseta*. Except *Lecane (Monostyla) bulla,* all species observed throughout the study period with the maximum quantity in summer season. The variation in the population density of this group ranged from 49 organisms/Liter (July) to 175 organisms/Liter (May) with annual average mean of 113 organisms/Liter.

Among Cladocera, *Indialona ganapati, Moina micrura, Diaphanosoma sarsi, D.excisum, Alona rectangular* and *Ceriodaphnia cornuta* were recorded. Indialona ganapati was observed throughout the study period. Cladocera constituted a significant component of zooplankton community for most part of the study period. They however, fluctuated from 11 organisms/Liter (August) to 155 organisms/Liter (May) with annual average of 63 organisms/Liter. *Moina micrura* was absent in two months and *Diaphanosoma sarsi, D.excisum, Alona rectangular* and *Ceriodaphnia cornuta* were not reported in one month each. The least contribution of group was noticed in rainy season.

Table 6.6: Monthly Analysis of Zooplankton Diversity in Harni (Katgaon (Year 2011-12)

Species/Month	June	July	August	September	October	November	December	January	February	March	April	May
Protozoa												
Diffugia spp.	02	00	06	04	06	08	10	13	38	33	27	30
Opercularia spp.	04	02	06	02	05	06	06	10	15	09	20	22
Total	**06**	**02**	**12**	**06**	**11**	**14**	**16**	**23**	**53**	**42**	**47**	**52**
Rotifera												
Brachionus calyciflorus	05	04	10	05	15	18	22	20	28	30	28	26
Brachionus falcatus	05	10	10	10	15	20	22	20	22	28	20	25
Brachionus diversicornis	05	05	05	08	18	18	22	25	19	22	19	34
Keratella tropica	10	10	10	12	10	22	18	18	22	20	25	20
Keratella quadrata	15	05	05	05	05	15	10	20	24	32	24	25
Lecane (monostyla) bulla	05	05	05	00	08	12	11	19	19	20	23	20
Trichocera porcellus	05	05	05	05	12	07	15	11	12	10	20	20
Filina longiseta	05	05	05	05	02	05	11	11	11	10	10	05
Total	**55**	**49**	**55**	**50**	**85**	**117**	**131**	**144**	**157**	**172**	**169**	**175**
Cladocera												
Indialona ganapati	04	02	02	04	02	05	08	15	15	20	32	30
Moina micrura	02	05	00	00	04	04	15	20	15	19	18	25
Diaphanosoma sarsi	04	04	00	04	02	05	04	10	14	20	30	20
Diaphanosoma excisum	02	05	02	00	02	05	04	20	15	15	22	25
Alona rectangular	02	00	05	05	05	05	10	12	15	20	18	25
Ceriodaphnia cornuta	02	02	02	00	05	05	15	15	15	20	25	30
Total	**16**	**18**	**11**	**13**	**20**	**29**	**56**	**92**	**89**	**114**	**145**	**155**

(Contd...)

Species/Month	June	July	August	September	October	November	December	January	February	March	April	May
Copepoda												
Diaptomus marshianus	05	04	10	12	12	15	18	15	20	20	26	20
Phylladiaptomus lindbergi	05	05	04	05	10	12	15	15	18	20	18	22
Mescyclops leukarti	10	10	04	05	10	10	16	20	22	22	26	24
Mesocyclops hyalinus	05	04	04	10	15	15	10	18	20	26	24	25
Cyclops viridis	04	04	04	10	15	18	15	18	20	20	25	20
Total	**29**	**27**	**26**	**42**	**62**	**70**	**74**	**86**	**100**	**108**	**119**	**111**
Ostracoda												
Cypris obensa	00	00	05	05	12	10	15	10	20	20	25	28
Cyclocypris globosa	00	00	05	05	15	15	15	15	18	25	22	25
Candocypria osborni	00	00	10	10	08	10	18	20	20	25	22	30
Total	**00**	**00**	**20**	**20**	**35**	**35**	**48**	**45**	**58**	**70**	**69**	**83**

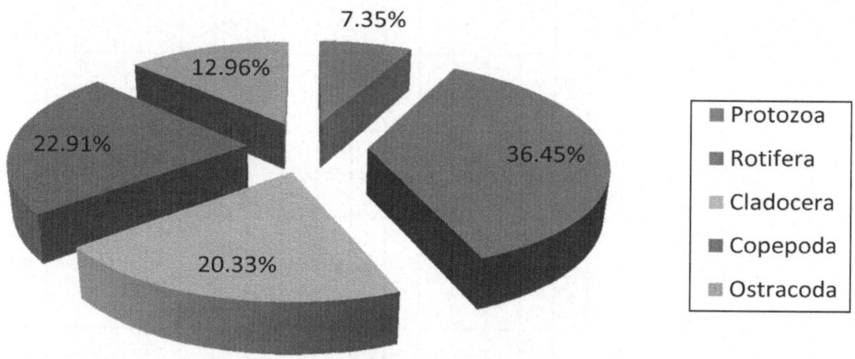

Fig. 6.1: **Percentage Contribution of Zooplankton in Harni (Katgaon) Reservoir (Year 2011-12)**

The members of Copepoda recorded were *Diaptomus marshianus, Phylladiaptomus lindbergi, Mesocylcops leukarti, Mesocylops hyalinus* and *Cyclops viridis*. All these species were observed in good numbers throughout the year with density varying from 26 organisms/Liter (August) to 119 organisms/Liter (April) with annual average density of 71 organisms/Liter. Most of the copepod species occurring in the reservoir were abundant in summer season when reservoir becomes shallow with less water.

The group Ostracoda was represented by *Cypris obensa, Cyclocypris globosa* and *Candocypria osborni*. All these species were absent in June and July. The population density of ostracoda ranged from nil (June and July) to 83 organims/Liter (May) with annual average of 40 organisms/Liter. The peak abundance of Ostracoda was observed in summer season.

In second year (2012-13) of investigation, a total of 25 species of zooplankton were identified, among them 3 species belong to Protozoa, 8 species to Rotifera, 6 species to Cladocera, 5 species to Copepoda and 3 species to Ostracoda (Table 6.7). Among the zooplanktonic group rotifera was dominant (39.34%), followed by Cladocera (23.50%), Copepoda (21.73%), Ostracoda (8.79%) and Protozoa (6.64%) (Fig. 6.2). Zooplankton density was comparatively higher in summer and lower in rainy season.

Protozoa was represented by three species i.e., *Paramecium caudatum, Diffugia spp* and *Opercularia spp.Paramecium caudatum* and *Diffugia spp* were dominant which were recorded in all months. Proportion of this group in relation to other zooplankton groups was lowest. *Opercularia spp* were reported only in two months of summer i.e., April and May.The annual average was 23 organisms/Liter and total number of individuals varied between 4 organisms/Liter (July) to 53 organims/Liter (February). The population of this group exhibited peak during summer season, while least population was recorded in monsoon season.

Table 6.7: Monthly Analysis of Zooplankton Diversity in Harni (Katgaon) Reservoir (Year 2012-13)

Species/Month	June	July	August	September	October	November	December	January	February	March	April	May
Protozoa												
Paramecium caudatum	02	02	05	04	10	05	10	15	15	20	22	22
Diffugia spp.	04	02	05	04	02	05	12	12	18	18	20	28
Opercularia spp.	00	00	00	00	00	00	00	00	00	00	05	10
Total	**06**	**04**	**10**	**08**	**12**	**10**	**22**	**27**	**33**	**38**	**47**	**60**
Rotifera												
Brachionus calyciflorus	15	12	05	10	15	15	15	20	25	25	30	35
Brachionus falcatus	10	10	08	10	15	18	20	22	22	25	22	30
Brachionus diversicornis	00	12	10	14	12	15	15	18	28	28	30	32
Keratella tropica	08	05	15	00	10	22	20	22	30	30	35	28
Keratella quadrata	09	00	00	05	05	12	22	20	30	26	26	30
Lecane (monostyla) bulla	00	08	04	04	05	10	28	25	20	25	28	28
Trichocera porcellus	10	10	05	08	06	10	10	22	35	35	22	32
Filina longiseta	12	05	05	05	06	10	22	25	32	21	29	32
Total	**64**	**62**	**42**	**56**	**74**	**112**	**152**	**174**	**222**	**215**	**222**	**247**
Cladocera												
Indialona ganapati	00	00	04	15	18	15	12	15	12	20	30	20
Moina micrura	05	02	04	10	10	10	05	18	14	28	25	18
Diaphanosoma sarsi												
Diaphanosoma excisum	05	10	05	08	15	12	20	15	18	22	30	15
Alona rectangular	10	05	15	05	12	14	18	15	20	20	30	25
Ceriodaphnia cornuta	02	04	04	04	10	14	18	15	15	25	20	22
Total	**26**	**26**	**37**	**52**	**80**	**75**	**83**	**93**	**94**	**140**	**155**	**120**

(Contd...)

Species/Month	June	July	August	September	October	November	December	January	February	March	April	May
Copepoda												
Diaptomus marshianus	04	08	10	04	05	10	18	20	25	20	22	20
Phylladiaptomus lindbergi	10	05	05	05	10	10	18	22	20	30	22	20
Mescyclops leukarti	02	04	10	04	12	10	20	20	28	32	25	25
Mesocyclops hyalinus	04	04	05	05	12	08	15	24	25	30	28	22
Cyclops viridis	08	08	10	12	12	15	20	22	23	25	30	25
Total	**28**	**29**	**40**	**30**	**51**	**53**	**91**	**108**	**101**	**137**	**127**	**112**
Ostracoda												
Cypris obensa	08	00	04	04	04	05	10	15	18	20	20	22
Cyclocypris globosa	00	00	00	05	05	10	10	18	12	18	24	25
Candocypria osborni	00	00	00	00	05	10	05	15	18	15	20	22
Total	**08**	**00**	**04**	**09**	**14**	**25**	**25**	**48**	**48**	**53**	**64**	**69**

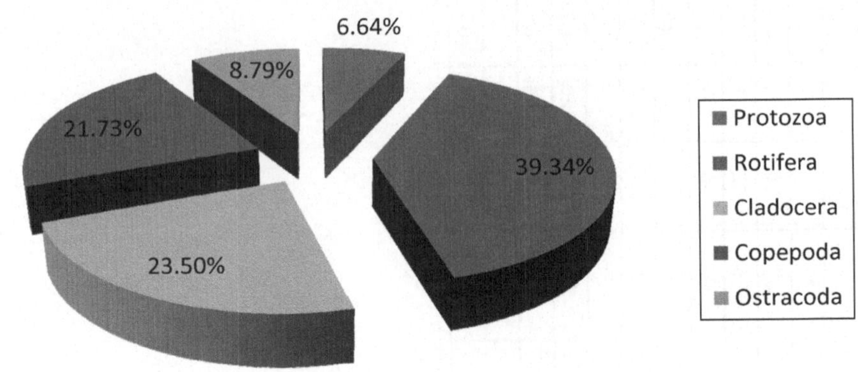

Fig. 6.2: **Quantitative Occurance of Zooplankton in Harni (Katgaon) Reservoir (Year 2012-13)**

The composition of rotifera population showed higher population during summer season, while lower population observed in monsoon. This perhaps may be due to influence of copious quantity rainwater and turbidity which gets drained into the reservoir. This group was represented by 8 species. *Brachionus calyciflorus, B.falcatus, Trichocera precellus* and *Filinia longiseta* were observed throughout the year, while *Brachionus diversicornis, Keratella tropica,* and *Lecane (Monostyla) bulla* were absent in one month each. *Keratella quadrata* was not observed in two months of rainy season (July and August).The annual average of this group was 137 organisms/Liter.Its density varied from 42 organisms/Liter (August) to 247 orgnisns/Liter (May).

In the cladocera group, *Indialona ganapati, Moina micrura, Diaphanosoma sarsi, D.excisum, Alona rectangular* and *Ceriodaphnia cornuta* were recorded. The density of cloadocerans varied from 26 organisms/Liter (June and July) to 155 organisms/Liter (April) with annual average of 82 organisms/Liter. *Indialona ganapati* was not seen in two months of rainy season (June and July) where as other species showed their presence round the year. All the members of this group showed higher population during summer season.

Among Copepods *Diaptomus marshianus, Phylladiaptomus lindbergi, Mesocyclops leukarti, Mesocyclops hyalinus* and *Cyclops viridis* were observed. All these species were observed round the second year of investigation. The number of individual varied from 28 organisms/Liter to 137 organisms/ Liter with mean of 76 organisms/Liter.

The Ostracod population fluctuated between nil (July) to 69 organisms/ Liter (May) with an average of 31organisms/Liter. This group was represented by three species i.e., *Cypris obensa, Cyclocypris globosa* and *Candocypria osborni*. All these members were totally absent in July.*Candocypria osborni* was not observed in entire rainy season, *Cyclocypris globosa* in three months of rainy season and *Cypris obensa* in July.

In third year of investigation, a total of 25 species of zooplankton belonging to Protozoa (3 species), Rotifera (8 species), Cladocera (6 species), Copepoda (5 species) and Ostracoda (3 species) were recorded from Harni (Katgaon) reservoir (Table 6.8).

Protozoans were represented by *Paramecium caudatum,Diffugia spp*,and *Opercularia spp*.This group contributed to 8.39% of the total zooplankton (Fig. 6.3). *Paramecium caudatum* was dominant and observed in all the seasons. *Diffugia spp* were not recorded in June and August and *Opercularia spp* in June. The population density of protozoans ranged from 4 organisms/Liter (June) to 60 organisms/Liter (January and February) with annual average of 32 organisms/Liter. The density of all protozoans was found to be maximum in summer season.

Rotifers contributed to 37.80% of the total zooplankton population, *Brachionus calyciflorus, B, falcatus, B.diversicornis, Keratella tropica, Lecane (Monostyla) bulla, Trichocera porcellus* and *Filinia logiseta* were observed round the third year of investigation. *Keratella quadrata* was absent in one month (April).Rotifers were dominant in summer season with density of 64 organisms/Liter (August) to 231 organisms/Liter (February).The average rotifer density was 145 organisms/Liter.

Cladocera contributed to 26.45% of the total zooplankton with annual average of 101 organisms/Liter.The population density of this group ranged from 19 organisms/Liter (September) to 182 organisms/Liter (April).Among cladocera, *Indialona ganapati, Alona rectangular* and *Ceriodaphnia cornuta* were recorded round the third year of investigation, while *Moina micrura, Diaphanosoma sarsi* and *D.excisum* were not recorded in September.

Copepods were represented by 5 species with its contribution to 20.08% of the zooplankton. *Diaptomus marshianus, Phylladiaptomus lindbergi,* and *Mesocyclops hyalinus* were present in all months, while *Mesocyclops leukarti* and *Cyclops viridis* were absent in September and June respectively. The copepod contribution ranged from 21 organisms/Liter (June and August) to 149 organisms/Liter (March) with an average of 77 organisms/Liter.

Ostracods contributed to 7.28% of the total zooplankton and represented by three species. *Cypris obensa* and *Candocypria osborni* were present in eleven months and *Cyclocypris globosa* in ten months.

The ostracod strength ranged from 4 organisms/Liter (June) to 55 organisms/Liter (February) with annual average of 28 organisms/Liter. All members of this group showed maxima in summer and minima in rainy season.

Phytoplankton diversity: A total fo 21 species of phytoplankton belonging to Chlorophyceae 98 species), Cyanophyceae (5 species), Bacillariophyceae (6 species) and Euglenophyceae (2 species) were recorded from Harni (Katgaon) reservoir (Table 6.9).

Table 6.8: Monthly Analysis of Zooplankton Diversity in Harni (Katgaon) Reservoir (Year 2013-14)

Species/Month	June	July	August	September	October	November	December	January	February	March	April	May
Protozoa												
Paramecium caudatum	04	02	04	02	10	12	10	12	15	15	10	15
Diffugia spp.	00	02	00	02	10	15	08	12	20	20	15	20
Opercularia spp.	00	02	04	08	08	12	12	15	25	25	22	18
Total	**04**	**06**	**08**	**12**	**28**	**39**	**30**	**39**	**60**	**60**	**47**	**53**
Rotifera												
Brachionus calyciflorus	04	08	10	10	12	15	20	20	30	25	25	28
Brachionus falcatus	10	10	05	04	10	18	22	22	28	22	28	25
Brachionus diversicornis	04	12	05	12	15	21	19	28	24	26	30	35
Keratella tropica	12	04	04	10	12	15	20	26	22	32	28	25
Keratella quadrata	12	12	08	10	15	20	20	25	32	32	00	30
Lecane (monostyla) bulla	08	05	12	12	15	18	20	22	35	35	30	28
Trichocera porcellus	10	05	10	10	19	20	18	24	30	28	22	25
Filina longiseta	05	10	10	08	08	20	14	20	30	30	30	25
Total	**65**	**66**	**64**	**76**	**106**	**147**	**153**	**187**	**231**	**230**	**193**	**221**
Cladocera												
Indialona ganapati	05	05	05	10	04	05	18	25	20	30	32	35
Moina micrura	10	10	10	00	05	05	22	15	20	28	30	30
Diaphanosoma sarsi	05	05	10	00	05	15	20	20	28	28	35	28
Diaphanosoma excisum	10	10	05	00	10	20	20	25	24	30	35	25
Alona rectangular	12	12	10	04	15	15	18	22	25	30	25	30
Ceriodaphnia cornuta	05	05	05	05	15	18	20	19	30	30	25	30
Total	**47**	**47**	**45**	**19**	**54**	**78**	**118**	**126**	**147**	**176**	**182**	**178**

(Contd...)

Species/Month	June	July	August	September	October	November	December	January	February	March	April	May
Copepoda												
Diaptomus marshianus	10	04	02	05	05	05	10	19	32	30	25	20
Phylladiaptomus lindbergi	05	10	05	04	12	12	18	19	30	32	30	28
Mescyclops leukarti	04	08	05	00	15	10	21	16	25	30	32	26
Mesocyclops hyalinus	02	05	04	02	10	18	12	15	25	22	25	28
Cyclops viridis	00	05	05	02	12	15	15	21	32	35	35	30
Total	**21**	**22**	**21**	**13**	**54**	**60**	**76**	**90**	**144**	**149**	**142**	**132**
Ostracoda												
Cypris obensa	04	00	04	04	15	10	05	05	20	18	15	10
Cyclocypris globosa	00	00	04	02	10	10	10	08	20	15	20	10
Candocypria osborni	00	05	05	08	05	05	10	15	15	18	15	15
Total	**04**	**05**	**13**	**14**	**30**	**25**	**25**	**28**	**55**	**51**	**50**	**35**

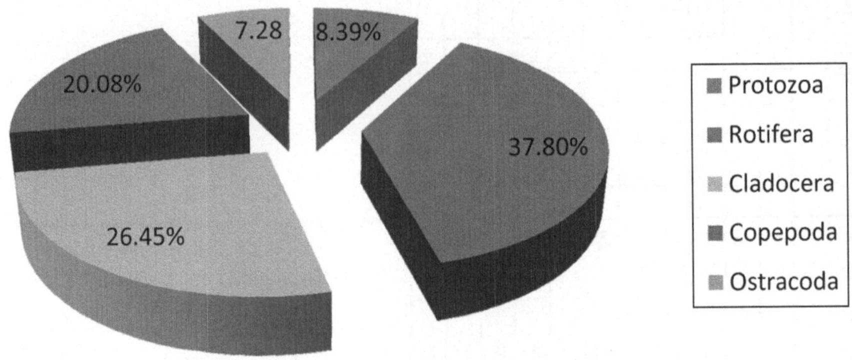

Fig. 6.3: **Quantitative Occurance of Zooplankton in Harni (Katgaon) Reservoir (Year 2013-14)**

During first year of study (2011-12), the phytoplankton consisted of 35.36% of Chlorophyceae, 30.26% of Bacillariophyceae, 25.33% of Cyanophyceae and 9.05% of Euglenophyceae (Fig. 6.4).

Chlorophyceae members were the dominant forms, followed by Bacillariophyceae, Cyanophyceae and Euglenophyceae.It was revealed that the class Chlorophyceae was dominant with annual average of 167 units/ Liter, followed by Bacillariophyceae (143 units/Liter), Cyanophyceae (120 units/Liter) and Euglenophyceae (43 units/Liter).

In case of Chlorophyceae, *Pediastrum simplex, Ankistrodesmus falcatus, Chlorella vulgaris, Closterium limneticum* and *Cosmarium contrctum* were observed in all the months. *Pediastrum duplex* and *Scendesmus armatus* were absent in September and august respectively, while *Ulothrix zonata* was not seen in two months i.e., June and September.

Among blue green algae, *Oscillatoria limnosa. Oscillatoria chlorine* and *Anabaena constricta* were observed throughout the first year of investigation with maximum and minimum in summer and monsoon season respectively.Sharma and Pant (1979) also recorded the maximum abundance of blue green lgae during summer months in Kumaon Lakes. This obviously may be due to the availability of sufficient sunlight and high water temperature.The variation in the population density of blue green algae ranged from 50 to 195 units/Liter and contributed to 25.33% of the total phytoplankton population.*Merismopedia punctata* and *Microcystis aerugenose* were recorded in eleven months.These species were not seen in one month of monsoon season.

The diatoms were represented by *Navicula gracilis, Navicula viridula, Nitzschia subtilis, Bacillaria paradoxa, Diatmos vuloare* and *Synedra affinis*. Out of these 6 species, *Navicula gracilis* and *Diatoms vuloare* were observed throughout the first year of invrstigation. The density of this group ranged from 40 to 220 units/Liter with annual average of 143 units/Liter.

Table 6.9: Monthly Analysis of Phytoplankton Diversity in Harni (Katgaon) Reservoir (Year 2011-12)

Species/Month	June	July	August	September	October	November	December	January	February	March	April	May
Chlorophyceae												
Ulothrix zonata	00	25	20	00	35	30	25	35	35	55	45	40
Pediastrum duplex	25	25	00	00	25	25	30	30	40	45	35	35
Pediastrum simplex	05	10	10	05	15	15	20	20	20	30	25	30
Scendesmus armatus	10	10	00	10	15	10	15	15	15	15	20	15
Ankistrodesmus falcatus	15	10	10	15	20	10	15	20	15	25	20	20
Chlorella vulgaris	15	10	15	15	10	10	20	15	20	20	25	20
Closterium limneticum	10	20	15	25	25	15	20	25	30	35	30	35
Cosmarium contractum	20	20	15	15	15	20	25	35	35	45	40	35
Total	**100**	**130**	**85**	**85**	**160**	**135**	**170**	**195**	**210**	**270**	**240**	**230**
Cyanophyceae												
Oscillatoria limnosoa	20	25	25	15	25	25	35	35	35	40	40	45
Oscillatoria chlorine	15	10	05	05	20	25	25	30	30	35	35	45
Anabaena constricta	15	20	20	20	05	25	20	25	30	35	30	35
Merismopedia punctata	25	25	20	00	10	20	25	25	20	30	30	35
Microcystis aerugenose	15	15	00	10	15	15	20	20	35	35	35	35
Total	**90**	**95**	**70**	**50**	**75**	**110**	**125**	**135**	**150**	**175**	**170**	**195**

(Contd...)

Species/Month	June	July	August	September	October	November	December	January	February	March	April	May
Bacillariophyceae												
Navicula gracilis	20	25	25	10	30	35	35	40	40	50	50	45
Navicula viridula	10	15	30	00	35	30	40	40	45	40	35	40
Nitzschia subtilis	20	25	00	15	20	35	35	40	40	45	45	40
Bacillaria paradoxa	05	10	00	10	00	15	20	20	25	25	30	25
Diatoms vuloare	10	10	25	05	20	25	30	35	35	40	35	35
Synedra affinis	00	00	00	00	10	05	10	15	15	20	15	15
Total	**65**	**85**	**80**	**40**	**115**	**145**	**170**	**190**	**200**	**220**	**210**	**200**
Euglenophyceae												
Euglena stellata	10	10	00	05	10	10	15	15	20	20	25	30
Euglena viridis	20	20	20	00	15	25	30	35	35	50	40	55
Total	**30**	**30**	**20**	**05**	**25**	**35**	**45**	**50**	**55**	**70**	**65**	**85**

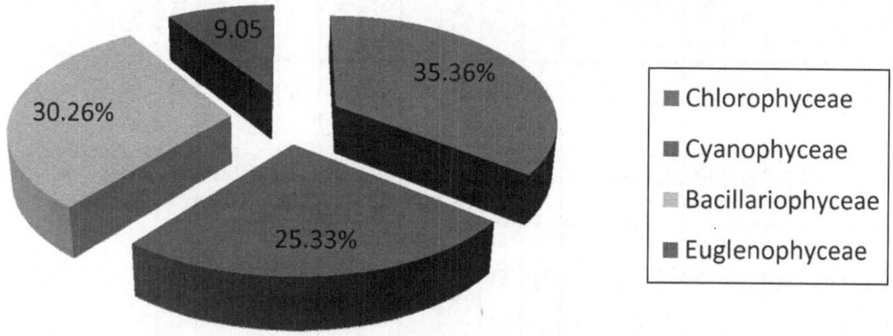

Fig. 6.4: **Quantitative Occurance of Phytoplankton of Harni (Katgaon) Reservoir (2011-12)**

Synedra affinis was totally absent in rainy season. *Bacillaria paradoxa* was absent in two months i.e., August and October, while *Navicula viridula* and *Nitzschia subtilis* were absent in September and August respectively.

Euglenophyceae was recorded by two species i.e., *Euglena stellata* and *Euglena viridis*. Both species were recorded in eleven months and absent in one month of rainy season. The population density of Euglenophyceae ranged from 5 to 85 units/Liter with annual average of 43 units/Liter. The contribution of this group was 9.05% of the total phytoplankton population.

During second year of investigation (2012-13) a total number of 21 species i.e., 8 species of Chlorophyceae, 5 species of Cyanophyceae, 6 species of Bacillariophyceae and 2 species of Euglenophyceae were recorded in Harni (Katgaon) reservoir (Table 6.10). The phytoplankton consisted of 37.98 % of Chlorophyceae, 31.27 % of bacillariophyceae, 24.05 % of Cyanophyceae and 6.73 % of Euglenophyceae (Fig. 6.5).

Chlorophyceae members were the dominating forms, followed by Bacillariophyceae, Cyanophyceae and Euglenophyceae. The class Chlorophyceae was dominant with annual average of 191 units/Liter, followed by Bacillariophyceae (157 units/liter), cyanophyceae (121 units/ Liter) and euglenophyceae (34 units/Liter)

Green algae were represented by *Ulothrix zonata, Pediastrum duplex, Pediastrum simplex, Scendesmus armatus, Akistrodesmus falcatus, Chorella vulgaris, Clostrium limneticum* and *Cosmarium contractum*. The density of this group ranged from 60 to 335 units/Liter with annual average of 191 units/Liter. *Ulothrix zonata, Pediastrum duplex, Closterium limneticum* and *Cosmarium contractum* were observed throughout the second year of investigation.

Chlorella vulgaris, Scendesmus armatus and *Pediastrum simplex* were absent in four, three and two months of rainy season, while *Ankistrodesmus falcatus* was not seen in one month (August).

Table 6.10: Monthly Analysis of Phytoplankton Diversity in Harni (Katgaon) Reservoir (Year 2012-13)

Species/Month	June	July	August	September	October	November	December	January	February	March	April	May
Chlorophyceae												
Ulothrix zonata	10	10	05	05	05	15	15	20	20	35	35	45
Pediastrum duplex	15	15	25	25	25	30	30	30	35	35	40	40
Pediastrum simplex	20	25	00	00	30	30	35	35	45	40	55	55
Scendesmus armatus	00	00	00	20	25	35	40	40	35	40	45	40
Ankistrodesmus falcatus	05	10	00	05	25	35	35	35	40	30	40	45
Chlorella vulgaris	00	00	00	00	10	10	15	15	20	35	30	35
Closterium limneticum	05	05	15	10	10	20	35	30	40	35	40	40
Cosmarium contractum	20	15	15	10	15	20	25	20	30	30	40	35
Total	**75**	**80**	**60**	**75**	**145**	**195**	**230**	**225**	**265**	**280**	**325**	**335**
Cyanophyceae												
Oscillatoria limnosoa	10	15	15	25	25	35	35	25	35	45	35	45
Oscillatoria chlorine	10	15	05	25	25	35	30	35	35	40	40	40
Anabaena constricta	05	10	15	00	20	25	25	30	35	35	35	35
Merismopedia punctata	10	15	00	15	20	20	35	35	40	35	45	45
Microcystis aerugenose	05	05	00	00	10	10	20	25	25	35	25	25
Total	**40**	**60**	**35**	**65**	**100**	**125**	**145**	**150**	**170**	**190**	**180**	**190**

(Contd...)

Species/Month	June	July	August	September	October	November	December	January	February	March	April	May
Bacillariophyceae												
Navicula gracilis	10	15	15	20	20	20	30	35	30	30	35	35
Navicula viridula	20	20	15	15	15	15	20	30	35	35	40	30
Nitzschia subtilis	05	15	20	00	25	25	25	25	40	40	30	35
Bacillaria paradoxa	10	10	25	25	35	35	45	40	45	35	35	40
Diatoms vuloare	15	15	00	10	00	20	25	25	25	30	55	40
Synedra affinis	25	25	35	30	00	30	35	30	40	45	45	35
Total	**85**	**100**	**110**	**100**	**95**	**145**	**180**	**185**	**215**	**215**	**240**	**215**
Euglenophyceae												
Euglena stellata	10	00	15	00	15	20	20	25	20	25	25	25
Euglena viridis	10	10	00	10	10	15	15	20	25	30	25	35
Total	**20**	**10**	**15**	**10**	**25**	**35**	**35**	**45**	**45**	**55**	**50**	**60**

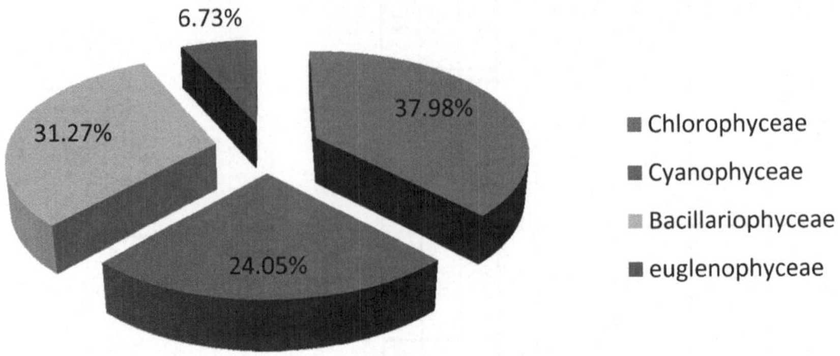

***Fig. 6.5:* Quantitative Occurance of Phytoplankton in Harni (Katgaon) Reservoir (Year 2012-13)**

The blue green algae were represented by *Oscillatoria limnosa, Oscillatoria chlorine, Anabaena constricta, Mersimopedia punctata* and *Microcystis aerogenose. Oscillatoria limnosa* and *Oscillatoria chlorine* were observed throughout the second year with minima in rainy season and maxima in summer season. *Anabaena constricta* and *Merismopedia punctata* were present in eleven months and absent in September and august respectively. *Microcystis aerogenose* was observed in 10 months and was absent in two months of rainy season i.e., august and September. The density of this group was between 35 to 190 units/Liter with annual averge of 121 units/Liter. This group contributed to 24.05% of the total phytoplankton population of second year of investigation.

The diatoms were represented by six species i.e., *Navicula gracilis, Navicula viridula, Nitzschia subtilis, Bacillaria paradoxa, Diatoms vuloare* and *Synedra affinis. Diatoms vuloare* and *Synedra affinis* were absent in October, while other species showed their presence throughout the second year of investigation. The population density of diatoms ranged from 85 to 240 units/Liter with annual average of 157 units/Liter. This group contributed to 31.27% of the total phytoplankton.

The class Euglenophyceae was represented by two species i.e., *Euglena stellata* and *Euglena viridis. Euglena stellata* was present in ten months and was absent in two months of rainy season i.e., July and September. Its density was between nil to 25 units/Liter. *Euglena viridis* was observed in eleven months and not recorded in august. Its density ranged from nil to 35 units/Liter. The density of Euglenophyceae ranged from 10 to 60 units/Liter with annual average of 34 units/Liter. This group contributed to 6.73% of the phytoplankton population.

During third year of investigation, total phytoplankton density was higher during summer season. Agale *et al.* (2013) also observed maximum density of phytoplankton in summer.

Chlorophyceae appeared as the dominant group of phytoplankton.The phytoplankton consisted of 39.62% of Chlorophyceae, 30.49% of Bacillariophyceae, 26.57% of Cyanophyceae and 3.32 o% of Euglenophyceae (Fig. 6.6).

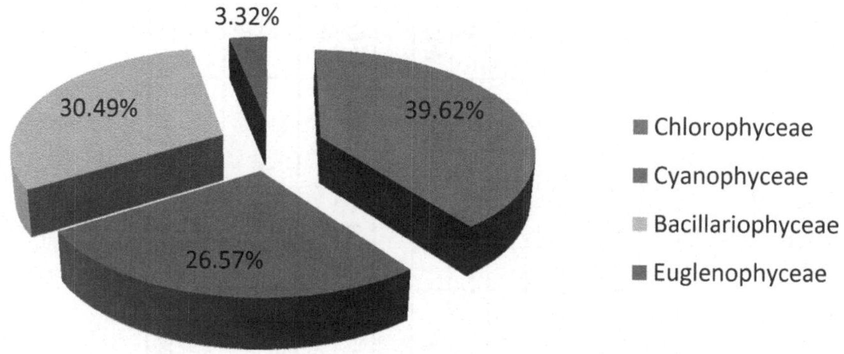

Fig. 6.6: **Quantitative Occurance of Phytoplankton in Harni (Katgaon) Reservoir (Year 2013-14)**

A Panoramic View of Harni (Katgaon) Reservoir

A total of 21 species of phytoplankton belonging to Chlorophyceae (8 species), Cyanophyceae (5 species), Bacillariophyceae (6 species) and Euglenophyceae (2 species) were recorded during third year of investigation (Table 6.11). During present investigation total phytoplankton density ranged from 195 units/Liter in September to 790 units/Liter in May.

Table 6.11: Monthly Analysis of Phytoplankton Diversity in Harni (Katgaon) Reservoir (Year 2013-14)

Species/Month	June	July	August	September	October	November	December	January	February	March	April	May
Chlorophyceae												
Ulothrix zonata	15	15	05	05	10	15	20	20	25	25	30	30
Pediastrum duplex	25	20	15	15	15	25	20	25	35	35	35	25
Pediastrum simplex	25	25	15	00	30	35	35	45	45	45	55	45
Scendesmus armatus	15	15	10	10	10	15	15	15	15	20	15	15
Ankistrodesmus falcatus	15	20	25	00	25	25	35	45	45	55	45	40
Chlorella vulgaris	15	05	05	05	15	25	25	35	35	40	40	40
Closterium limneticum	30	35	35	00	30	35	35	35	40	35	40	45
Cosmarium contractum	30	35	35	30	35	40	40	45	55	50	45	55
Total	**170**	**170**	**145**	**65**	**170**	**215**	**225**	**265**	**295**	**305**	**305**	**295**
Cyanophyceae												
Oscillatoria limnosoa	20	25	25	20	25	35	35	40	35	40	40	40
Oscillatoria chlorine	15	15	10	00	05	10	25	25	40	30	35	35
Anabaena constricta	20	25	00	15	20	25	25	25	35	35	35	35
Merismopedia punctata	20	25	20	00	20	35	35	40	45	45	55	45
Microcystis aerugenose	25	25	20	25	35	35	45	45	55	45	45	55
Total	**100**	**115**	**75**	**60**	**105**	**140**	**165**	**175**	**210**	**195**	**210**	**210**

(Contd...)

Species/Month	June	July	August	September	October	November	December	January	February	March	April	May
Bacillariophyceae												
Navicula gracilis	20	20	25	00	25	35	35	35	40	45	40	45
Navicula viridula	25	20	20	20	25	30	25	35	35	40	45	35
Nitzschia subtilis	15	15	10	10	25	25	35	35	45	35	35	55
Bacillaria paradoxa	20	25	15	00	00	35	35	45	35	55	50	50
Diatoms vuloare	25	25	20	20	00	10	15	25	25	35	35	35
Synedra affinis	15	25	25	20	20	25	25	35	30	35	35	35
Total	**120**	**130**	**115**	**70**	**95**	**160**	**170**	**210**	**210**	**245**	**240**	**255**
Euglenophyceae												
Euglena stellata	05	05	00	00	00	10	05	10	10	10	15	15
Euglena viridis	10	10	10	00	10	10	15	10	15	15	15	15
Total	**15**	**15**	**10**	**00**	**10**	**20**	**20**	**20**	**25**	**25**	**30**	**30**

Chlorophyceae was the most dominant group of phytoplankton in respect to abundance with mean value of 219 units/Liter. A total of 8 species of Chlorophyceae were observed. Among these *Ulothrix zonata,Pedistrum duplex, Scendesmus armatus, Chlorella vulgaris* and *Cosmarium contractum* were recorded in all months with maximum density in summer and minimum density in rainy season. *Pediastrum simplex, Ankistrodesmus falcatus* and *Closterium limneticum* were absent in September. The density of this group was in the range of 65 units/Liter (September) to 305 units/Liter (March and April) with annual average of 219 units/Liter.

The Bacillariophyceae ranked as the second highest among phytoplankton group in respect to abundance and number of species (6). The range of Bacillariophyceae was from 70 to 255 units/Liter with annual average of 168 units/Liter. The occurrence of Bacillariophyceae was highest in summer and lowest in rainy season. Out of six species, *Navicula viridula,Nitzschia subtilis* and *Synedra affinis* were recorded throughout the third year of investigation, while *Navicula gracilis* and *Diatmos vuloare* were absent in September and October respectively. *Bacillaria paradoxa* was absent in two months i.e., September and October.

The class Cyanophyceae was represented by five species. The abundance of Cyanophyceae was found to highest in summer season and lowest in rainy season. *Oscillatoria limnosa* and *Microcystis aerugenose* were recorded throughout the third year of inverstigation, while *Oscillatoria chlorine* and *Merismopedia punctata* were absent in September and *Anabaena constricta* in August. The density of this group ranged from 60 units/Liter (September) to 210 units/Liter (April and May) with annual average of 147 units/Liter.

Euglenophyceae was the least dominant group of phytoplankton in respect of both abundance and number of species. Euglenophyceae was represented by two species i.e., *Euglena stellata* and *Euglena viridis*. This group was absent in month of September and its density ranged from nil (September) to 30 units/Liter (April and May) with annual average of 18 units/ Liter.*Euglena stellata* was absent in three months i.e., August, September and October and *Euglena viridis* in one month i.e., September. Euglenophyceae was the most abundance group during summer season.

In present investigation Chlorophyceae was found to be the main component of phytoplankton population, followed by Bacillariophyceae, Cyanophyceae and Euglenophyceae.

In the present study, the population density of phytoplankton was higher during summer months in the three years' investigation period (2011-12 to 2013-14), followed by winter and rainy months. These findings corroborate with Shukla *et al.* (2013).

CHAPTER - 7

Gharni Reservoir

The Gharni reservoir was impounded on river Gharni in Shirur Anantpal tehsil of Latur district. The reservoir is located at latitude 18°22′30″ and longitude 76°49′15″. The total water spread area of reservoir is 949 ha at FRL with a catchment area of 243.66 sq.km. The gross storage capacity of the reservoir is 25.9 mm^3. The fishery of the reservoir is managed by Gharni Matsyavysaik Sahakari Society, Gharni. The co-operative society is formed by the 35 fishermen living around the reservoir. The seed of Indian major carps with exotics like *Cyprinus carpio* and *Ctenopharyngodon idella* is regularly stocked in the reservoir.

Total 22 fish species were recorded from different spots during the study period. During the present investigation 11 species of Cypriniformes (including 2 exotic species i.e., *Cyprinus carpio* and *Ctenopharyngodon idella*) from the reservoir, 5 species from Siluriformes, 2 species each from Clupeiformes and Perciformes, 1 species each from Mastacembeliformes, and Mugiliformes (Table 7.2). Cypriniformes contributed maximum of 50% fish species, followed by Siluriformes (22.72%), Clupeiformes (9.09%), Perciformes (9.09%), Mugiliformes (4.55%) and Mastacembeliformes (4.55%) (Fig. 7.1).

The details of the fish production from the reservoir for the period of 2011-12 to 2013-14 is shown in Table 7.3.The study of the data reveals that the maximum fish production was recorded at 66400 kg during 2011-12. It gave an average fish production of 69.96 kg/ha/yr. The minimum production was during 2013-14 kg, at 44400 kg, giving an average fish production of 46.78 kg/ha/yr. During the entire study period the catch of local fishes showed the higher catches than those of stocked species. The maximum fish catch was recorded during the summer season. The fish catch composition showed similarity with the species of the few reservoirs in Maharashtra as recorded by Sakhare (2001) and Sakhare and Joshi (2002).

Table 7.1: Morphometry of Gharni Reservoir

Year of Construction	1969
River	Gharni
Location	Sirur
District	Latur
Location	Latitude 180 22'30" Longitude 760 49'15"
Basin	Godavari
Subbasin	Manjara
Year of completion	1969
Rainfall (mm)	724
Type of dam	Earthen
Purpose	Irrigation
Length of dam (m)	956
Height of dam (m)	15.24
Catchment area (sq.km)	243.46
Gross storage capacity at FRL (MCM)	25.08
Live storage capacity (MCM)	22.46
Dead storage capacity (MCM)	2.62
Full Resevoir Level (m)	594.05
Water spread area (ha)	949
Irrigation potential (ha)	2834

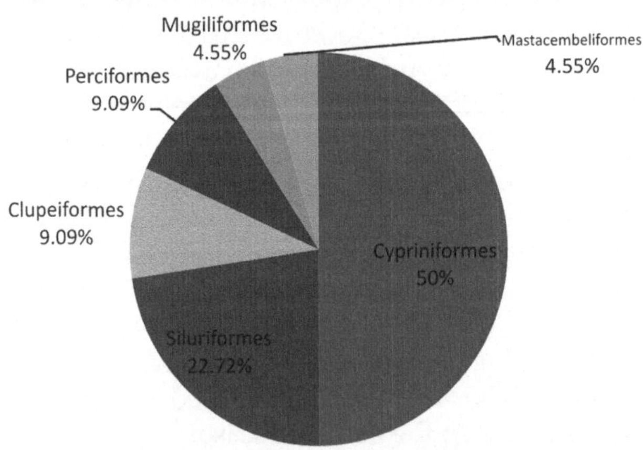

Fig. 7.1: **Percentage Contrubution of Different Groups of Fishes in Gharni Reservoir**

Table 7.2: Fish Fauna of Gharni Reservoir

Order: Clupeiformes **Suborder:Notopteroidei** **Family: Notopteridae** 1. *Notopterus notopterus (Pallas)*
2. *Notopterus chitala (Ham.)*
Order: Cypriniformes **Suborder: Cyprinoidei** **Family: Cyprinidae** 3. *Catla catla (Ham.)*
4. *Labeo rohita (Ham.)*
5. *Labeo boggut (Sykes)*
6. *Cirrhinus mrigala (Ham.)*
7. *Cyprinus carpio(Linn)*
8. *Ctenopharyngodon idella (Ham.)*
9. *Amblypharyngodon mola (Ham.)*
10. *Puntius sarana sarana (Ham.)*
11. *Puntius chola (Ham.)*
12. *Rasbora daniconius (Ham.)*
Family: Cobitidae 13. *Nemacheilus botia (Ham.)*
Order: Siluriformes **Family: Bagridae** 14. *Mystus cavasius (Ham.)*
15. *Mystus seenghala (Sykes)*
16. *Mystus vittatus (Bloch)*
Family: Claridae 17. *Clarias batrachus (Linn.)*
Family: Heterpneustidae 18. *Heteropnesutes fossilis (Bloch)*
Order: Mugiliformes **Family: Mugilidae** 19. *Mugil cephalus (Linn.)*
Order: Mastacembeliformes 20. *Mastacembelus pancalus (Ham.)*
Order: Perciformes **Family: Anabantidae** 21. *Anabas testudineus (Bloch)*
Family: Ambassidae 22. *Chanda ranga (Ham.)*

During first year of investigation, local fishes formed to about 41.42% of the total catch, while *Catla catla, Labeo rohita, Cirrhinus mrigala, Ctenophyaryngodon idella* and *Cyprinus carpio* formed 14.76%, 10.54%, 2.56%, 13.40% and 17.32% of the total fish catch in reservoir. Exotics (*Ctenophyayngodon idella* and *Cyprinus carpio*) togetherly contributed to about 30.72% of the totoal catch.

During second year of investigation, local fishes formed 38% of the total catch, while *Catla catla, Labeo rohita, Cirrhinus mrigala, Ctenophryngodon idella* and *Cyprinus carpio* contributed to about 13.67%, 8.83%, 1.67%, 14.17% and 23.67% of the catch respectively. Exotic species i.e., *Ctenopharyngodon idella* and *Cyprinus carpio* togetherly contributed to 37.84% of the total fish catch.

During third year of investigation, local fishes dominated over the carps and contributed to 39% of the total fish landing. *Catla catla, Labeo rohita* and *Cirrhinus mrigala* formed 12.39%, 4.09% and 1.96% of the total fish catch. Exotic species such as *Ctenopharyngodon idella* and *Cyprinus carpio* contributed to 18.24 % and 24.32% of the total fish catch. These two species togetherly formed 42.56% of the total catch.

No earlier reports on the presence of Grass carp either in upstream or downstream of Gharni reservoir are available. The possibility of introduction in the reservoir appeared to be through stocking material brought from outside.

The study on fish catchand catch composition revealed that *Cyprinus carpio* contribute to about 21.77% of the total fish catch in reservoir. A more important disqualification is its propensities to compete with *Cirrhinus mrigala*.The stocking of *Cyprinus carpio* in Gharni reservoir has nearly eliminated *Cirrhinus mrigala.*

Peak fishing is mainly confined to certain seasons commencing from pre-monsoon months till the onset of floods. Fishing activity is generally low during monsoon and pre-monsoon months.Lentic sector, being very deep is often shunned by fishermen.

Physico-chemical environment: The year wise seasonal averages of various physico-chemical parameters are presented in Table 7.4.

Temperature is critical in growth, reproduction and sometimes survival. Each species of fish has an optimum temperature range for growth, as well as upper and lower lethal temperatures. Below the optimum temperature food consumption and food conversion decline until a temperature is reached at which growth ceases and food consumption is limited to a maintenance ration. Below this temperature is a lower lethal temperature at which death occurs. Above the optimum temperature food consumption increases while food conversion declines.

Table 7.3: Fish Catch Details of Gharni Reservoir of Latur District, Maharashtra

	Catla Catla	Labeo Rohita	Cirrhinus Mrigal	Cyprinus Carpio	Ctenopharyngodon Idella	Local Fishes	Total
2011-12	9800	7000	1700	11500	8900	27500	66400
%	14.76	10.54	2.56	17.32	13.40	41.42	
2012-13	8200	5300	1000	14200	8500	22800	60000
%	13.67	8.83	1.67	23.67	14.17	38	
2013-14	5500	1815	870	10800	8100	17315	44400
%	12.39	4.09	1.96	24.32	18.24	39	

The surface temperature values ranged from 17 to 28.5 °C during 2011-12, 17.5 to 29.5 °C during 2012-13 and 18.5 to 30.5 °C during 2013-14. The overall mean recorded as 23.18. The surface temperature values were maximum during summer and minimum in winter season. Steady change in the atmospheric temperature with the change in the seasons results in the corresponding change in the water temperature. High summer temperature and bright sunlight accelerate the process of decay of organic matter resulting into the liberation of large quantities of carbon dioxide and nutrients (Agarwal and Rajwar, 2010). The highest surface water temperature in summer months can be attributed to the direct relationship between bright sunshine, its duration and air temperature (Hussain, 1977).

Carbon dioxide is one of the most important substances in the life of organisms. The monthly variation in free carbon dioxide ranges from 00 mg/l to 1.7 mg/l with an average of 0.47 mg/l. It was found to be absent in winter and rainy season. Free CO_2 content in water sample was negligible in majority of the months, might be due to pollution and photosynthetic activity of phytoplankton.

Total alkalinity is the measure of the capacity of water to neutralize of strong acid. The alkalinity in water is generally imparted by the salts of carbonates, bicarbonates, phosphates, nitrate, borates, and silicates etc. together with the hydroxyl ions in free state. The seasonal variation in total alkalinity ranged from 130 mg/l to 270 mg/l, with an average of 194.71 mg/l. The alkalinity was maximum in the summer months while minimum in the rainy season. Alkalinity was maximum in summer season due to increase in bicarbonate in water while minimum in rainy season due to increase in water level causing dilution.

Hardness is governed by the concentration of calcium and magnesium salts largely combined with bicarbonates and carbonates giving temporary hardness while sulfate, chloride and other anions of mineral acids causing permanent hardness. The monthly variations in total hardness ranges between 77.3 mg/l to 110 mg/l, with an average values 89.86 mg/l. The maximum amount of hardness was recorded in the summer and minimum amount of total hardness recorded in the winter season. The higher value of hardness was during summer may be due to decrease in water level and evaporation of water.

Chloride is an important parameter in accessing the water quality. It controls the salinity of water and osmotic stress on biotic communities. Chloride content indicated the presence of organic matter presumably of animal origin and mostly this may also bring about an increase in the ammonical nitrogen. The seasonal variation in chloride values ranges from 35.4 mg/l to 63.5 mg/l, with an average values 51.95 mg/l. The maximum amount of chlorides was recorded in summer season while minimum amount of chloride was recorded winter. Higher chloride concentration during summer season due to high temperature.

The quantity of total dissolved solids is dependent on the stratification of the lake. It is also dependent on the water inlet that comes to the lake. Thus, the dissolved solids content of standing water is dependent on the catchment area. The dissolved solids are also fixed by phytoplankton. Major nutrients like nitrogen, phosphrous, iron, silicon and others may be depleted and so limit production or alter the composition of algal community.

Total dissolved solids are the solids present in water in the dissolved state. The total dissolved solids ranged from 105.5 mg/l to 149 mg/l, with an average 126.83 mg/l. It was recorded maximum in the summer season while it was recorded minimum in the winter.

Zooplankton diversity: In first year of investigation, total 25 species of zooplankton were identified from Gharni reservoir (Table 7.5). Rotifers were dominant (37.14%), followed by Cladocera (27.74%), Copepoda (15.17%), Ostracoda (11.10%) and Protozoa (8.85%) (Fig.7.2). Zooplanktons of all major groups were observed in summer season. The summer population maxima of zooplankton were co-related with higher temperatures, lower transparency and high standing crop of primary producers leading to greater availability of food. Similar findings were expressed by Salve and Hiware (2010) and Joshi (2011). During present investigation, the zooplankton population was low in monsoon season. It might also be due to fall of temperature and dilution in concentration of minerals and salts in reservoir water (Chakraborty 2004; Dutta *et al.* 2010, Okogwo *et al.* 2010 and Bhat *et al.* 2014).

Protozoans were represented by 3 species. *Paramecium caudatum* and *Opercularia spp* were absent in June, while *Diffugia spp* were absent in July and September. The concentration of group ranged from 5 organisms/liter (June) to 62 organisms/Liter (April) with annual average of 32organisms/liter.

Rotifers were represented by 8 species which made-up about-up 37.14% of the total zooplankton count, with an annual average of 131 organisms/ Liter. The rotifer density ranged from 21 organisms/Liter (June) to 222 organisms/Liter (April).Their densities were highest in the summer and decreased in monsoon season. Among rotifers *Brachionus calyciflorus, B.falcatus, Keratella tropica* and *K.quadrata* were observed round the year. *Brachionus diversicornis* and *Trichocera porcellus* were absent in July and June respectively. *Lecane (Monostyla) bulla* and *Filinia logiseta* were not observed in two months of rainy season i.e., *Lecane (Monostyla) bulla* in June and July and *Filinia longiseta* in June and September.

Cladocera was represented by 6 species. *Indialona ganapati* was observed throughout the year with its peak in summer season. *Moina micrura* was not detected in June and September, while *Diaphanosoma sarsi, D.excisum, Alona rectangular* and *Ceriodaphnia cornuta* were absent in one month each. Density of this group ranged from 20 organisms/Liter (September) to 193 organisms/ Liter (April) with average density of 98 organisms/Lite (Table 7.5).

Table 7.4: Seasonal Fluctuation in Water Quality Parameters of Gharni Reservoir

Season/Year	Water Temp.(°C)	Transparency (cm)	pH	TDS (mg/l)	DO (mg/l)	CO_2 (mg/)	TA (mg/l)	Cl^- (mg/l)	TH (mg/l)
2011-12									
Monsoon	23.5	70	8.4	125	8.9	Nil	130	60.5	99.5
Winter	17	85.5	8.5	105.5	8.0	Nil	190	35.4	80.5
Summer	28.5	95	8.5	140	5.8	1.4	270	63.5	110
Mean	23	83.5	8.46	123.5	7.56	0.46	196.6	53.13	96.66
2012-13									
Monsoon	23.5	45	8.5	120.5	8.4	Nil	130	55.5	86.5
Winter	17.5	80	8.4	110.5	7.5	Nil	210	34.7	77.3
Summer	29.5	80.5	8.3	130.5	5.2	1.7	250	60.3	88.5
Mean	23.5	68.5	8.4	120.5	7.03	0.56	196.6	50.16	84.1
2013-14									
Monsoon	20.2	52	8.4	138	8.0	Nil	140.5	55.5	88
Winter	18.5	65	8.4	122.5	7.5	Nil	170	42.8	78.5
Summer	30.5	70.5	8.4	149	6.7	1.2	262	59.4	100
Mean	23.06	62.5	8.4	136.5	7.4	0.4	190.8	52.56	88.83
Grand Mean	32.18	71.5	8.42	126.8	7.33	0.47	194.7	51.95	89.86

Table 7.5: Monthly Analysis of Zooplankton Diversity in Gharni Reservoir (Year 2011-12)

Species/Month	June	July	August	September	October	November	December	January	February	March	April	May
Protozoa												
Paramecium caudatum	00	04	04	05	10	10	15	10	15	18	22	18
Diffugia spp.	05	00	02	00	08	12	10	15	18	15	20	18
Opercularia spp.	00	02	02	04	05	04	12	15	16	20	20	20
Total	**05**	**06**	**08**	**09**	**23**	**26**	**37**	**40**	**49**	**53**	**62**	**56**
Rotifera												
Brachionus calyciflorus	05	05	12	10	18	20	22	26	22	30	32	32
Brachionus falcatus	04	15	10	05	10	18	18	30	30	28	26	28
Brachionus diversicornis	02	00	10	10	18	12	12	18	38	32	35	26
Keratella tropica	08	10	18	15	15	18	20	22	32	32	35	36
Keratella quadrata	02	04	04	04	20	18	22	28	30	30	30	29
Lecane (monostyla) bulla	00	00	02	02	22	15	20	28	28	28	28	30
Trichocera porcellus	00	02	02	00	05	10	12	10	12	15	18	20
Filina longiseta	00	02	02	00	05	10	12	10	12	15	18	20
Total	**21**	**38**	**63**	**51**	**118**	**116**	**138**	**172**	**204**	**207**	**222**	**219**
Cladocera												
Indialona ganapati	04	08	10	05	12	12	14	20	24	28	30	30
Moina micrura	00	05	10	00	08	11	12	15	24	25	35	28
Diaphanosoma sarsi	04	10	05	00	10	10	15	22	28	30	32	35
Diaphanosoma excisum	04	12	05	00	10	10	15	22	28	30	32	35
Alona rectangular	00	04	04	10	08	15	18	20	25	38	32	30
Ceriodaphnia cornuta	15	02	00	05	12	15	20	22	26	30	32	29
Total	**27**	**41**	**34**	**20**	**62**	**73**	**94**	**119**	**149**	**173**	**193**	**187**

(Contd…)

Species/Month	June	July	August	September	October	November	December	January	February	March	April	May
Copepoda												
Diaptomus marshianus	04	10	05	10	10	10	10	15	18	20	25	28
Phylladiaptomus lindbergi	00	00	00	00	12	10	12	12	15	22	22	28
Mescyclops leukarti	04	10	10	12	12	10	15	15	18	24	28	26
Mesocyclops hyalinus	04	05	10	05	10	10	12	15	20	20	20	28
Cyclops viridis	12	25	25	27	44	40	49	57	71	86	95	110
Total	**27**	**41**	**34**	**20**	**62**	**73**	**94**	**119**	**149**	**173**	**193**	**187**
Ostracoda												
Cypris obensa	00	04	04	04	10	10	14	12	14	20	20	28
Cyclocypris globosa	00	05	10	10	10	12	12	14	14	28	25	30
Candocypria osborni	00	05	10	05	05	15	15	14	20	19	26	25
Total	**00**	**14**	**24**	**19**	**25**	**37**	**41**	**40**	**48**	**67**	**71**	**83**

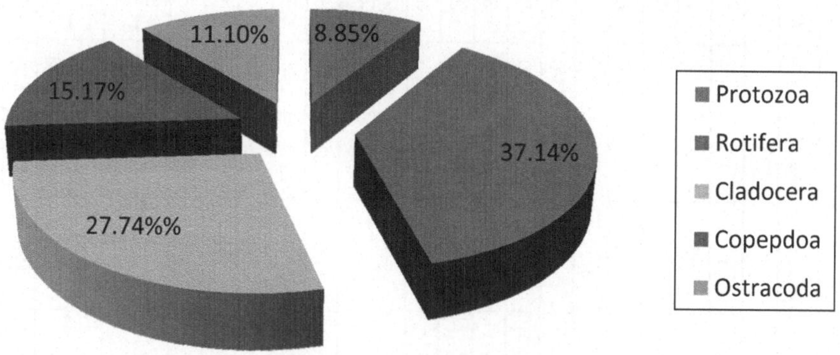

Fig. 7.2: **Quantitative Occurance of Zooplankton in Gharni Reservoir (Year 2011-12)**

Copepods were represented by 5 species. *Phylladiaptomus lindbergi* was not observed in entire rainy season, while other species were present round the year. The population density of group reached its peak in May with 110 organisms/Liter while in June it was least with 12 organisms/Liter. The annual average of copepods was 53 organisms/Liter. Normally the monsoon is associated with lower population densities due to its dilution effect and decreased photosynthetic activity by primary producers. Similar results have been shown by Bais and Agarwal (1993) and Joshi (2011).

Ostracods represented by three species, ranged from nil (June) to 83 organisms/Liter (May) with average density of 39 organisms/Liter. In June, ostracods were totally absent, while in other months they were seen with maxima in summer.

During second year of investigation (2012-13) 25 species belonging to 5 groups were identified (Table 7.6). The zooplankton maxima was recorded in summer season, followed by winter and monsoon. Rotifers dominated the zooplanktons (36.34%) followed by Cladocera (30.09%), Copepoda (20.60%), Ostracoda (8.05%) and Protozoa (4.92%) (Fig.7.3).

Protozoans were represented by three species i.e., *Paramecium caudatum, Diffugia spp* and *Opercularia spp.Paramecium caudatum* and *Diffugia spp* were recorded round the year with maxima in summer and minima in rainy season. *Opercularia spp* were not observed in two months of rainy season (June and September). Protozoan density was in the range of 6 organisms/Liter to 32 organisms/Liter with an average density of 19 organisms/Liter.

Rotifers were represented by eight species. Except *Filinia longiseta* all species were observed round the year. *Filinia longiseta* was absent in August. Rotifer density ranged from 55 organisms/Liter (August) to 241 organisms/Liter (April) with average density of 139 organims/Liter.

Table 7.6: Monthly Analysis of Zooplankton Diversity in Gharni Reservoir (Year 2012-13)

Species/Month	June	July	August	September	October	November	December	January	February	March	April	May
Protozoa												
Paramecium caudatum	04	04	02	04	08	05	08	08	10	10	12	10
Diffugia spp.	02	02	04	05	05	05	05	08	08	10	12	10
Opercularia spp.	00	02	02	00	05	05	08	10	10	10	08	05
Total	**06**	**08**	**08**	**09**	**18**	**15**	**21**	**26**	**28**	**30**	**32**	**25**
Rotifera												
Brachionus calyciflorus	02	04	04	04	15	15	15	18	28	22	28	30
Brachionus falcatus	02	02	04	05	15	12	15	18	20	28	30	35
Brachionus diversicornis	05	15	11	09	10	14	16	18	20	25	32	32
Keratella tropica	08	10	10	10	12	12	16	20	25	25	32	32
Keratella quadrata	05	10	10	10	14	13	18	22	27	28	25	30
Lecane (monostyla) bulla	15	10	08	10	12	18	14	27	27	30	28	25
Trichocera porcellus	10	12	08	12	18	12	18	27	30	30	34	28
Filina longiseta	15	08	00	10	12	16	15	25	28	32	32	30
Total	**62**	**71**	**65**	**60**	**108**	**112**	**127**	**175**	**205**	**220**	**241**	**232**
Cladocera												
Indialona ganapati	10	05	05	05	15	18	20	22	25	30	32	37
Moina micrura	05	10	05	10	10	15	18	25	28	30	30	35
Diaphanosoma sarsi	00	10	10	04	12	20	22	28	28	22	35	30
Diaphanosoma excisum	10	02	05	00	10	18	20	22	30	30	35	28
Alona rectangular	05	10	15	10	18	18	20	25	32	32	25	35
Ceriodaphnia cornuta	08	12	10	08	15	15	18	25	32	38	38	35
Total	**38**	**49**	**50**	**37**	**80**	**104**	**118**	**147**	**175**	**189**	**195**	**200**

(Contd…)

Species/Month	June	July	August	September	October	November	December	January	February	March	April	May
Copepoda												
Diaptomus marshianus	05	10	05	10	12	15	18	18	18	24	22	35
Phylladiaptomus lindbergi	10	05	05	05	15	15	15	20	20	20	24	30
Mesocyclops leukarti	05	00	02	05	10	18	18	18	22	28	28	32
Mesocyclops hyalinus	02	04	08	05	08	12	20	20	22	30	30	28
Cyclops viridis	02	02	08	05	12	12	18	20	25	25	30	28
Total	**24**	**21**	**28**	**30**	**57**	**72**	**89**	**96**	**107**	**127**	**142**	**153**
Ostracoda												
Cypris obensa	02	02	04	05	05	10	10	15	18	20	15	15
Cyclocypris globosa	00	04	05	05	08	08	10	15	20	20	15	18
Candocypria osborni	04	02	05	05	08	05	12	12	18	18	12	20
Total	**06**	**08**	**14**	**15**	**21**	**23**	**32**	**42**	**56**	**58**	**42**	**53**

Table 7.7: Monthly Analysis of Zooplankton Diversity in Gharni Reservoir (Year 2013-14)

Species/Month	June	July	August	September	October	November	December	January	February	March	April	May
Protozoa												
Paramecium caudatum	04	02	04	05	08	10	12	15	30	30	35	35
Diffugia spp.	10	00	04	00	05	12	10	20	28	28	35	35
Opercularia spp.	00	04	05	05	05	10	15	22	22	32	30	30
Total	**14**	**06**	**14**	**10**	**18**	**32**	**37**	**57**	**80**	**90**	**100**	**90**
Rotifera												
Brachionus calyciflorus	08	02	02	05	08	10	18	18	26	30	30	35
Brachionus falcatus	04	10	10	10	10	12	15	12	30	25	28	30
Brachionus diversicornis	02	05	08	10	05	15	10	15	22	25	28	30
Keratella tropica	05	04	05	10	10	15	12	18	20	20	35	28
Keratella quadrata	02	04	05	05	12	18	15	18	22	18	25	28
Lecane (monostyla) bulla	08	02	04	00	10	15	18	22	28	25	32	35
Trichocera porcellus	02	06	04	02	08	15	18	25	22	30	22	30
Filina longiseta	02	02	00	00	10	12	20	29	25	30	35	30
Total	**33**	**34**	**38**	**42**	**73**	**112**	**126**	**157**	**195**	**203**	**235**	**246**
Cladocera												
Indialona ganapati	04	05	05	04	04	20	12	15	18	20	25	35
Moina micrura	00	04	05	00	05	12	15	20	26	25	28	28
Diaphanosoma sarsi	00	04	05	08	05	12	18	20	20	22	22	35
Diaphanosoma excisum	12	10	05	10	12	15	15	22	20	28	32	32
Alona rectangular	00	10	12	10	10	00	15	18	22	28	30	30
Ceriodaphnia cornuta	18	10	10	00	10	14	20	20	25	25	25	28
Total	**34**	**43**	**42**	**32**	**46**	**73**	**95**	**115**	**131**	**148**	**162**	**188**

(Contd…)

Species/Month	June	July	August	September	October	November	December	January	February	March	April	May
Copepoda												
Diaptomus marshianus	05	06	02	04	05	12	10	12	22	22	30	30
Phylladiaptomus lindbergi	04	00	02	00	05	10	12	15	22	25	32	28
Mescyclops leukarti	04	00	00	04	04	05	10	15	25	25	29	28
Mesocyclops hyalinus	04	05	05	05	05	10	10	18	20	28	30	29
Cyclops viridis	02	02	05	02	04	08	15	20	20	28	32	33
Total	**19**	**13**	**14**	**11**	**23**	**45**	**47**	**80**	**109**	**128**	**153**	**148**
Ostracoda												
Cypris obensa	04	00	00	05	05	08	00	05	10	15	20	18
Cyclocypris globosa	04	02	00	04	05	08	18	12	10	15	20	20
Candocypria osborni	04	02	00	05	05	10	08	12	12	18	18	25
Total	**12**	**04**	**00**	**14**	**15**	**26**	**26**	**29**	**32**	**48**	**48**	**63**

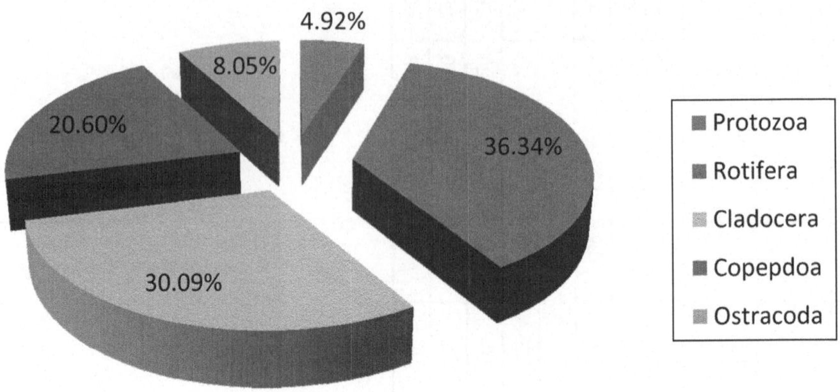

Fig. 7.3: **Quantitative Occurance of Zooplankton in Gharni Reservoir (Year 2012-13)**

Cladocera represented by six species, which had summer maxima and monsoon minima. When the dynamics of the cladocera group was observed, there was always a summer maxima. *Indialona ganapati, Moina micrura* and *Alona rectangular* had peaks in May representing 37 organisms/Liter, 35 organisms/Liter and 35 organisms/Liter respectively. *Diaphanosoma sarsi* and *D.excisum* had peaks of abundance in April, while *Ceriodaphnia cornuta* was found to be most dominant during March and April with 38 organisms/ Liter. *Diaphanosoma sarsi* and *D.excisum* were not recorded in June and September respectively.

Copepods were represented by five species, out of which *Mesocyclops leukarti* was not detected in July. Other species showed their presence round the year. *Diaptomus marshianus, Phylladiaptomus lindbergi* and *Mesocyclops leukarti* had peaks in May representing 35 organisms/Liter, 30 organisms/Liter and 32 organisms/Liter respectively. *Mesocyclops hyalinus* and *Cyclops viridis* had peak of abundance in April representing 38 organisms/Liter and 30 organisms/Liter respectively. The copepod density ranged from 21 organisms/Liter (July) to 153 organisms/Liter (May) with average density of 79 organisms/Liter.

Ostracods were representing by three species. *Cypris obensa* and *Candocypria osborni* were recorded round the year with peak in March (20 organisms/Liter) and May (20 organisms/Liter). *Cyclocypris globosa* was dominated in February and March with density of 20 organisms/Liter. The density of this group varied from 6 organisms/Liter (June) to 58 organisms/ Liter (March) with average value of 31 organisms/liter.

In third year of investigation (2013-14) the total population of zooplankton in the reservoir was found to range from a minimum of 100 organisms/Liter (July) to 735organisms/Liter (May) (Table 7.7). Zooplanktom activity was minimum in rainy season and maximum in summer. The annual zooplankton population in the reservoir is apportioned between Rotifers (35.09%), Cladocerans (26.05%), Copepods (18.55%), Protozoans (12.87%) and Ostracods (7.44%) (Fig. 7.4).

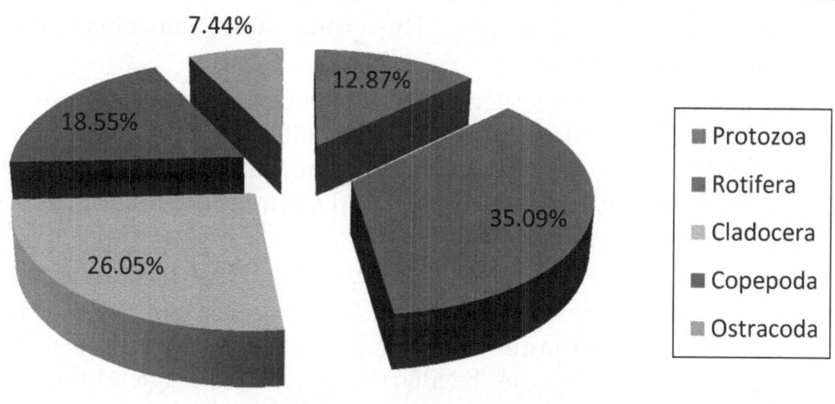

Fig. 7.4: **Quantitative Occurance of Zooplankton in Gharni Reservoir (Year 2013-14)**

Protozoans were represented by three species. *Paramecium caudatum* was recorded throughout the year with maximum density of 35 organisms/ Liter in April and minimum of 2 organisms/Liter in July. *Diffugia spp* were not recorded in July and September and showed maximum density of 35 organisms/Liter in April and May. *Opercularia spp* were absent in June and showed maximum density in March (32 organisms/Liter). Protozoan density ranged from 6 organisms/Liter in July to 100 organisms/Liter in April.

Rotifers were represented by eight species. *Brachionus calyciflorus, B.falcatus, B.diversicornis, Keratella tropica, K.quadrata* and *Trichocera porcellus* were recorded round the third year of investigation. *Lecane (Monostyla) bulla* was not found in September and *Filinia longiseta* in August and September. The density of rotifers ranged from 33 organisms/Liter (June) to 246 organisms/Liter (May) with annual average density of 125 organisms/Liter. Rotifer density in summer was more when compared to other seasons.

Cladocerans were represented by six species. The density of this group ranged from 32 organisms/Liter (September) to 188 organisms/Liter (May) with annual average of 92 organisms/Liter. In case of cladocera, *Indialona ganapati* and *Diaphanosoma excisum* were present round the year.*Moina micrura* was absent in two months of rainy season i.e., June and September, *Diaphanosoma sarsi* in one month i.e., June and *Ceriodaphnia cornuta* in one month i.e., September. *Alona rectangular* was also absent in two months i.e., June and November.

Copepods were represented by 5 species. *Diaptomus marshianus, Mesocyclops hyalinus* and *Cyclops viridis* were observed throughout the third year of investigation, while *Phylladiaptomus lindbergi* and *Mesocyclops leukarti* were absent in two months of rainy season. The copepod density fluctuated from 11 organisms/Liter (September) to 153 organisms/Liter (April) with mean density of 66 organisms/Liter. This group showed maxima in summer and minima in rainy season.

Ostracods were represented by three species. Ostracods were totally absent in August. Their density ranged from nil (August) to 63 organisms/ Liter (May) with an average density of 26 organisms/Liter. *Cypris obensa* was absent in three months (July, August and December), while other species were absent in one month i.e., August.

Phytoplankton diversity: The first year study of the phytoplankton sampled in Gharni reservoir showed 18 species (Table 7.8). The phytoplankton assemblage was respresented by four classes viz., Chlorophyceae, Cyanophyceae, Bacillariophyceae and Euglenophyceae.

The class Chlorophyceae was represented by maximum species. It was represented by 7 species. The class was represented by species such as *Zygnema sp, Pediastrum duplex, Scendesmus armatus, Oedogonium patulum, Ankistrodesmus falcatus, Chlorella vulgaris* and *Cosmarium contractum.*

The class Cyanophyceae was represented by five species. It was represented by *Oscillatoria limnosa, Oscillatoria chlorine, Anabaena constricta, Merismopedia punctata* and *Microcystis aerugenose.*

The class Bacillariophyceae was represented by three species i.e., *Navicula gracilis, Nitzschia subtilis* and *Bacillaria paradoxa.*

The class Euglenophyceae was represented by three species.It was represented by *Euglena pisciformis, Euglena viridis* and *Euglena stellata.*

During first year of investigation (2011-12), the phytoplankton consisted of 41.12% of Chlorophyceae, 23.50% of Cyanophycee, 18.14% of Bacillariophyceae and 17.24% of Euglenophyceae (Fig.7.5). It was revelaed that the class Chlorophyceae was dominant with annual average of 134 units/ Liter, followed by Cyanophyceae (77 units/Liter), Bacillariophyceae (59 units/ Liter) and Euglenophyceae (56 units/liter).

In case of Chlorophyceae, *Zygnema sp, Pediastrum duplex* and *Scendesmus armatus* were recorded throughout the first year of investigation. The density of Chlorophyceae ranged from 40 units/Liter to 215 units/Liter with minima in rainy season and maxima in summer. *Oedogonium patulum* and *Cosmarium contractum* were absent in one month of rainy season, while *Ankistrodesmus falcatus* was not observed in two months of rainy season i.e., August and September. *Chlorella vulgaris* was totally absent in rainy season.

Table 7.8: Monthly Analysis of Phytoplankton Diversity in Gharni Reservoir (Year 2011-12)

Species/Month	June	July	August	September	October	November	December	January	February	March	April	May
Chlorophyceae												
Zygnema sp	10	15	15	20	25	25	20	25	25	25	30	25
Pediastrum duplex	15	10	10	15	15	35	30	25	30	30	35	35
Scendesmus armatus	15	05	05	15	25	20	25	25	30	35	35	25
Oedogonium patulum	05	00	10	15	15	25	20	35	30	35	40	30
Ankistrodesmus falcatus	10	25	00	00	15	15	25	20	25	35	35	35
Chlorella vulgaris	00	00	00	00	05	05	05	10	15	15	10	10
Cosmarium contractum	25	20	00	15	10	10	15	10	25	20	25	25
Total	**80**	**75**	**40**	**80**	**110**	**135**	**140**	**150**	**180**	**195**	**210**	**215**
Cyanophyceae												
Oscillatoria limnosoa	10	10	05	05	10	10	15	10	15	25	15	15
Oscillatoria chlorime	05	05	05	05	05	10	10	15	25	25	25	25
Anabaena constricta	15	05	05	00	10	15	10	15	20	30	30	20
Merismopedia punctata	15	10	05	10	15	15	20	20	25	30	35	30
Microcystis aerugenose	15	10	10	15	15	20	20	20	20	25	20	20
Total	**60**	**40**	**30**	**35**	**55**	**70**	**75**	**80**	**105**	**135**	**125**	**110**

(Contd…)

Species/Month	June	July	August	September	October	November	December	January	February	March	April	May
Bacillariophyceae												
Navicula gracilis	20	10	20	20	25	25	25	30	35	35	35	35
Nitzschia subtilis	05	05	10	10	15	15	25	25	20	45	25	35
Bacillaria paradoxa	00	00	00	00	05	10	15	15	20	35	35	25
Total	**25**	**15**	**30**	**30**	**45**	**50**	**65**	**70**	**75**	**115**	**95**	**95**
Euglenophyceae												
Euglena pisciformis	05	05	00	00	10	10	15	25	25	30	25	25
Euglena viridis	00	00	00	05	15	10	25	35	35	40	40	35
Euglena stellata	00	00	10	15	10	20	30	30	40	35	35	35
Total	**05**	**05**	**10**	**20**	**35**	**40**	**70**	**90**	**100**	**105**	**100**	**95**

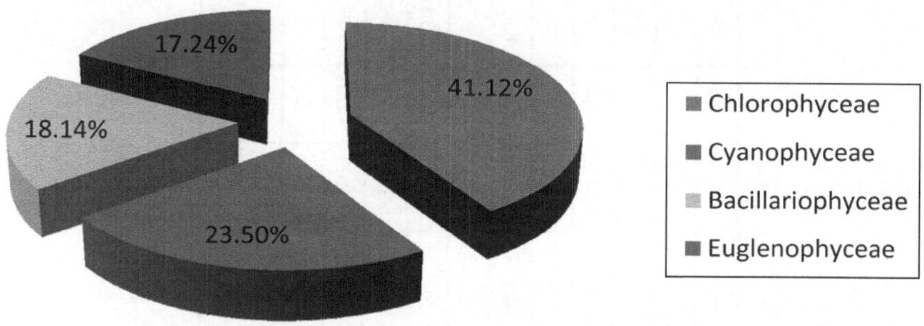

***Fig. 7.5:* Quantitative Occurance of Phytoplankton in Gharni Reservoir (2011-12)**

Among Cyanophyceae, *Oscillatoria limnosa, Oscillatoria chlorine, Anabaena constricta, Mersmopedia punctata* and *Microcystis aerugenose* were recorded. *Oscillatoria limnosoa, Oscillatoria chlorine, Merismopedia punctata* and *Microcystis aerugenose* were observed in all seasons, while *Anabaena constricta* was not seen in September. The variation in the population density of Cyanophyceae ranged from 30 to 135 units/Liter and contributed to 23.50% of the total phytoplankton population. The density of *Oscillatoria limnosa* ranged from 5 to 25 units/Liter, *Oscillatria chlorine* 5 to 25 units/liter, *Anabaena constricta* nil to 30 units/Liter, *Merismopedia punctata* 5 to 35 units/liter and *Microcystis aerugenose* 10 to 25 units/Liter.

The class Bacillariophyceae was represented by three species i.e., *Navicula gracilis, Nitzschia subtilis* and *Bacillaria paradoxa.Naavicula gracilis* and *Nitzschia subtilis* were observed throughout the first year of investigation with minima in rainy season and maxima in summer. *Bacillaria paradoxa* was absent in rainy season. The population density of *Navicula gracilis,Nitzschia subtilis* and *Bacillaria paradoxa* varied from 10 to 35 units/Liter, 5 to 45 units/liter and nil to 35 units/liter.This group contributed to about 18.14% of the total phytoplankton population with annual average of 59 units/Liter.

The class Euglenophyceae contributed to about 17.24% of the total phytoplankton population with annual average of 56 units/Liter. *Euglena pisciformis* and *Euglena stellata* were absent in two months of rainy season, while *Euglena viridis* was not seen in three months of rainy season i.e., June, July and August. Density of this group ranged from 5 to 105 units/Liter with minima in rainy season and maxima in summer season.

During the second year (2012-13) of investigation, a total number of 18 species (7 species of Chlorophyceae, 5 species of Cyanophyceae, 3 species of Bacillariophyceae and 3 species of Euglenophyceae) of phytoplankton were recorded in Gharni reservoir (Table 7.9). The phytoplankton consisted of 33.29% of Chlorophyceae, 33.42% of Cyanophyceae, 19% of Bacillariophyceae and 14.29% of Euglenophyceae (Fig. 7.6).

Table 7.9: Monthly Analysis of Phytoplankton Diversity in Gharni Reservoir (Year 2012-13)

Species/Month	June	July	August	September	October	November	December	January	February	March	April	May
Chlorophyceae												
Zygnema sp	10	05	05	05	05	05	10	10	10	15	10	10
Pediastrum duplex	15	10	15	10	15	15	15	10	15	20	20	15
Scendesmus armatus	10	10	15	20	25	25	20	25	30	35	35	30
Oedogonium patulum	05	05	00	00	00	10	05	10	15	20	25	20
Ankistrodesmus falcatus	10	10	05	05	15	15	20	25	25	30	25	25
Chlorella vulgaris	05	05	00	00	05	10	15	15	10	25	25	20
Cosmarium contractum	20	15	15	10	20	25	25	30	35	35	30	30
Total	**75**	**60**	**55**	**50**	**85**	**105**	**110**	**125**	**140**	**180**	**170**	**150**
Cyanophyceae												
Oscillatoria limnosoa	20	15	15	05	15	25	25	35	35	30	30	30
Oscillatoria chlorime	25	20	20	05	30	35	35	40	40	35	35	35
Anabaena constricta	15	10	10	00	15	15	25	25	35	35	35	30
Merismopedia punctata	15	15	00	00	10	10	20	25	25	25	20	15
Microcystis aerugenose	10	15	00	00	20	20	25	25	35	35	30	30
Total	**85**	**75**	**45**	**10**	**90**	**105**	**130**	**150**	**170**	**160**	**150**	**140**

(Contd...)

Species/Month	June	July	August	September	October	November	December	January	February	March	April	May
Bacillariophyceae												
Navicula gracilis	10	05	00	15	25	25	30	30	30	35	25	25
Nitzschia subtilis	10	05	10	15	10	20	25	30	25	45	40	30
Bacillaria paradoxa	05	05	00	20	20	15	20	30	35	25	25	25
Total	**25**	**15**	**10**	**50**	**55**	**60**	**75**	**90**	**90**	**105**	**90**	**80**
Euglenophyceae												
Euglena pisciformis	10	05	05	10	15	15	20	25	35	35	25	30
Euglena viridis	00	00	00	00	10	10	15	15	20	25	30	25
Euglena stellata	05	05	00	00	05	05	15	20	35	30	30	30
Total	**15**	**10**	**05**	**10**	**30**	**30**	**50**	**60**	**90**	**90**	**85**	**85**

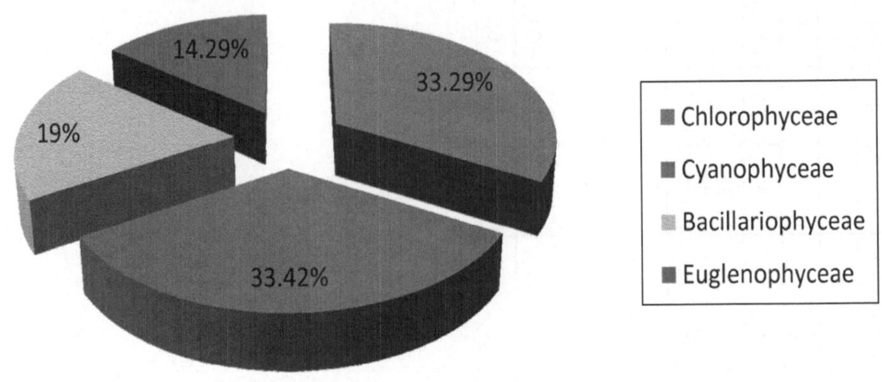

Fig. 7.6: **Quantitative Occurance of Phytoplankton in Gharni Reservoir (2012-13)**

In case of Chlorophyceae, *Zygnema sp, Pediastrum duplex, Scendesmus armatus, Ankistrodesmus falcatus and Cosmarium contractum* were recorded throughout the second year of investigation. *Chlorella vulgaris* was observed in ten months and absent in two months of rainy season i.e., August and September, while *Oedogonium patulum* was not observed in three months of rainy season. The density of this group fluctuated from 50 to 180 units/Liter.

Cyanophyceae was represented by 5 species, out of which two species (*Oscillatoria limnosa* and *Oscillatoria chlorine*) were observed throughout the second year of investigation. *Merismopedia punctata* and *Microcystis aerugenose* were absent in august and September, while *Anabaena constricta* was absent in September. The density of this group ranged from 10 to 170 units/Liter.

In case of Bacillariophyceae, *Nitzschia subtilis* was recorded throughout the second year of investigation. *Navicula gracilis* and *Bacillaria paradoxa* were not observed in month of August. The density of this group ranged from 10 to 105 units/Liter with annual average of 62 units/Liter.

The class Euglenophyceae was represented by three species i.e., *Euglena pisciformis, Euglena viridis* and *Euglena stellata*. The population density was between 5 to 90 units/Liter with annual average of 47 units/Liter. *Euglena pisciformis* was observed throughout the second year of study period, while *Euglena viridis* was absent in entire rainy season. *Euglena stellata* was absent two months of rainy season i.e., August and September.

During third year of investigation (2013-14), the phytoplankton consisted of 41.57% of Chlorophyceae, 33.61% of Cyanophyceae, 16.16% of Bacillariophyceae and 8.66% of Euglenophyceae (Fig. 7.7). The phytoplankton productivity fluctuated seasonally and the maximum number of 560 units/Liter was recorded during the month of February and March and minimum number of 95 units/Liter during the month of September (Table 7.10).

Table 7.10: Monthly Analysis of Phytoplankton Diversity in Gharni Reservoir (Year 2013-14)

Species/Month	June	July	August	September	October	November	December	January	February	March	April	May
Chlorophyceae												
Zygnema sp	15	20	15	00	10	15	20	25	25	35	35	30
Pediastrum duplex	05	15	15	00	15	20	20	25	25	35	35	35
Scendesmus armatus	20	20	10	05	25	25	25	30	35	30	35	35
Oedogonium patulum	25	20	10	05	30	25	30	35	35	40	35	30
Ankistrodesmus falcatus	20	20	10	05	15	20	20	25	30	30	35	35
Chlorella vulgaris	00	00	00	00	10	20	15	25	35	35	35	30
Cosmarium contractum	10	00	00	00	15	15	20	25	30	30	30	25
Total	**95**	**95**	**60**	**15**	**120**	**140**	**150**	**190**	**215**	**235**	**240**	**220**
Cyanophyceae												
Oscillatoria limnosoa	15	10	00	10	15	20	25	20	35	30	35	35
Oscillatoria chlorine	20	10	00	00	20	20	25	25	30	30	30	30
Anabaena constricta	25	20	20	05	20	15	35	35	45	45	40	35
Merismopedia punctata	20	15	20	15	25	25	30	35	40	35	35	35
Microcystis aerugenose	10	15	00	10	15	25	30	35	40	35	30	30
Total	**90**	**70**	**40**	**40**	**95**	**105**	**145**	**150**	**190**	**175**	**170**	**165**

(Contd...)

Species/Month	June	July	August	September	October	November	December	January	February	March	April	May
Bacillariophyceae												
Navicula gracilis	10	10	05	10	10	15	20	20	30	25	25	20
Nitzschia subtilis	05	05	00	10	15	20	25	25	35	35	30	30
Bacillaria paradoxa	10	05	05	15	20	25	30	35	35	30	25	20
Total	**25**	**20**	**10**	**35**	**45**	**60**	**75**	**80**	**100**	**90**	**80**	**70**
Euglenophyceae												
Euglena pisciformis	00	00	10	00	15	15	20	20	35	35	20	30
Euglena viridis	10	05	05	05	10	10	15	10	15	20	20	15
Euglena stellata	00	00	00	00	00	00	00	00	05	05	10	10
Total	**10**	**05**	**15**	**05**	**25**	**25**	**35**	**30**	**55**	**60**	**50**	**55**

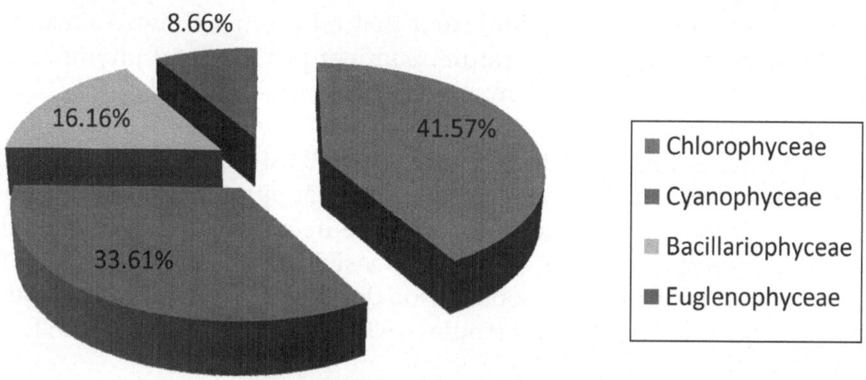

***Fig. 7.7:* Quantitative Occurance of Phytoplankton in Ghrani Reservoir (2013-14)**

In case of Chlorophyceae, *Scendesmus armatus, Oedogonium patulum* and *Ankistrodesmus falcatus* were recorded in all months. Their number was high in summer and low in monsoon season. *Chlorella vulgaris* was not seen in rainy season. Similarly *Cosmarium contractum* was also absent in three months of rainy season. *Zygnema sp* and *Pediastrum duplex* were not recorded in month of September. The density of this group ranged from 15 units/Liter (September) to 240 units/Liter (April) with annual average of 148 units/Liter.

The class Cyanophyceae was represented by five species, out of which two species (*Anabaena constricta* and *Merismopedia punctata*) were seen throughout the third year of investigation. *Oscillatoria limnosoa* and *Microcystis aerugenose* were absent in August. *Oscillatoria chlorine* was absent in two months of rainy season i.e., August and September. The density of this group ranged from 40 units/Liter (August and September) to 190 units/Liter.

Among Bacillariophyceae, *Navicula gracilis* and *Bacillaria paradoxa* were recorded throughout the study period, while *Nitzschia subtilis* was absent in one month i.e., August. The density of Bacillariophyceae ranged from 10 units/liter to 100 units/Liter. It was maximum in February and minimum in August. The annual average of this group was 57 units/Liter.

In case of Euglenophyceae three species were recorded, out of which only one i.e., *Euglena viridis* was recorded throughout the third year of investigation. *Euglena stellta* was not seen in monsoon and winter season. *Euglena pisciformis* was absent in three months of rainy season. The density of this group fluctuated from 5 units/Liter to 60 units/Liter with annual average of 31 units/Liter.

Phytoplankton community of Gharni reservoir comprised of 18 species of which 7 belong to Chlorophyceae, 5 to Cyanophyceae, 3 to

Bacillariophyceae and 3 to Eugelnophyceae. Individual phytoplankton population dynamics clearly indicated that all groups showed maxima in summer with increasing temperature. Summer peak in total phytoplankton population was due to higher temperature (Chandrakiran *et al.*, 2014). Decline in phytoplankton population in monsoon was a result of flushing due to incessant rain in regions which also hamper light penetration decreasing photosynthesis (Chandrakiran *et al.*, 2014). Similar opinion was also proposed by various workers who suggested that the heavy rainfall, over flooding, dilution and turbidity are the factors responsible for the reduced population of phytoplankton during monsoon season despite of increased nutrient levels during the period (Tripathi and Pandey 1990; Kumar and Gupta 2002; Laskar and Gupta 2013).

CHAPTER - 8

Siddeshwar Reservoir

It was constructed on Purna River at Siddheshwar village in the Aundha Taluka, Hingoli district. Siddheshwar dam serve as an important source of several benefits and facilities to the region of Hingoli, Parbhani and Nanded districts. It is situated at northern part of Marathwada region of Maharashtra. The location of dam is at 19035′-19040′ N latitude 7605′-770E longitude. It was commissioned in 1975 across the river Purna. Its water spread area is 2574 ha. The salient features of the reservoir are given in Table 8.1.

The result of the present study revealed the occurrence of twenty three fish species belonging seven orders (Table 8.2). The analysis of data indicated that the order cypriniformes was dominant with 10 fish species followed by order siluriformes 5, and perciformes 3. The order clupeiformes and mastacembeliformes each with two species have been recorded, while order channiformes was represented by a single species.

In the present study order Cypriniformes formed the major fish species, constituting 43.48% of the fish fauna, followed by Siluriformes 21.75%, Perciformes 13.04%, Clupeiformes 8.69 %, Masatcembeliformes 8.69 % and Channiformes 4.35%.

Among cyprinidae *Catla catla, Labeo rohita, Cirrhinus mrigala, Cyprinus carpio, Amblypharyngodon mola, Osteobrama cotio, Puntius sarana sarana, Puntius ticto ticto, Puntius sophore* and *Rasbora daniconius* were recorded.

The order perciformes contributed 3 fish species, and represented by 3 species i.e., *Oreochromis mossambicus, Glossogobius giuris* and *Chanda ranga.*

Among order clupeiformes *Notopterus notopterus* and *Notopteurs chitala* were recorded, while order mastacembeliformes was also represented by two species i.e., *Mastacembelus armatus* and *Mastacembelus pancalus.*

Table 8.1: Salient Features of Siddeshwar Reservoir

Basin Name	Godavari
River	Purna
Dam type	Earthen
Purpose of dam	Irrigation
Year of completion	1968
Rainfall at reservoir site (mm)	638
Length of dam (m)	6658
Height of dam (m)	38.26
Type of spillway	Ogee
Length of spillway (m)	304.8
Type of spillway gates	Radial
Number of spillway gates	14
Catchment Area (sq.km)	7770
Full reservoir Level (m)	413.11
Minimum Drawn Down Level (m)	410.26
Maximum water level (m)	414.94
Gross Storage Capacity at FRL (mcm)	250.85
Live Storage Capacity (mcm)	80.96
Dead Storage Capacity (mcm)	169.89
Submergence Area (Th Ha)	4.058
Number of villages affected	15

The total fish production from the reservoir and its composition during three years' period are shown in Table 8.3. The results show that the catches from the reservoir during three years varied widely with average total catch of 27683.33 kg. The catches for the year 2011-12 were higher as compared with catches of remaining two years. The total catch from the six fish species, *Catla catla, Labeo rohita, Cirrhinus mrigala, Cyprinus carpio, Channa gachua* and *Oreochromis mossambicus* formed 39.86 per cent of the total average catch for the three years. Among these, the two exotics (*Cyprinus carpio* and *Oreochromis mossambicus*) formed 7.16% of the total catch. Similarly other species (*Notopterus notopterus, Notopterus chitala, Amblypharyngodon mola, Osteobrama cotio, Puntius sarana sarana, Puntius ticto ticto, Puntius sophore, Rasbora daniconius, Mystus cavasius, Mystus seenghala, Mystus vittatus, Wallago attu, Channa gachua, Mastacembelus armatus. Mastacembelus pancalus, Glossogobius giuris* and *Chanda ranga*) formed 60.14% of the total catches. On whole the contribution of the exotic fishes remained 1980.66 kg (7.16%) of the total catches.

Table 8.2: Fish Diversity of Siddeshwar Reservoir

Order: Clupeiformes **Suborder: Notopteroidei** **Family: Notopteridae** 1. *Notopterus notopterus (Pallas)*
2. Notopterus chitala (Ham.)
Order: Cypriniformes **Suborder: Cyprinoidei** **Family: Cyprinidae**
3. *Catla catla (Ham.)*
4. *Labeo rohita (Ham.)*
5. *Cirrhinus mrigala (Ham.)*
6. *Cyprinus carpio(Linn)*
7. *Amblypharyngodon mola (Ham.)*
8. *Osteobrama cotio (Ham.)*
9. *Puntius sarana sarana (Ham.)*
10. *Puntius ticto ticto (Ham.)*
11. *Puntius sophore (Ham.)*
12. *Rasbora daniconius (Ham.)*
Order: Siluriformes **Family: Bagridae**
13. *Mystus cavasius (Ham.)*
14. *Mystus seenghala (Sykes)*
15. *Mystus vittatus (Bloch)*
Family: Claridae 16. *Clarias batrachus (Linn.)*
Family: Siluridae 17. *Wallago attu (Bloch and Schneider)*
Order: Channiformes **Family: Channidae** 18. *Channa gachua (Haml.)*
Order: Mastacembeliformes 19. *Mastacembelus pancalus (Ham.)* 20. *Mastacembelus armatus (Lacepede)*
Order: Percioformes **Family: Cichlidae** 21. *Oreochromis mossambicus (Peters)*
Family: Gobiidae 22. *Glassogobius giuris (Ham.)*
Family: Ambassidae 23. *Chanda ranga (Ham.)*

Table 8.3: Details of Fish Caches in Siddeshwar Reservoir

Year	*Catla catla*	*Labeo rohita*	*Cirrhinus mrigala*	*Cyprinus carpio*	*Oreochromis mossambicus*	*Channa gachua*	Others	Total
2011-12	3940	4203	2120	1505	602	1280	16450	30100
2012-13	3050	3050	385	1285	680	1000	16000	25450
2013-14	4250	2300	500	1350	520	1080	17500	27500
Average	27683.33	3746.66	3184.33	1001.66	1380	600.66	1120	16650
%	13.53	11.50	3.62	4.98	2.18	4.05	60.14	100

Fishing efforts mainly entailed gill net operations and were exercised by respective fish contractors. The categories of fish documented in this study comprised Indian major carps (*Catla catla, Labeo rohita, Cirrhinus mrigala*) and the exotics (*Oreochromis mossambicus* and *Cyprinus carpio*). Fishing operations covered a widespread area and the annual data were pooled in a way to enable unbiased and representative fish catch sampling and data collected from district fishery development office, Hingoli. Common carp (*Cyprinus carpio*) constituted 5% of total catch and *Oreochromis mossambicus* 2%. The catla fishery in reservoir was adversely affected by the accidental entry of *Oreochromis mossambicus*. The contribution of the catla in meager. Exotic species (*O.mossambicus* and *C.carpio*) together formed 7% of the total catch in Siddeshwar reservoir.

Physico-chemical environment: Water temperature may affect chemical as well as biological water characteristics. Rates of many biological and chemical processes vary with temperature. Biological water quality may vary with temperature due to varying species survival rates in different temperatures.

A chemical characteristic that varies with the temperature of water is dissolved oxygen content. The saturation value of dissolved oxygen in water is inversely related to water temperature (Mark, 2006). Therefore, in temperate climates, levels are typically higher in the winter and lower in the summer.

The surface temperature values ranged from 21 to 27 °C during 2011-12, 21.5 to 26.8 °C during 2012-13 and 23.5 to 27 °C during 2013-14. The overall mean recorded as 24.53.The surface temperature values were maximum during summer and minimum in winter season.

Transparency is a characteristic of water that varies with the combined effect of colour and turbidity. It measures the depth to which light penetrates in the water body. In the present investigation the value of transparency varied from 42 cm to 80 cm (Table 8.4). The transparency of reservoir water was found to be lowest (42 cm) during rainy season and highest (80 cm) in summer. Reduced transparency during rainy season may be due to erosion of soil carried by runoff from the catchment areas. Jain and Sharma (2000) and Sharma *et al.* (2012) also reported lowest transparency in rainy season.

During the period of observation the pH of the water was always > 8, a complete absence of free carbon dioxide being indicated. The pH ranged from 8.4 to 8.7 without showing any marked seasonal variations.

The total dissolved solids are naturally present in water or are the result of mining or some industrial treatment of water. Total dissolved solids contains minerals and organic molecules that provide benefits such as nutrients or contaminants such as toxic metals and organic pollutants. Changes in total dissolved solids concentrations in natural waters often result from industrial effluent, changes to the water balance (by limiting inflow, by increased water use or icreased precipitation), or by salt water intrusion (Phyllis and Lawrence, 2007).

Table 8.4: Seasonal Fluctuation in Water Quality Parameters of Siddeshwar Reservoir

Season/Year	Water Temp.(ºC)	Transparencey (cm)	pH	TDS (mg/l)	DO (mg/l)	CO_2 (mg/)	TA (mg/l)	Cl^- (mg/l)	TH (mg/l)
2011-12									
Monsoon	24	46	8.5	180	9.2	Nil	158.5	19	110
Winter	21	70	8.5	172	6.8	Nil	120	18.9	98
Summer	27	80	8.4	190	5.9	Nil	135.5	20.2	100
Mean	24	65.33	8.46	180.6	7.3	Nil	138	19.36	102.66
2012-13									
Monsoon	24.5	42	8.7	200	9.0	Nil	142	19.3	98
Winter	21.5	58	8.5	198	7.9	Nil	110	18.5	122
Summer	26.8	72	8.6	215	6.8	Nil	135	20	100.5
Mean	24.26	57.33	8.6	204.3	7.9	Nil	129	19.26	106.83
2013-14									
Monsoon	25.5	42.5	8.5	188	10.2	Nil	150.5	19.8	105
Winter	23.5	62.5	8.5	179	7.5	Nil	120	20.2	110
Summer	27	70.5	8.7	210	6.2	Nil	142.8	18.8	98.8
Mean	25.33	58.50	8.56	192.3	7.96	Nil	137.7	19.60	104.6
Grand Mean	24.53	60.38	8.54	192.4	7.72	Nil	134.9	19.40	104.69

In the present investigation, the total dissolved solids ranged between 172 to 190 mg/l, 198 to 215 mg/l and 179 to 210 mg/l in first, second and third year respectively. The maximum total dissolved solids recorded in summer which decreased during rainy season due to dilution of reservoir water and minimum values were recorded during winter probably because of stagnation. These findings support the observations made by Tripathi and Pandey (1990).

Dissolved oxygen in natural water depends on the physical, chemical and biological activities in the water body. Dissolved oxygen content, plays a vital role in supporting aquatic life and is susceptible to slight environmental changes. Dissolved oxygen is an important limnological parameter indicating level of water quality and organic pollution in the water body (Wetzel and Likens, 2006). In present study concentration of dissolved oxygen in Siddeshwar reservoir varied from 5.9 to 10.2 mg/l with minimum in summer and maximum in rainy season. The present study reports a gradual decrease in dissolved oxygen from winter to summer. The seasonal variation of dissolved oxygen in water depends upon the temperature of the water body which influences the oxygen solubility in water (Sharma *et al.* 2012).

Alkalinity of water is a measure of weak acid present in it ad of the cations balanced against them (Sverdrap *et al.*1942). The observation of alkalinity reveals that the seasonal variation ranged from 110 mg/l to 158.5 mg/l. Seasonally the values were highest in the monsoon season, decreases in summer months and were recorded lowest in winter (Table 8.4).

The absence of free carbon dioxide in the surface layer of the reservoir in all three years can be attributed to its removal by phytoplankton for photosynthesis. The absence of free carbon dioxide resulted in an increase in pH.

The chloride content of the surface water was low, from 18.5 to 20.2 mg/l. There was no sharp rise in chloride content at any time during the period of investigation, and thus it can conclude that the water was free from pollution. There was no seasonal variation observed in the chloride content of reservoir.

The hardness of surface water is mainly due to carbonates of calcium and magnesium. The total hardness of the water ranged from 98 to 122 mg/l. There were no seasonal variations.

Zooplankton Diversity: A total of 25 species of zooplankton were recorded from Siddeshwar reservoir. Out of 25 species, 3 species belonged to protozoa, 8 to rotifera,6 to cladocera, 5 to copepoda and 3 to ostracoda.

During 2011-12 rotifera dominated the zooplankton poplation (35.49%) followed by Cladocera (32.15%), Copepoda (15.20%), Ostracoda (13.47%) and Protozoa (3.69%). Summer months exhibited higher population of zooplankton (Fig. 8.2). All zooplankton groups showed maxima in summer and minima in monsoon. The order of dominance in first year of investigation is rotifera>cladocera>copepoda>ostracoda>protozoa.

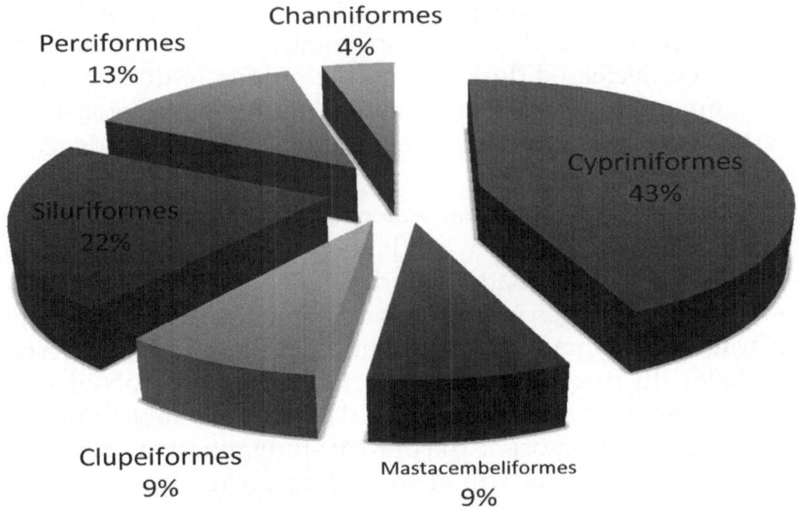

Fig. 8.1: **Orderwise Contribtuion of Fish Species of Siddeshwar Reservoir**

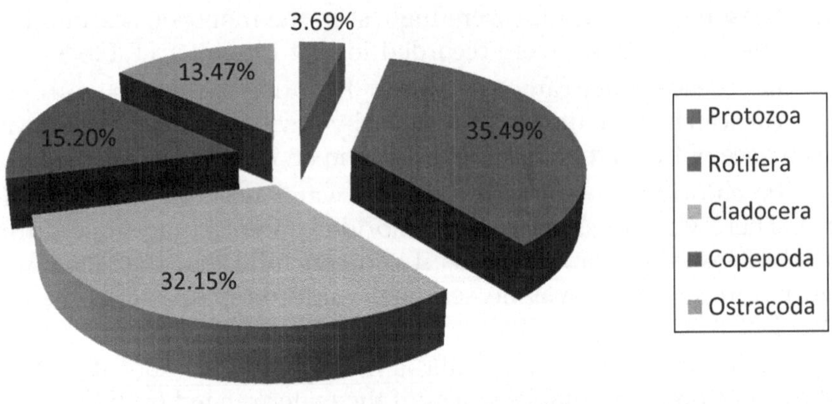

Fig. 8.2: **Quantitative Occurance of Zooplankton in Siddeshwar Reservoir (Year 2011-12)**

Among protozoa, *Paramecium caudatum* and *Opercularia spp* were recorded in nine months.these species were absent in rainy season. *Diffugia spp* were present in eleven months. The protozoan density ranged from 2 organisms/Liter (June, July and September) to 26 organisms/Liter (January) with annual average of 12 organisms/Liter.

Rotifers were represented by 8 species (Table 8.5). The annual average of this group was 112 organisms/Liter.Its density ranged from 54 organisms/ Liter (August) to 218 organisms/Liter (May). The peak period of rotifers was observed during summer season,followed by winter and monsoon.*Brachionus calyciflorus* was present in ten months,while other group members were recorded round the year.

The cladoceran species recorded during first year of investigation include *Indialona ganapati, Moina micrura, Diaphanosoma sarsi, D.excium, Alona rectangular* and *Ceriodaphnia cornuta.* The species composition and abundance of each zooplankton group varied from time to time and season. Density, diversity and composition of zooplankton also exhibit seasonal variation.

Copepods were represented by 5 species with annual average mean of 48 organisms/Liter. Its density varied from 10 organisms/Liter (September) to 93 organisms/Liter (February). *Diaptomus marshianus, Mesocyclops leukarti, Mesocyclops hyalinus* and *Mesocyclops leukarti* were absent in one month each.

Ostracods were represented by three species with annual average of 43 organisms/Liter. Density of this group observed from 13 organisms/Liter (June) to 92 organisms/Liter (March). *Cypris obensa* and *Cyclocypris globosa* were observed round the year while *Candocypria osborni* was present in eleven months. The ostracod peak was observed during summer followed by winter and monsoon.

In second year of investigation rotifers were dominant showing highest percentage (35.92%) composition and diversity followed by Cladocera (24.60%), Copepoda (22.38%), Ostracoda (12.38%) and Protozoa (4.73%). The quantitative zooplankton analysis showed that zooplankton density is more in summer followed by winter and monsoon season (Fig. 8.3). The quantitative relationship amongst the groups of zooplankton is Rotifera> Cladocera> Copepoda> Ostracoda> protozoa. The species composition and abundance of each zooplankton group varied from season to season.

Under protozoa, *Paramecium caudatum* was absent in rainy season, *Diffugia spp* in three months of rainy season and *Opercularia spp* in June. The annual average of group was 16 organisms/Liter. The protozoans were totally absent in June and maximum density was recorded in March (47 organisms/Liter).

In rotifers, *Brachionus calciflorus, B.falcatus, Lecane (Monostyla) bulla* and *Filinia longiseta* were recorded in all months, while *Brachionus diversicornis* was absent in August, *Keratella tropica* in September and *K.quadrata* in three months of rainy season (June, August and September). *Trichocera porcellus* was absent in June and July. The rotifer density ranged from 32 organisms/ Liter (June) to 217 organisms/Liter (March) with annual average of 118 organisms/Liter.

Table 8.5: Monthly Analysis of Zooplankton Diversity in Siddheshwar Reservoir (2011-2012)

Species/Month	June	July	August	September	October	November	December	January	February	March	April	May
Protozoa												
Paramecium caudatum	00	00	02	00	04	02	02	04	05	08	05	02
Diffugia spp.	02	02	02	00	02	05	06	12	10	02	02	05
Opercularia spp.	00	00	00	02	04	02	05	10	05	10	08	10
Total	**02**	**02**	**04**	**02**	**10**	**09**	**13**	**26**	**20**	**20**	**15**	**17**
Rotifera												
Brachionus calyciflorus	05	00	00	15	14	12	18	15	14	20	28	25
Brachionus falcatus	08	12	05	08	08	14	15	10	12	18	18	22
Brachionus diversicornis	10	05	10	10	05	15	11	05	14	20	20	25
Keratella tropica	05	02	05	10	15	17	12	08	12	18	15	30
Keratella quadrata	10	10	05	14	12	12	05	10	15	28	25	30
Lecane (monostyla) bulla	12	10	05	14	11	14	15	14	12	25	20	32
Trichocera porcellus	10	12	10	15	15	12	10	12	10	25	22	29
Filina longiseta	05	10	14	11	12	10	10	15	15	28	25	25
Total	**65**	**61**	**54**	**97**	**92**	**106**	**96**	**94**	**104**	**182**	**173**	**218**
Cladocera												
Indialona ganapati	10	15	15	05	20	12	20	22	30	39	28	25
Moina micrura	02	12	05	12	14	18	15	27	32	30	20	20
Diaphanosoma sarsi	18	05	10	10	20	15	25	20	30	25	22	28
Diaphanosoma excisum	12	04	08	10	15	17	20	24	25	25	26	17
Alona rectangular	05	06	08	12	12	24	18	27	20	23	18	22
Ceriodaphnia cornuta	04	04	02	08	08	10	15	18	26	23	20	18
Total	**61**	**46**	**48**	**57**	**69**	**96**	**113**	**138**	**163**	**165**	**134**	**130**

(Contd…)

Species/Month	June	July	August	September	October	November	December	January	February	March	April	May
Copepoda												
Diaptomus marshianus	04	05	02	02	05	08	05	10	20	12	15	19
Phylladiaptomus lindbergi	04	04	10	00	02	05	05	08	24	20	14	18
Mescyclops leuckarti	00	05	05	04	08	05	10	12	18	18	20	24
Mesocyclops hyalinus	02	03	04	02	05	04	08	15	20	20	11	16
Cyclops viridis	05	10	05	02	02	04	10	15	11	22	19	12
Total	**15**	**27**	**26**	**10**	**22**	**26**	**38**	**60**	**93**	**92**	**79**	**89**
Ostracoda												
Cypris obensa	04	10	12	05	05	05	05	12	28	25	26	26
CyclocyprisGlobosa	05	02	04	04	10	10	12	20	24	25	35	30
Candocypria osborni	04	05	00	05	12	05	12	10	22	30	32	30
Total	**13**	**17**	**16**	**14**	**27**	**20**	**29**	**42**	**74**	**81**	**92**	**86**

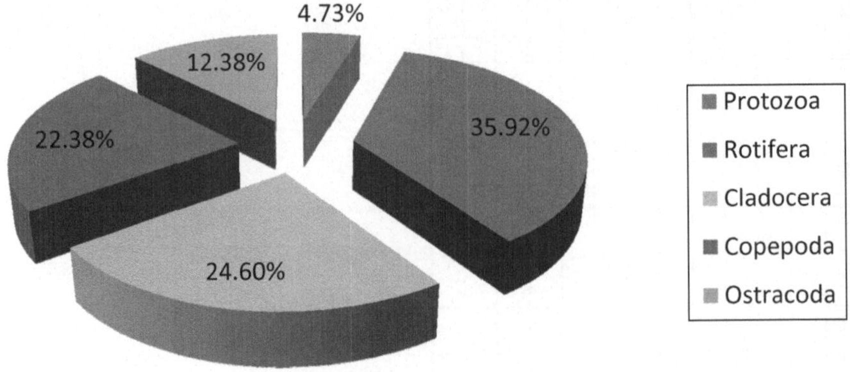

Fig.8.3: **Quantative Occurance of Zooplankton in Siddeshwar Reservoir (Year 2012-13)**

Among cladocerans, *Indialona ganapati, Moina micrura, Diaphanosoma excisum, Alona rectangular* and *Ceriodaphnia cornuta* were recorded throughout the year, while *Diaphanosoma sarsi* was not detected in April. The density of this group ranged from 36 organisms/liter (August) to 153 organisms/Liter (May) with an annual average of 81 organisms/liter (Table 8.6).

Copepods were represented by 5 species.All these species encountered round the year with maximum density in summer and minimum density in monsoon season. The annual average density was recorded at 73 organisms/Liter.

Among ostracods *Cyclocypris globosa* and *Candocypria osborni* were not detected in June and July respectively. *Cypris obensa* was recorded in all months. The density of ostracods ranged from 6 organisms/liter (July) to 92 organisms/Liter (May) with an annual average of 41 organisms/Liter.

In third year of investigation, altogether 25 species belonging to five groups of zooplankton were identified. During this period Rotifera dominated the zooplankton population (32.11%), followed by Cladocera (27.37%), Copepoda (23.57%), Ostracoda (10.51%) and Protozoa (6.44%) (Fig.8.4).

Protozoans were represented by 3 species. *Opercularia spp* were recorded in all months with minima in rainy season and maxima in summer. *Paramecium caudatum* was not detected in June and *Diffugia spp* in July and August. The density of group fluctuated from 4 organisms/Liter (July and August) to 42 organisms/Liter (April) with average of 20 organisms/Liter (Table 8.7).

Rotifers were represented by 8 species, out of which 5 species (*Brachionus calciflorus, B.falcatus, B.diversicornis. Keratella tropica* and *K.quadrata*) were observed in all months, while *Lecane (Monostyla) bulla, Trichocera porcellus* and *Filinia longiseta* were absent in one month each. Rotifer density in Siddeshwar reservoir varied from 23 organisms/Liter (June) to 200 organisms/Liter (April) with average density of 99 organisms/Liter (Table 8.7).

Table 8.6: Monthly Analysis of Zooplankton Diversity in Siddheshwar Reservoir (Year 2012-13)

Species/Month	June	July	August	September	October	November	December	January	February	March	April	May
Paramecium caudatum	00	00	00	00	05	06	05	10	10	12	12	12
Diffugia spp.	00	00	00	05	05	02	04	05	08	15	10	03
Opercularia spp.	00	04	02	02	02	04	02	02	12	20	02	05
Total	**00**	**04**	**02**	**07**	**12**	**12**	**11**	**17**	**30**	**47**	**24**	**20**
Rotifera												
Brachionus calyciflorus	05	05	05	10	10	15	12	15	18	25	32	30
Brachionus falcatus	05	05	10	05	15	15	10	14	25	35	26	24
Brachionus diversicornis	05	08	00	05	10	12	15	20	28	20	30	32
Keratella tropica	10	10	10	00	15	14	20	18	25	29	22	20
Keratella quadrata	00	05	00	00	10	20	15	12	29	33	25	25
Lecane (monostyla) bulla	05	04	05	10	10	10	10	14	26	22	30	23
Trichocera porcellus	00	00	05	10	08	12	14	10	28	28	25	20
Filina longiseta	02	02	05	02	10	14	20	15	15	25	19	30
Total	**32**	**39**	**40**	**42**	**88**	**112**	**116**	**118**	**194**	**217**	**209**	**204**
Cladocera												
Indialona ganapati	10	10	12	10	05	05	15	15	15	22	20	26
Moina micrura	04	12	10	05	08	08	10	18	24	20	18	24
Diaphanosoma sarsi	08	05	05	05	10	05	12	14	24	22	00	25
Diaphanosoma excisum	05	05	04	05	12	12	18	20	19	19	18	20
Alona rectangular	10	03	03	14	14	15	10	15	22	22	30	30
Ceriodaphnia cornuta	05	05	02	02	10	10	09	10	25	25	29	28
Total	**42**	**40**	**36**	**41**	**59**	**55**	**74**	**92**	**129**	**130**	**115**	**153**

(Contd...)

Species/Month	June	July	August	September	October	November	December	January	February	March	April	May
Copepoda												
Diaptomus marshianus	05	10	05	04	15	14	12	15	20	26	22	30
Phylladiaptomus lindbergi	05	04	05	05	16	12	14	09	18	24	22	20
Mescyclops leukarti	02	08	02	02	12	15	18	20	22	18	25	18
Mesocyclops hyalinus	10	03	08	15	14	11	14	15	25	22	25	20
Cyclops viridis	05	10	14	12	20	10	18	15	28	26	25	20
Total	**27**	**35**	**34**	**38**	**77**	**62**	**76**	**74**	**113**	**116**	**119**	**108**
Ostracoda												
Cypris obensa	05	04	02	02	05	07	10	15	25	30	26	30
Cyclocypris globosa	00	02	05	02	05	12	15	20	25	20	22	32
Candocypria osborni	04	00	04	04	10	15	10	10	28	25	25	30
Total	**09**	**06**	**11**	**08**	**20**	**34**	**35**	**45**	**78**	**75**	**73**	**92**

Table 8.7: Monthly Analysis of Zooplankton Diversity in Siddheshwar Reservoir (Year 2013-14)

Species/Month	June	July	August	September	October	November	December	January	February	March	April	May
Protozoa												
Paramecium caudatum	00	02	02	05	04	05	04	05	10	15	20	10
Diffugia spp.	02	00	00	04	05	08	05	08	10	10	10	12
Opercularia spp.	04	02	02	02	07	07	07	05	15	15	12	15
Total	**06**	**04**	**04**	**11**	**16**	**20**	**16**	**18**	**35**	**40**	**42**	**37**
Rotifera												
Brachionus calyciflorus	05	05	02	05	10	05	05	15	15	19	20	25
Brachionus falcatus	02	05	04	02	12	08	10	15	20	24	30	19
Brachionus diversicornis	02	02	05	04	08	08	12	15	20	20	30	26
Keratella tropica	02	05	05	05	10	06	15	10	15	30	28	20
Keratella quadrata	02	02	05	05	10	15	10	12	14	20	22	30
Lecane (monostyla) bulla	02	0	02	10	12	20	08	05	19	20	25	20
Trichocera porcellus	00	05	02	10	10	15	10	10	20	24	25	27
Filina longiseta	08	00	02	05	10	10	15	15	25	30	30	25
Total	**23**	**24**	**27**	**46**	**82**	**81**	**85**	**97**	**148**	**187**	**200**	**192**
Cladocera												
Indialona ganapati	05	04	02	02	12	12	20	15	25	30	20	25
Moina micrura	02	00	05	03	14	15	20	20	20	32	18	25
Diaphanosoma sarsi	02	02	00	00	12	20	18	20	24	28	00	20
Diaphanosoma excisum	02	05	05	04	17	25	20	15	19	30	30	20
Alona rectangular	02	05	05	05	10	20	15	18	25	20	15	18
Ceriodaphnia cornuta	05	05	05	05	14	15	15	17	28	23	20	22
Total	**18**	**21**	**22**	**19**	**79**	**107**	**108**	**105**	**141**	**163**	**103**	**130**

(Contd…)

Species/Month	June	July	August	September	October	November	December	January	February	March	April	May
Copepoda												
Diaptomus marshianus	04	10	08	05	12	15	15	16	20	20	19	20
Phylladiaptomus lindbergi	05	05	05	02	20	14	18	20	25	22	18	25
Mescyclops leukarti	00	02	02	10	12	18	18	15	30	00	30	20
Mesocyclops hyalinus	04	08	05	12	04	18	13	12	35	25	00	22
Cyclops viridis	02	05	10	08	15	15	14	18	32	28	30	28
Total	**15**	**30**	**30**	**37**	**75**	**80**	**78**	**81**	**142**	**95**	**97**	**115**
Ostracoda												
Cypris obensa	05	02	02	05	05	05	05	10	15	18	15	19
Cyclocypris globosa	00	05	02	02	05	10	08	12	20	22	22	35
Candocypria osborni	00	00	00	10	02	05	10	12	24	20	30	28
Total	**05**	**07**	**04**	**17**	**12**	**20**	**23**	**34**	**59**	**60**	**67**	**82**

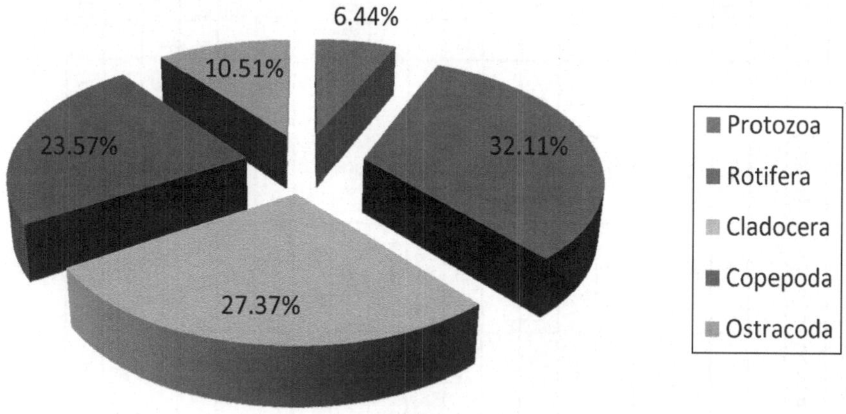

Fig. 8.4: **Quantative Occurance of Zooplankton in Siddeshwar Reservoir (Year 2013-14)**

Cladocera contributed next to rotifera in dominance and the density ranged between 18 organisms/Liter to 163 organisms/Liter (March) with an annual average of 85 organisms/liter. Seasonal distribution of cladoceran showed higher summer maxima. *Indialona ganapati, Diaphanosoma excisum, Alona rectangular* and *Ceriodaphnia* were recorded in all months. *Moina micrura* was absent in July and Diaphanosoma sarsi in August and September (Table 8.7).

Copepods contributed next to cladocera and represented by 5 species.*Diaptomus marshianus, Phylladiaptomus lindbergi* and *Cyclops viridis* were observed round the year, while *Mesocyclops leukarti* was absent in two months (June and March) and *Mesocyclops hyalinus* in one month (April). Seasonal distribution and density showed the maxima in February (142 organisms/Liter) and minima in June (15 organisms/Liter) with annual average of 73 organisms/Liter.

The ostracods also registered a seasonal periodicity. *Cypris obensa* was recorded in all months, while *Cyclocypris globosa* was observed in eleven months only.*Candocypria osborni* was recorded in nine months. It was absent in three months of rainy season. The ostracod population recorded maximum of 82 organisms/Liter in May and minimum of 4 organisms/Liter in August (Table 8.7).

Phytoplankton diversity: During the present study, four groups of phytoplankton namely, Cyanophyceae (Blue-green algae), Chlorophyceae (Green algae), Bacillariophyceae (Diatoms) and Euglenophyceae were recorded in the reservoir (Table 8.8).

A total of 21 species were found in the phytoplankton groups with Chlorophyceae having the highest of 10 species, while Cyanophyceae and Bacillariophyceae had 5 species each. Euglenophyceae was represented by a single species.

Table 8.8: Monthly Analysis of Phytoplankton Diversity in Siddeshwar Reservoir (Year 2011-12)

Species/Month	June	July	August	September	October	November	December	January	February	March	April	May
Chlorophyceae												
Zygnema sp	20	20	20	25	35	35	35	40	35	35	35	30
Ulotrix zonata	15	15	05	15	20	25	25	25	30	35	30	35
Pediastrum duplex	10	15	10	10	15	20	20	25	25	30	35	25
Pediastrum simplex	20	25	25	20	25	25	35	35	35	45	45	45
Scendesmus armatus	15	10	05	05	15	15	20	20	20	45	25	25
Oedogonium patulum	20	25	20	20	15	20	25	35	35	45	45	40
Ankistrodesmus falcatus	30	35	20	00	15	25	35	35	35	40	35	40
Chlorella vulgaris	35	40	30	20	25	40	45	45	55	55	45	50
Closterium limneticum	30	25	35	35	35	40	45	45	55	50	55	45
Cosmarium contractum	20	15	15	15	20	25	25	30	30	35	35	35
Total	**215**	**225**	**185**	**165**	**220**	**270**	**310**	**335**	**355**	**415**	**385**	**370**
Cyanophyceae												
Oscillatoria limnosoa	20	25	25	15	15	25	35	35	45	40	35	45
Oscillatoria chlorime	25	25	35	25	35	45	45	40	45	55	50	55
Anabaena constricta	10	15	15	00	10	15	15	25	20	25	35	35
Merismopedia punctata	25	25	15	15	20	20	35	35	45	45	40	40
Microcystis aerugenose	10	10	15	00	00	15	20	20	25	30	30	35
Total	**90**	**100**	**105**	**55**	**80**	**120**	**150**	**155**	**180**	**195**	**190**	**210**

(Contd...)

Species/Month	June	July	August	September	October	November	December	January	February	March	April	May
Bacillariophyceae												
Navicula gracilis	10	25	25	20	20	25	35	35	35	40	45	55
Navicula viridula	25	35	20	30	35	35	40	45	45	55	55	50
Nitzschia subtilis	20	25	25	35	35	35	40	55	50	45	40	45
Synedra affinis	25	35	35	30	25	35	55	45	40	45	50	50
Diatoms vuloare	30	30	35	25	20	35	35	40	45	45	40	45
Total	**110**	**150**	**140**	**140**	**135**	**165**	**205**	**220**	**215**	**230**	**230**	**245**
Euglenophyceae												
Euglena pisciformis	10	15	15	00	00	15	15	25	20	25	25	25
Total	**10**	**15**	**15**	**00**	**00**	**15**	**15**	**25**	**20**	**25**	**25**	**25**

During first year of investigation (2011-12), the phytoplankton consisted of 46.28% of Chlorophyceae, 291.86% of Cyanophyceae, 29.31% of Bacillariophyceae and 2.55% of Euglenophyceae (Fig. 8.5). It was revealed that the class Chlorophyceae was dominant with annual average of 288 units/ Liter, followed by Bacillariophyceae (182 units/Liter), Cyanophyceae (136 units/Liter) and Euglenophyceae (16 units/liter).

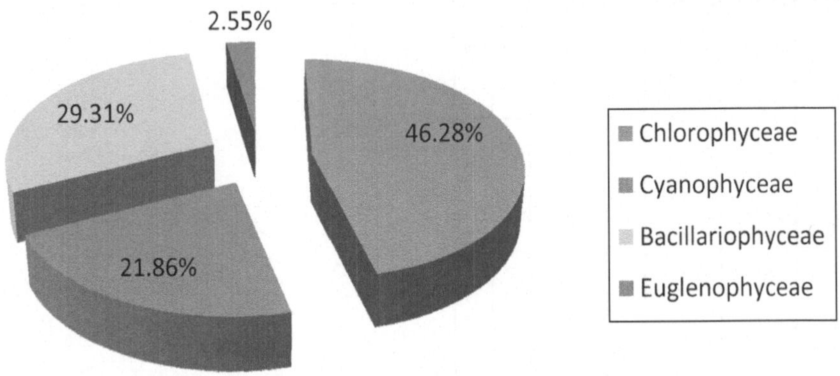

Fig. 8.5: **Quantitaqtive Occurance of Phytoplankton from Siddeshwar Reservoir (Year 2011-12)**

In case of Chlorophyceae, except *Ankistrodesmus falcatus* all species recorded throughout the first year of investigation. The density of this group ranged from 165 units/Liter to 415 units/Liter with minima in rainy season and maxima in summer.

Among Cyanophyceae, *Oscillatoria limnosoa,Oscillatoria chlorine,Anabaena constricta, Merismopedia punctata* and *Microcystis aerugenose* were recorded. *Oscillatoria limnosoa, Oscillatoria chlorine* and *Merismopedia punctata* were observed in all months, while Anabaena constricta was not seen in September and *Microcystis aerugenose* was absent in two months i.e., September and October. The density of this group varied from 55 to 210 units/Liter with annual average of 136 units/Liter.

The class Bacillariophyceae was represented by five species i.e., *Navicula gracilis, Navicula viridula, Nitzschia subtilis, Synedra affinins and Diatoms vuloare.* The density of this group ranged from 110 units/Liter (June) to 245 units/ Liter (May) with annual average of 182 units/Liter. All species were observed throughout the first year of investigation with minima in rainy season and maxima in summer season.

The class Euglenophyceae was represented by a single species i.e., *Euglena pisciformis*, which was present in ten months and absent in September and October.The density of this species fluctuated from nil (September and October) to 25 units/Liter (March, April and May).

During second year of investigation (2012-13), the phytoplankton consisted of 49.89% of Chlorophyceae, 23.34% of Bacillariophyceae, 24.73% of Cyanophyceae and 2.04% of Euglenophyceae (Fig.8.6).

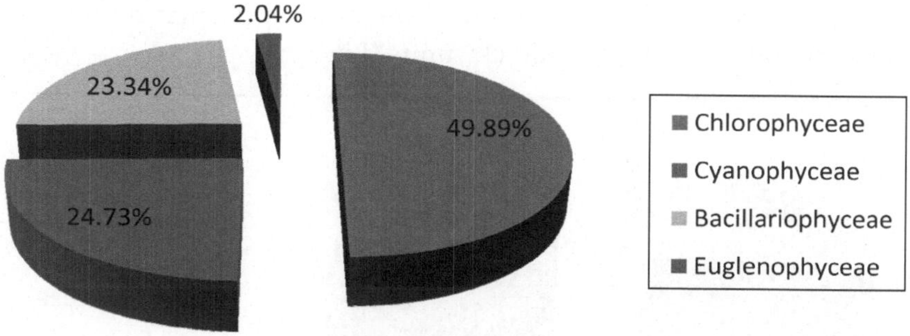

***Fig. 8.6:* Quantitative Occurance of Phytoplankton from Siddeshwar Reservoir (Year 2012-13)**

The phytoplankton density fluctuated seasonally and the minimum number of 130 units/Liter was recorded during the months of September and the maximum number of 635 units/Liter during the month of March.

In case of Chlorophyceae, out of 10 species, only six species were present throughout the second year of investigation, while 3 species viz., *Zygnema sp*, *Ankistrodesmus falcatus* and *Cosmarium contractum* were absent in August and September. *Oedogonium patulum* was not seen in September. The density of this group varied from 80 units/Liter (September) to 290 units/Liter (March) with annual average of 194 units/Liter.

The class Cyanophyceae was represented by five species i.e., *Oscillatoria limnosoa*, *Oscillatoria chlorine*, *Anabaena constricta*, *Merismopedia punctata* and *Microcystis aerugenose*. The population density of this group ranged from 25 units/Liter (August) to 170 units/Liter (March) with annual average of 96 units/Liter. Out of five species, *Merismopedia punctata* was observed throughout the second year of investigation. *Oscillatoria limnosa* and *Oscillatoria chlorine* were absent in September and *Anabaena constricta* and *Microcystis aerugenose* in August.

In case of class Bacillariophyceae five species were recorded, out of which only two species (*Navicula gracilis* and *Diatoms vuloare*) were observed in all months. *Navicula viridula* and *Synedra affinis* were not seen in three months. *Nitzschia subtilis* was absent in entire rainy season i.e., June to September. The density of this group varied from 20 units/Liter to 170 units/ Liter (May) with annual average of 91 units/Liter.

The class Euglenophyceae was represented by a single species i.e., *Euglena housepisciformis*. It was absent in two months (August and September). The density of this species ranged from nil to 15 units/Liter with annual average of 8 units/Liter.

During third year of invstigation (2013-14), the phytoplankton consisted of 47.48% of Chlorophyceae, 25.92% of Cyanophyceae, 24.38% of Bacillariophyceae and 2.22% of Euglenophyceae (Fig. 8.7). It was revealed that the class Chlorophyceae was dominant with annual average of 231 units/ Liter, followed by Cyanophyceae (126 units/Liter), Bacillariophyceae (119 units/Liter) and Euglenophyceae (11 units/Liter).

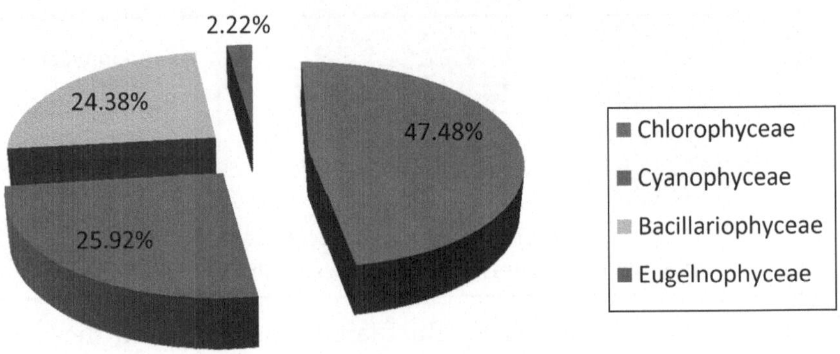

Fig. 8.7: **Quantitative Occurance of Phytoplankton from Siddeshwar Reservoir (2013-14)**

Spillways of Siddeshwar Reservoir

Table 8.9: Monthly Analysis of Phytoplankton Diversity in Siddeshwar Reservoir (Year 2012-13)

Species/Month	June	July	August	September	October	November	December	January	February	March	April	May
Chlorophyceae												
Zygnema sp	05	05	00	00	05	05	10	05	10	10	15	10
Ulotrix zonata	20	15	15	10	10	15	20	20	20	25	25	20
Pediastrum duplex	15	15	10	15	10	20	20	25	25	35	30	30
Pediastrum simplex	15	10	05	05	15	15	15	20	20	25	25	20
Scendesmus armatus	10	10	15	15	20	20	25	25	35	30	35	35
Oedogonium patulum	10	15	05	00	05	15	20	20	25	25	25	30
Ankistrodesmus falcatus	15	20	00	00	20	15	25	25	35	35	30	30
Chlorella vulgaris	20	15	10	10	10	15	15	20	25	30	25	35
Closterium limneticum	30	25	25	25	35	35	30	35	45	40	40	35
Cosmarium contractum	10	15	00	00	20	20	25	30	30	35	30	30
Total	**150**	**145**	**85**	**80**	**150**	**175**	**205**	**225**	**270**	**290**	**280**	**275**
Cyanophyceae												
Oscillatoria limnosoa	10	10	10	00	15	15	20	15	20	20	25	25
Oscillatoria chlorime	05	05	10	00	10	15	15	15	20	25	25	25
Anabaena constricta	10	15	00	15	20	25	30	35	45	55	40	35
Merismopedia punctata	05	05	05	05	15	25	20	25	35	35	30	30
Microcystis aerugenose	10	10	00	10	15	15	20	25	30	35	35	35
Total	**40**	**45**	**25**	**30**	**75**	**95**	**105**	**115**	**150**	**170**	**155**	**150**

(Contd...)

Species/Month	June	July	August	September	October	November	December	January	February	March	April	May
Bacillariophyceae												
Navicula gracilis	15	25	20	15	20	15	15	25	30	25	35	35
Navicula viridula	10	10	00	00	00	15	20	25	25	30	30	40
Nitzschia subtilis	00	00	00	00	05	15	20	20	25	30	35	30
Synedra affinis	05	00	00	00	10	10	15	15	25	45	35	35
Diatoms vuloare	10	15	15	05	10	15	20	20	30	35	30	30
Total	**40**	**50**	**35**	**20**	**45**	**70**	**90**	**105**	**135**	**165**	**165**	**170**
Euglenophyceae												
Euglena pisciformis	05	05	00	00	05	05	10	10	15	10	15	15
Total	**05**	**05**	**00**	**00**	**05**	**05**	**10**	**10**	**15**	**10**	**15**	**15**

Table 8.10: Monthly Analysis of Phytoplankton Diversity in Siddeshwar Reservoir (Year 2013-14)

Species/Month	June	July	August	September	October	November	December	January	February	March	April	May
Chlorophyceae												
Zygnema sp	15	10	10	00	10	15	20	20	25	25	35	25
Ulothrix zonata	25	20	20	15	20	25	25	35	35	40	45	40
Pediastrum duplex	10	05	05	05	15	15	20	20	30	35	35	30
Pediastrum simplex	15	10	00	10	15	15	15	20	20	20	20	20
Scendesmus armatus	00	00	00	00	10	15	15	20	25	35	35	30
Oedogonium patulum	15	20	35	30	35	35	35	45	45	45	40	45
Ankistrodesmus falcatus	20	15	00	00	20	25	25	30	35	40	45	45
Chlorella vulgaris	10	05	05	05	15	10	15	25	25	30	30	30
Closterium limneticum	25	00	25	00	30	35	30	40	45	45	40	35
Cosmarium contractum	00	00	00	00	30	35	35	45	55	55	50	45
Total	**135**	**85**	**100**	**65**	**200**	**225**	**235**	**300**	**340**	**370**	**375**	**345**
Cyanophyceae												
Oscillatoria limnosoa	15	15	10	10	15	15	20	25	30	35	45	40
Oscillatoria chlorime	25	15	10	10	20	25	35	35	45	45	55	45
Anabaena constricta	10	10	05	00	15	25	20	30	35	40	40	35
Merismopedia punctata	20	15	15	10	10	15	25	25	35	40	35	35
Microcystis aerugenose	20	10	00	00	25	35	30	35	40	40	45	50
Total	**90**	**65**	**40**	**30**	**85**	**115**	**130**	**150**	**185**	**200**	**220**	**205**

(Contd...)

Species/Month	June	July	August	September	October	November	December	January	February	March	April	May
Bacillariophyceae												
Navicula gracilis	15	20	15	00	10	20	25	25	30	30	35	35
Navicula viridula	20	15	10	10	15	25	25	35	30	40	55	45
Nitzschia subtilis	20	35	00	10	35	35	40	35	40	45	40	40
Synedra affinis	15	15	10	05	10	20	20	35	30	35	35	30
Diatoms vuloare	10	10	00	10	15	10	15	15	25	25	35	35
Total	**80**	**95**	**35**	**35**	**85**	**110**	**125**	**145**	**155**	**175**	**200**	**185**
Euglenophyceae												
Euglena pisciformis	10	10	05	05	05	10	10	15	10	15	20	15
Total	**10**	**10**	**05**	**05**	**05**	**10**	**10**	**15**	**10**	**15**	**20**	**15**

In case of Chlorophyceae, ten species were recorded during third year investigation (Table 8.10). Four species (*Ulothrix zonata, Pediastrum duplex, Oedogonium patulum* and *Chlorella vulgaris* were observed throughout the third year of investigation, while *Scendesmus armatus* and *Cosmarium contractum* were not seen in rainy season. *Ankistrodesmus falcatus* and *Closterium limneticum* were absent in two months of rainy season. *Zygnema sp* and *Pediastrum simplex* were absent in September and August respectively. The density of this group ranged from 65 units/Liter (September) to 375 units/Liter (April) (Table 8.10).

The class Cyanophyceae was represented by five species,out of which *Oscillatoria limnosoa, Oscillatoria chlorine* and *Merismopedia punctata* were observed throughout the third year of investigation, while *Anabaena constricta* was absent in one month (September) and *Microcystis aerugenose* in two months (August and September). The density of this group ranged from 30 units/ Liter (September) to 220 units/Liter (April).

In case of Bacillariophyceae five species were recorded. *Navicula viridula* and *Synedra affinis* were present throughout the third year of investigation. Navicula gracilis was absent in September. *Nitzschia subtilis* and *Diatoms vuloare* were absenr in August.The density of this group ranged from 35 units/Liter (August and September) to 200 units/Liter (April) (Table 8.10).

The class Euglenophyceae was represented by a single species i.e., *Euglena pisciformis*. It was recorded throughout the third year of investigation. Its density fulcuated from 5 units/Liter (September and October) to 20 units/ Liter (April).

CHAPTER - 9

Bhategaon Reservoir

The Bhategaon is one of the smallest reservoirs in Hingoli district of Maharashtra. The reservoir has water spread area of 23.50 ha. The salient features of reservoir are depicted in Table 9.1.

Table 9.1: Salient Features of Bhategaon Reservoir

Year of Construction	1966
Basin	Godavari
River	Penganga
Location	Bhategaon
District	Hingoli
Rainfall (mm)	819.40
Length of dam (m)	452
Height of dam(m)	13.45
Catchment area(sq.km)	15.36
Gross Storage capacity (mcm)	1.54
Live storage capacity (mcm)	1.39
Dead storage capacity(mcm)	0.15
Water spread area (ha)	46.50
Irrigation potential ((ha)	461

The Bhategaon reservoir harbours a variety of fish species (Table 9.2). Fish fauna consists of 23 species belonging to 5 orders. Among the collection, 11 species of cypriniformes, 5 species of siluriformes, 3 species of channiformes, 3 species of perciformes and 1 species of mastacembeliformes were recorded (Table 9.2). The fishery of reservoir was significantly dominated by Grass carp (*Ctenopharyngodon idella*), contributing over 10% of the total fish cathches.

The major carnivores (although present in sparse density) were *Channa gachua, Channa striatus, Channa marulius* and *Mystus spp*. The landing size of Grass carp was around 1 to 1.5 kg (mean 1kg). High fish production recorded in Bhategaon reservoir is primarily due to the shallowness of the habitat, high trophic status and overwhelming dominance of Grass carp.

Table 9.2: Fish Fauna of Bhategaon Reservoir

Order: Cypriniformes **Suborder: Cyprinoidei** **Family: Cyprinidae** 1. *Chela phulo (Ham.)*
2. *Catla catla (Ham.)*
3. *Labeo rohita (Ham.)*
4. *Cirrhinus mrigala (Ham.)*
5. *Ctenopharyngodon idella (Ham.)*
6. *Amblypharyngodon mola (Ham.)*
7. *Osteobrama cotio (Ham.)*
8. *Puntius sarana sarana (Ham.)*
9. *Puntius chola (Ham.)*
10. *Puntius sophore (Ham.)*
11. *Rasbora daniconius (Ham.)*
Order: Siluriformes **Family: Bagridae** 12. *Mystus cavasius (Ham.)*
13. *Mystus seenghala (Sykes)*
14. *Mystus vittatus (Bloch)*
Family: Claridae 15. *Clarias batrachus (Linn.)*
16. *Ompak bimaculatus (Bloch)*
Order: Channiformes **Family: Channidae** 17. *Channa gachua (Haml.)*
18. *Channa striatus (Bloch)*
19. *Channa marulius (Ham.)*
Order: Mastacembeliformes 20. *Mastacembelus pancalus (Ham.)*
Order: Perciformes **Family: Anabantidae** 21. *Anabas testudineus (Bloch)*
Family: Gobiidae 22. *Glassogobius giuris (Ham.)*
Family: Ambassidae 23. *Chanda ranga (Ham.)*

In Bhategaon reservoir stocking is done @ one lakh fry per year. In the species composition, *Catla catla* with 35% was the dominant species, followed by *Labeo rohita* (25%), *Cirrhinus mrigala* (20%), and *Ctenopharyngodon idella* (20%).

In first year (2011-12) of the investigation the fish yield was 2400 kg (102.12 kg/ha/yr). The percentage contribution was the highest (87.92%) in case of Indian majora carps, followed by Grass carp (10.42%) and local fishes (1.66%) (Table 9.3).

Table 9.3: Fish Catch in Bhategaon Reservoir (in kilograms)

Year	Indian Major Carps (kg)	Grass Carp (kg)	Local Fishes (kg)	Total Catch (kg)	Fish Production (kg/ha/yr)
2011-12	2110 (87.92%)	250 (10.42%)	40 (1.66%)	2400	102.12
2012-13	2500 (78.13%)	410 (12.81%)	290 (9.06%)	3200	136.17
2013-14	1840 (89.76%)	150 (7.31%)	60 (2.93%)	2050	87.23

In second year (2012-13), fish yield further increased to3200 kg (136.17 kg/ha/yr). This increase in fish yield was mainly due to reduction in water level making it easy to harvest the fish. Indian major carps were dominant constituting 78.13% followed by Grass carp constituting 12.81% and local fishes contributing 9.06% of the total fish catch (Table 9.3).

In third year of investigation (2013-14) total fish catch was registered at 2050 kg (87.23 kg/ha/yr). The percentage contribution was the highest (89.76%) in case of Indian major carps, followed by grass carp (7.31%) and local fishes (2.93%) (Table 9.3).

The Grass carp seed is purchased from the hatchery constructed in the vicinity of reservoir. The weed infested and shallowness of the reservoir is favourable for the growth of Grass carp. The fish is found effective for cleaning the submerged vegetation. Hence, it is concluded that the Grass carp is ideal and suitable candidate for the Bhategaon reservoir. It is also preferred by local consumers. The introduction has been used successfully to control submerged weeds in reservoir.

At first the Grass carp were not much preferred by the people. Now a days as the fishes slowly adopt itself to the soil of the area, their demands are becoming higher in the market. The fish is found to grow faster in comparison to Indian major carps due to availability of soft aquatic grass. The fish contribute the highest percentage of catch composition of the reservoir at present. Grass carp was transplanted in this weedy infested reservoir. Its transplantation was considered a welcome addition to enhance fish production from culture ponds as well as to effectively control aquatic weeds.

The fish, though selective, voraciously weeds, terrestrial fodder grasses and horticultural wastes and grows fast. In view of its food spectrum being totally different from that of other carps there is no adverse impact of grass carp when cultures with other carps. This attribute makes it an ideal fish for culture mostly in weed infested reservoirs and also for culture in combination with other carps.

Physico-chemical Environment: The range of variation of temperature is smaller as changes occur more slowly in water than in air. Water has several unique properties that combine to control temperature changes like high specific heat, high latent heat of fusion, highest known latent heat of evaporation.

During the present study highest water temperature was recorded during summer and minimum during winter season. The annual averages of temperature were obtained at 27 °C in 2011-12, 28.43 °C in 2012-13 and 26.9 °C in 2013-14 (Table 9.4). The highest temperature recorded in summer season is due to direct relationship between bright sunshine, its duration and air temperature. The results of present study on water temperature agree with the temperature pattern of other water bodies in different parts of India (Devi 1997; Sakhare 2007, Jetithor 2010).

Water temperature plays an important role in either decreasing or increasing the concentration of certain chemical characteristics of water. The occurrence of aquatic organisms of a given water body is also directly or indirectly linked with the variation in temperature ranges.

Water transparency is a physical measurable variable and is quite significant for production. Transparency is inversely proportional to turbidity created by suspended inorganic and organic matter. During the present three year study period transparency expressed in cms ranged between 40.5 to 110 cm (Table 9.4). The water was less transparent during monsoon as compared to winter and summer. The low values recorded in rainy season may be due to the heavy rains and winds of high velocity and high values recorded during winter and summer months were probably due to low and moderate velocity of winds. According to Das (1996) high secchi disc transparencies indicate insufficient phytoplankton productivity to support enough fish food organisms for good fish production.

The pH values were relatively constant with small fluctuations in the range of 8.0 to 8.7 (Table 9.4). The values were slightly higher during winter period. Hussain (1977) observed small and irregular pH fluctuations. Devi (1985) also found irregular and small pH fluctuations in Mir-Alam tank in Andhar Pradesh. The present results also indicated that Bhategaon reservoir appeared to be alkaline. This may be due to unpolluted condition of the water and also perhaps due to the photosynthetic activity of algae which were in abundance in the reservoir. The study gave evidence to the findings of Devi (1985), Devi (1997) and Rao (1982).

Table 9.4: Seasonal Fluctuation in Water Quality Parameters of Bhategaon Reservoir

Season/Year	Water Temp. (°C)	Transparencey (cm)	pH	TDS (mg/l)	DO (mg/l)	CO_2 (mg/1)	TA (mg/l)	Cl^- (mg/l)	TH (mg/l)
2011-12									
Monsoon	27	40.5	8.0	160	9.4	Nil	113	30.7	138
Winter	22	80.5	8.4	180	6.3	Nil	175	45.2	110.5
Summer	32	110	8.2	210.5	5.2	0.5	217	39.2	142
Mean	27	77	8.2	183.5	6.9	0.16	168.3	38.36	130.16
2012-13									
Monsoon	28	56	8.2	170	8.5	Nil	110	31.2	140
Winter	23.3	98	8.7	190.3	7.8	Nil	140	44.7	122
Summer	34	98.5	8.4	200	4.9	Nil	250	35.4	158
Mean	28.43	84.16	8.4	186.7	7.06	Nil	166.6	37.1	140
2013-14									
Monsoon	24.5	60	8.4	150	10.3	Nil	100	33.2	132
Winter	26	70.5	8.6	150.2	7.8	Nil	155	39.7	110
Summer	30.2	80.5	8.6	180	5.8	1.30	230	34.8	134
Mean	26.9	70.33	8.53	162.7	7.96	0.43	161.6	35.9	125.33
Grand Mean	27.44	77.16	8.37	177.6	7.32	0.19	165.5	37.12	131.83

The trophy of water body reflects in the concentration and composition of its total dissolved solids in water. The underwater climate of a water body is also dependent upon the nature, size, shape, colour, density and dispersion of the suspended particles. Total dissolved solids mainly controlled by the atmospheric temperature, rainfall, water level and pH.

In the present investigation total dissolved solids were in the range of 150 to 210.5 mg/l (Table 9.4). Total dissolved solids were maximum during summer season during the entire study period. These values were lowest during monsoon period. During present investigation large amount of dissolved solids have been observed in summer when the water level comes down considerably due to evaporation. The increase in the concentration could be directly related to the surface area of the reservoir.

The trophy of water body reflects in the concentration and composition of its total dissolved solids in water. The underwater climate of a water body is also dependent upon the nature, size, shape, colour, density and dispersion of the suspended particles. Total dissolved solids mainly controlled by the atmospheric temperature, rainfall, water level and pH.

In the present investigation total dissolved solids were in the range of 150 to 210.5 mg/l (Table 9.4). Total dissolved solids were maximum during summer season during the entire study period. These values were lowest during monsoon period. During present investigation large amount of dissolved solids have been observed in summer when the water level comes down considerably due to evaporation. The increase in the concentration could be directly related to the surface area of the reservoir.

Oxygen is a prime limiting factor in waters with a heavy load of organic material. The value of dissolved oxygen isone of the most important index of the purity of a stream. The oxygen supplied in water comes chiefly from two sources, from the air and from photosynthesis by aquatic plants. The amount of oxygen obtained by water from the atmosphere depends mainly on the temperature, the atmospheric pressure and the salinity of the water. The solubility of oxygen increases by low temperatures and salinities.

During present investigation, higher values of dissolved oxygen were recorded in rainy season and minimum in summer. Maximum concentration of dissolved oxygen was recorded in third year in the range of 5.8 to 10.3 mg/l with an average of 7.96.

Many authors (Pejaver *et al.* 2004; Khatavkar *et al.* 2004; Jetithor 2010; Meshram 2013) have discussed the seasonal fluctuation in the dissolved oxygen content of the lakes and reservoirs in India.

Carbon dioxide was absent in monsoon and winter seasons two years (first and third year), while it was totally absent in second year of investigation. Its average value was calculated at 0.19 mg/l.

The total alkalinity ranged from 100 mg/l to 250 mg/l with average of 165.55 mg/l. It was maximum in summer and minimum in rainy season.

Chloride is one of the important anions of fresh water and marked quantitative accumulations of this anion over a period of time is indicative of anthropogenic pollution. The minimum chloride values were found during monsoon months, due to dilution by the monsoon floods with the decrease of inflow in winter, chloride concentration rose due to increase in evapotranspiration. Devi (1985) expressed similarity in Mir-alam lake.

The chloride content was high during winter months and low during monsoon months. The range of chlorides were found to be 30.7 to 45.2 mg/l in first year, 31.2 to 44.7 mg/l in second year and 33.2 to 39.7 mg/l in third year of investigation (Table 9.4).

Higher values of total hardness were recorded in summer, followed by monsoon and winter. Its average value was 131.83 mg/l.

Zooplankton diversity: During 2011-12, rotifera dominated the zooplankton population (31.46%) followed by cladocera (27.65%), copepoda (23.20%), protozoa (11.95%) and ostracoda (5.74%) are presented in Fig. 9.1. Total 25 different species of zooplankton were identified. Summer months exhibited higher population of zooplankton (Table 9.5). All zooplankton groups showed maxima in summer and minima in monsoon.

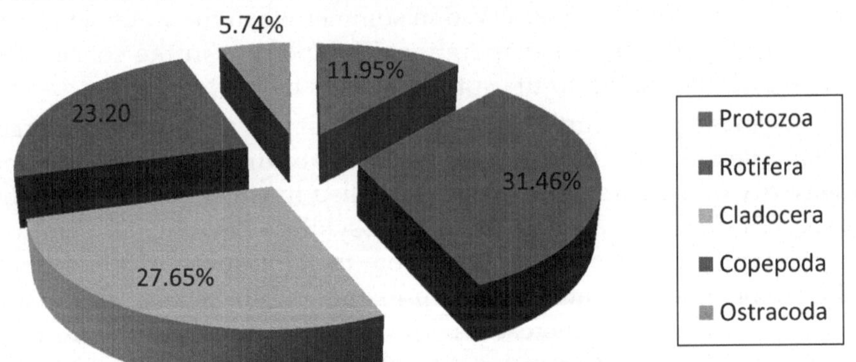

Fig. 9.1: **Quantitative Occurance of Zooplankton in Bhategaon Reservoir (Year 2011-12)**

Protozoans were represented by 3 species (Table 9.5). The species *Paramecium caudatum* and *Diffugia spp* accounted for 11 months, while *Opercularia spp* was present in ten months only. The maximum density of protozoa was recorded in April (62 organisms/Liter) and minimum population during August (8 organisms/Liter). The annual average of this group was 36 organisms/Liter.

Table 9.5: Monthly Analysis of Zooplankton Diversity in Bhategaon Reservoir (Year 2011-12)

Species/Month	June	July	August	September	October	November	December	January	February	March	April	May
Protozoa												
Paramecium caudatum	10	10	04	00	05	12	18	15	25	18	15	20
Diffugia spp.	05	00	04	05	10	14	10	20	10	20	24	22
Opercularia spp.	00	12	00	05	10	09	12	18	18	08	20	10
Total	**15**	**28**	**08**	**10**	**25**	**35**	**40**	**53**	**53**	**46**	**62**	**52**
Rotifera												
Brachionus calyciflorus	02	15	05	15	10	15	08	12	22	11	20	25
Brachionus falcatus	04	20	05	10	02	15	10	10	10	16	18	25
Brachionus diversicornis	05	05	10	02	05	15	10	16	20	20	25	18
Keratella tropica	05	05	10	02	05	15	10	16	20	20	25	18
Keratella quadrata	04	10	04	04	06	18	12	14	15	20	18	20
Lecane (monostyla) bulla	02	06	12	05	02	15	11	10	08	18	20	28
Trichocera porcellus	03	00	02	00	04	08	10	08	12	25	17	25
Filina longiseta	05	05	05	06	10	04	10	05	20	22	20	20
Total	**30**	**66**	**53**	**47**	**44**	**99**	**79**	**90**	**125**	**152**	**158**	**181**
Cladocera												
Indialona ganapati	02	05	05	15	05	18	20	16	15	20	09	10
Moina micrura	02	10	12	10	10	22	10	10	12	20	18	25
Diaphanosoma sarsi	07	14	05	15	07	28	22	14	16	12	10	05
Diaphanosoma excisum	05	09	08	17	09	32	10	12	08	11	14	16
Alona rectangular	10	11	15	10	15	16	19	25	08	11	14	16
Ceriodaphnia cornuta	10	10	15	19	10	20	18	16	08	20	20	20
Total	**36**	**59**	**60**	**86**	**56**	**136**	**99**	**91**	**81**	**101**	**93**	**90**

(Contd…)

Species/Month	June	July	August	September	October	November	December	January	February	March	April	May
Copepoda												
Diaptomus marshianus	10	10	10	10	10	14	15	15	15	20	14	18
Phylladiaptomus lindbergi	10	05	05	05	20	15	18	12	15	20	14	16
Mescyclops leukarti	08	12	05	08	15	10	10	14	18	05	18	22
Mesocyclops hyalinus	04	12	15	10	10	08	05	14	18	05	18	22
Cyclops viridis	10	05	05	10	15	18	16	12	15	22	18	18
Total	**42**	**44**	**40**	**43**	**70**	**65**	**64**	**67**	**78**	**102**	**106**	**108**
Ostracoda												
Cypris obensa	05	05	10	05	05	05	08	07	10	04	05	12
Cyclocypris globosa	05	05	04	04	00	08	10	05	05	10	08	00
Candocypria osborni	00	02	00	05	00	06	10	08	10	05	04	10
Total	**10**	**12**	**14**	**14**	**05**	**19**	**28**	**20**	**25**	**19**	**17**	**22**

Rotifers were represented by 8 species (Table 9.5), and species *Trichocera porcellus* recorded for 10 months only, while other species were recorded round the year. The peak period of rotifers was observed during month of May (18 organisms/Liter) and it was minimum during month of June (30 organisms/liter).The annual average of this group was 94 organisms/Liter.

Cladocerans were represented by 6 species (Table 9.5), and all members of this group were present round the year of investigation. The peak period of cladocerans was observed during month of March (10 organisms/Liter) and it was minimum during month of June (36 organisms/Liter).The annual average of this group was 82 organisms/Liter.

Copepod was represented by 5 species (Table 9.5). The maxima was 108 organisms/Liter during May and minima was 40 organisms/Liter during August. The annual average of this group was 69 organisms/Liter. All members of copepoda were present throughout the investigation of first year.

Ostracoda was represented by 3 species. The highest density was observed during December (28 organisms/liter),while lowest density was recorded during October (05 organisms/Liter). *Cypris obensa* was recorded in all months, while *Cyclocypris globosa* and *Candocypria osborni* were not seen in two months (October and May) and three months (June,August and October) respectively.

During 2012-13, zooplanktons were represented by protozoa, rotifera, cladocera, copepoda and ostracoda. Among zooplankton rotifera dominated, followed by cladocera, copepoda, protozoa and ostracoda.

The monthly variations in total zooplankton population during year 2012-13 is presented in Table 9.6.

Protozoa accounted for about 8.55%, and were represented by 3 species (Table 9.6). The highest density was observed in the month of April (43 organisms/Liter). Throughout the summer months, protozoan population was maximum. However, during rainy season, the population was comparatively less. The average annual density of this group was 22 organisms/Liter.

Rotifers were represented by 8 species and accounted for about 38.82% (Fig. 9.2). *Filinia longiseta* was present in 11 months, while other members of this group were observed throughout the second year of investigation. The peak period of rotifers was observed in month of March (163 organims/liter) and it was minimum in the month of September (53 organisms/Liter). The annual average density of this group was 101 organisms/Liter.

Cladocerans accounted for 24.90% and were represented by 6 species (Table 9.6). The species *Indialona ganapati, Moina micrura* and *Alona rectangular* were recorded round the year,while *Diaphanosoma sarsi* and *D.excisum* were present in eleven months, and *Ceriodaphina cornuta* in 10 months. The maximum cladoceran population (99 organisms/Liter) was recorded during February.

Table 9.6: Monthly Analysis of Zooplankton Diversity in Bhategaon Reservoir (Year 2012-13)

Species/Month	June	July	August	September	October	November	December	January	February	March	April	May
Protozoa												
Paramecium caudatum	05	00	05	00	05	05	10	12	25	20	05	02
Diffugia spp.	08	05	04	10	02	04	05	10	05	15	18	20
Opercularia spp.	00	00	05	00	05	02	08	15	04	05	20	02
Total	**13**	**05**	**14**	**10**	**12**	**11**	**23**	**37**	**34**	**40**	**43**	**24**
Rotifera												
Brachionus calyciflorus	10	06	12	14	11	10	15	10	15	14	19	19
Brachionus falcatus	05	10	05	05	10	11	12	10	20	18	14	10
Brachionus diversicornis	05	10	05	02	02	12	15	08	22	25	20	18
Keratella tropica	05	05	04	07	10	12	15	14	20	28	22	20
Keratella quadrata	10	05	12	05	15	14	15	12	18	19	18	20
Lecane (monostyla) bulla	09	10	05	05	12	12	14	08	17	15	18	17
Trichocera porcellus	05	12	04	10	08	20	11	10	18	24	15	15
Filina longiseta	10	00	08	05	08	12	16	15	25	20	18	22
Total	**59**	**58**	**55**	**53**	**76**	**103**	**113**	**87**	**155**	**163**	**144**	**141**
Cladocera												
Indialona ganapati	10	05	05	10	05	12	10	14	15	05	10	10
Moina micrura	04	05	04	05	10	15	15	18	20	15	20	15
Diaphanosoma sarsi	05	05	04	00	05	19	12	15	15	15	22	25
Diaphanosoma excisum	02	00	08	02	07	11	14	16	16	18	20	16
Alona rectangular	02	08	02	05	08	15	17	10	15	20	18	16
Ceriodaphnia cornuta	02	00	00	05	10	12	08	09	18	15	15	15
Total	**25**	**23**	**23**	**27**	**45**	**84**	**76**	**82**	**99**	**88**	**105**	**97**

(Contd...)

Species/Month	June	July	August	September	October	November	December	January	February	March	April	May
Copepoda												
Diaptomus marshianus	05	05	08	05	05	15	10	12	15	10	16	20
Phylladiaptomus lindbergi	10	08	02	02	10	10	12	14	10	15	22	15
Mescyclops leukarti	02	10	05	10	05	12	05	05	10	20	05	15
Mesocyclops hyalinus	00	05	02	00	10	11	10	05	10	20	05	15
Cyclops viridis	10	05	08	10	10	15	14	12	10	19	20	22
Total	**27**	**33**	**25**	**27**	**40**	**63**	**51**	**48**	**65**	**72**	**75**	**86**
Ostracoda												
Cypris obensa	05	05	07	05	08	02	08	10	18	18	05	08
Cyclocypris globosa	00	04	05	10	02	10	12	10	15	15	08	02
Candocypria osborni	08	09	12	15	14	16	35	25	43	38	15	15
Total	**13**	**09**	**12**	**15**	**14**	**16**	**35**	**25**	**43**	**38**	**15**	**15**

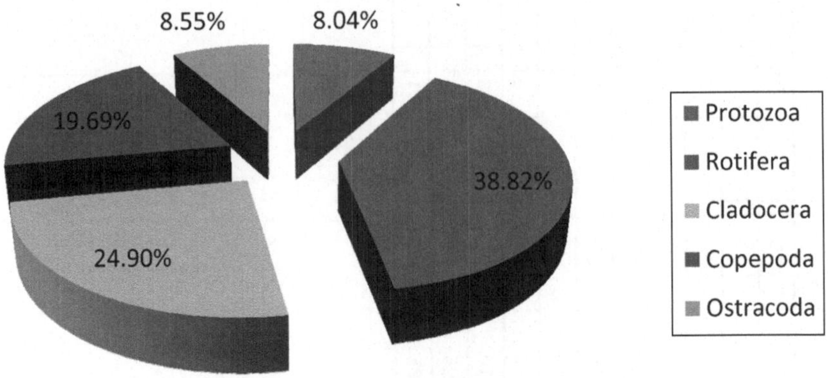

***Fig. 9.2*: Quantitative Occurance of Zooplankton in Bhategaon Reservoir ((2012-13)**

Copepoda accounted for 19.69% and were represented by 5 species (Table 9.6). The average annual density was 51 organisms/Liter with maxima in May (86 organims/Liter) and minima in August (25 organisms/liter). Except *Mesocyclops hyalinus* all group members were present round the year. *Mesocyclops hyalinus* was absent in two months of rainy season (June and September).

Ostracoda came 5th in order of occurrence, and were represented by three species with summer maxima. Their total contribution among zooplankton was about 8.04%.*Candocypria osborni* was absent in July and August, while *Cyclocypris globosa* was absent in June. *Cypris obensa* was recorded in all months.

During third year (2013-14) of investigation rotifera dominated the zooplankton population (37.46%), followed by cladocera (26.39%), copepoda (19.16%), ostracoda (9.80%) and protozoa (7.19%). Total 25 different species of zooplankton were identified. Summer months exhibited higher population of zooplankton (Fig. 9.3). All the zooplanktonic groups showed the summer maxima and minima in monsoon.

Protozoans were represented by 3 species (Table 9.7). Protozoan density recorded a maximum of 53 organisms/Liter in May and minimum of 6 organisms/Liter in August. *Paramecium caudatum* was observed in all months, while *Diffugia spp* and *Opercularia spp* were absent in one month each. The average annual density was 22 organisms/Liter.

Among rotifera, *Brachionus calciflorus, B.falcatus, B.diversicrnis, Keratella tropica, K.quadrata* and *Lecane (Monostyla) bulla* were present round the year, while *Trichocera precellus* and *Filinia logiseta* were absent in August and July respectively. The maximum density was recorded in May (191 organisms/ Liter) and minimum in August (47 organisms/Liter) with annual average density of 116 organisms/liter.

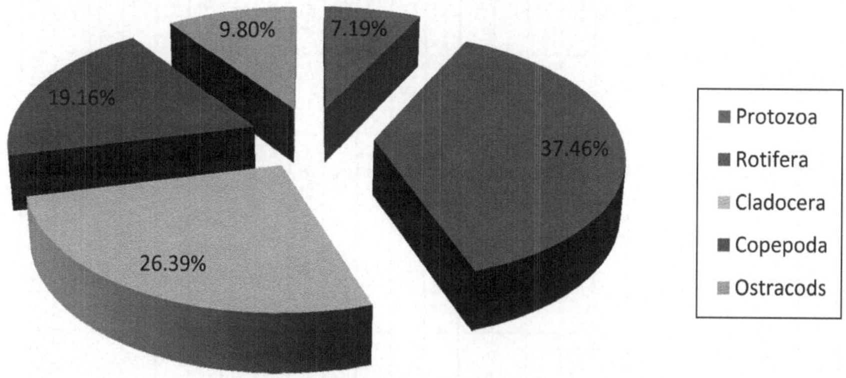

Fig. 9.3: **Quantitative Occurance of Zooplankton in Bhategaon Reservoir (2013-14)**

Cladocera represented by 6 species. Density of group recorded a maxima of 122 organisms/Liter in May and a minimum of 37 organisms/liter in July with annual average density of 82 organisms/Liter. Three members of this group (*Indialona ganapati, Diaphanosoma sarsi* and *Alona rectangular*) were recorded round the third year of investigation, while *Moina micrura* was not seen in two months (July and December), *Diaphanosoma excisum* in September and *Ceriodaphnia cornuta* in July.

Copepoda represented by 5 species. *Cyclops viridis* showed presence throughout the year, while *Diaptomus marshianus, Phylladiaptomus lindbergi, Mesocyclops leukarti* and *Mesocyclops hyalinus* were observed in eleven months only.The minimum density of 18 organims/Liter was recorded in July and maximum of 108 organisms/Liter in May with annual average of 59 organisms/Liter.

Ostracods were presened by 3 members. *Cyclocypris globosa* showed presence in all months, while *Cypris obensa* and *Candocypria osborni* were absent in one month each. The density of ostracods ranged from 8 organisms/Liter (July) to 50 organisms/liter (February) with annual average of 30 organims/ Liter.

Phytoplankton diversity: The study of the phytoplankton sampled in Bhategaon reservoir showed 21 species (Table 9.8). The phytoplankton assemblage was represented by four classes viz., Chlorophyceae, Cyanophyceae, Bacillariophyceae and Euglenophyceae.

The class Chlorophyceae was represented by maximum species. It was reported by 10 species. The class was represented by *Zygnema sp, Ulothrix zonata, Pediastrum duplex, Pediastrum simplex, Scendesmus armatus, Oedogonium patulum, Ankistrodesmus falcatus, Chlorella vulgaris, Closterium limneticum* and *Cosmarium contractum.*

Table 9.7: Monthly Analysis of Zooplankton Diversity in Bhategaon Reservoir (Year 2013-14)

Species/Month	June	July	August	September	October	November	December	January	February	March	April	May
Protozoa												
Paramecium caudatum	04	05	02	05	05	08	06	08	10	10	10	10
Diffugia spp.	05	02	04	00	04	05	05	05	12	12	14	15
Opercularia spp.	00	04	00	04	02	07	05	12	10	14	15	18
Total	**09**	**11**	**06**	**09**	**11**	**20**	**16**	**25**	**32**	**36**	**39**	**53**
Rotifera												
Brachionus calyciflorus	04	02	05	10	07	10	12	10	12	20	16	10
Brachionus falcatus	04	15	05	05	08	14	15	18	15	22	22	19
Brachionus diversicornis	10	10	05	05	12	14	14	15	19	18	28	32
Keratella tropica	12	02	10	10	10	12	12	16	20	30	15	25
Keratella quadrata	10	04	05	12	05	15	18	19	26	18	25	35
Lecane (monostyla) bulla	10	08	05	05	12	20	20	18	20	15	22	17
Trichocera porcellus	05	15	00	10	15	15	18	15	22	30	22	30
Filina longiseta	10	00	12	15	20	15	18	16	18	22	25	23
Total	**65**	**56**	**47**	**72**	**89**	**115**	**127**	**127**	**152**	**175**	**175**	**191**
Cladocera												
Indialona ganapati	08	10	10	10	14	12	10	18	20	20	12	20
Moina micrura	04	00	10	15	11	15	00	17	25	14	25	19
Diaphanosoma sarsi	12	10	18	05	19	14	16	11	17	20	20	18
Diaphanosoma excisum	05	07	05	00	13	18	12	18	18	20	21	20
Alona rectangular	04	10	02	05	18	19	12	16	20	30	20	25
Ceriodaphnia cornuta	05	00	05	12	08	12	16	10	18	15	22	20
Total	**38**	**37**	**50**	**47**	**85**	**90**	**66**	**90**	**118**	**119**	**120**	**122**

(Contd…)

Species/Month	June	July	August	September	October	November	December	January	February	March	April	May
Copepoda												
Diaptomus marshianus	08	00	05	05	11	10	05	20	16	15	20	25
Phylladiaptomus lindbergi	00	10	05	10	16	15	12	17	25	18	20	30
Mescyclops leukarti	05	00	05	15	05	15	10	18	20	20	32	20
Mesocyclops hyalinus	05	04	02	05	00	05	12	17	22	16	10	18
Cyclops viridis	02	04	12	10	05	10	05	10	09	12	18	15
Total	**20**	**18**	**29**	**45**	**37**	**55**	**44**	**82**	**92**	**81**	**100**	**108**
Ostracoda												
Cypris obensa	05	02	00	02	10	15	10	12	14	18	11	18
Cyclocypris globosa	05	04	06	05	05	10	12	14	16	15	22	05
Candocypria osborni	00	02	04	08	10	05	17	18	20	14	16	14
Total	**10**	**08**	**10**	**15**	**25**	**30**	**39**	**44**	**50**	**47**	**49**	**37**

Table 9.8: Monthly Analysis of Phytoplankton Diversity in Bhategaon Reservoir (Year 2011-12)

Species/Month	June	July	August	September	October	November	December	January	February	March	April	May
Chlorophyceae												
Zygnema sp	10	05	00	05	15	10	15	25	35	35	45	25
Ulothrix zonata	15	00	00	00	20	20	25	25	25	30	25	25
Pediastrum duplex	20	00	10	10	00	15	20	20	35	35	25	20
Pediastrum simplex	25	15	10	10	15	20	20	25	25	20	20	20
Scendesmus armatus	20	15	15	00	10	15	15	25	25	35	25	15
Oedogonium patulum	10	05	05	05	00	00	00	25	25	30	30	25
Ankistrodesmus falcatus	15	05	05	00	10	15	15	20	25	25	35	25
Chlorella vulgaris	20	15	15	10	15	10	15	15	25	25	35	30
Closterium limneticum	25	15	10	00	10	25	20	25	30	30	30	25
Cosmarium contractum	10	05	05	10	10	15	15	25	25	35	25	20
Total	**170**	**80**	**75**	**50**	**105**	**145**	**160**	**230**	**275**	**300**	**295**	**230**
Cyanophyceae												
Oscillatoria limnosoa	10	05	05	00	15	15	25	20	35	30	35	35
Oscillatoria chlorime	05	00	10	00	20	25	20	20	35	30	35	30
Anabaena constricta	15	10	00	10	20	35	35	45	40	40	40	40
Merismopedia punctata	20	15	15	00	15	20	15	20	25	25	35	35
Microcystis aerugenose	00	00	00	00	10	15	10	15	15	25	20	20
Total	**50**	**30**	**30**	**10**	**80**	**110**	**105**	**120**	**150**	**150**	**165**	**160**

(Contd...)

Species/Month	June	July	August	September	October	November	December	January	February	March	April	May
Bacillariophyceae												
Navicula viridula	05	00	00	05	10	10	15	15	20	20	15	15
Nitzschia subtilis	10	05	05	10	10	05	10	10	15	15	10	05
Synedra affinis	25	20	15	15	20	20	10	25	25	20	35	30
Diatoms vuloare	10	10	05	05	05	20	20	25	25	30	45	45
Bacillaria paradoxa	00	10	00	00	10	10	15	15	10	15	35	20
Total	**50**	**45**	**25**	**35**	**55**	**65**	**70**	**90**	**95**	**100**	**140**	**115**
Euglenophyceae												
Euglena pisciformis	00	05	05	10	10	15	10	15	15	15	10	05
Total	**00**	**05**	**05**	**10**	**10**	**15**	**10**	**15**	**15**	**15**	**10**	**05**

The class Cyanophyceae was represented by 5 species.It was represented by *Oscillatoria limnosa, Oscillatoria chlorine, Anabaena constricta, Merismopedia punctata* and *Microcystis aerugenose.*

The class Bacillariphyceae was represented by 5 species i.e., Navicula *viridula, Nitzschia subtilis, Synedra affinis, Diatoms vuloare* and *Bacillaria paradoxa.* The class Euglenophyceae was represented by a single species i.e., *Euglena pisciformes.*

During first year of investigation (year 2011-12) the phytoplankton consisted of 49.48% of Chlorophyceae, 27.13% of Cyanophyceae, 20.70% of Bacillariophyceae and 2.69% of Euglenophyceae (Fig. 9.4).

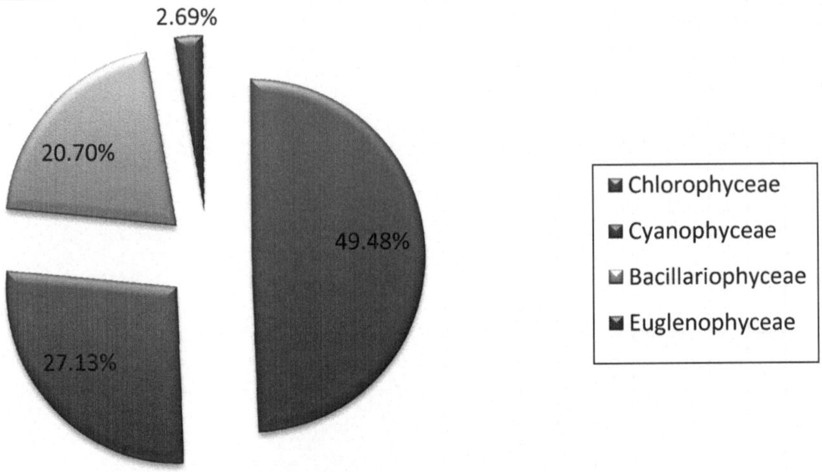

Fig.9.4: **Quantitative Occurance of Phytoplankton from Bhategaon Resevoir (Year 2011-12)**

In case of Chlorophyceae, *Pediastrum simplex, Chlorella vulgaris* and *Cosmarium contractum* were recorded throughout the year. Their number was high in summer and low in rainy season. *Zygnema sp, Scendesmus armatus, Ankistrodesmus falcatus,Pediastrum duplex* and *Clostrium limneticum* were absent in one month of rainy season,while *Ulothrix zonata* was absent in three months of rainy season (July, August and September) and *Oedogonium patulum* was absent in three months of winter season (October, November and December).

Among Cyanophyceae, *Oscillatoria limnosa, Oscillatoria chlorine, Anabaena constricta, Merismopedia punctata* and *Microcystis aerugenose* were recorded. *Oscillatoria limnosa, Anabaena constricta* and *Merismopedia punctata* were not observed in one month and *Oscillatoria chlorine* in two months of the rainy season. *Microcystis aerugenose* was absent in entire rainy season.

Among Bacillariophyceae, *Navicula viridula, Nitzschia subtilis, Synedra affinis, Diatoms vuloare* and *Bacillaria paradoxa* were recorded. *Nitzschia subtilis, Synedra affinis* and *Diatmos vuloare* were observed throughout the first year of investigation with maximum and minimum density in summer and monsoon respectively.*Navicula viridula* was not seen in two months i.e., July and August and *Bacillaria paradoxa* in three months (June, August and September).

The variation in the population density of Bacillariophyceae ranged from 25 to 140 units/liter and contributed to about 20.70% of the total phytoplankton population.

A single species i.e., *Euglena pisciformis* was represented by class Euglenophyceae, which was absent in first month of investigation i.e., July. The population density of *Euglena pisciformis* varied from nil to 15 units/liter. This group contributed to 2.69% of the total phytoplankton.

During the second year (2012-13) of investigation, a total number of 21 species (10 species of Chlorophyceae, 5 species of Cyanophyceae, 5 species of Bacillariophyceae and 1 species of Euglenophyceae were recorded in Bhategaon reservoir.The phytoplankton consisted of 39.80% of Chlorophyceae, 31.73% of Bacillariophyceae, 25.19% of Cyanophyceae and 3.28% of Euglenophyceae (Fig. 9.5). The class Chlorophyceae was dominant with annual average of 132 units/liter followed by Bacillariophyceae (105 units/liter), Cyanophyceae (83 units/liter) and Euglenophyceae (11 units/Liter).

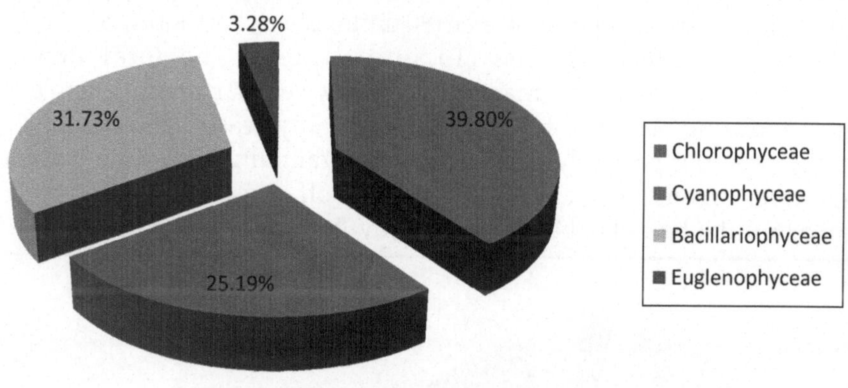

***Fig. 9.5:* Quantitative Occurancnce of Phytoplankton from Bhategaon Reservoir during (Year 2012-13)**

In case of Chlorophyceae, *Pediastrum duplex, Pediastrum simplex, Scendesmus armatus, Chlorella vulgaris* and *Cosmarium contractum* were recorded throughout the second year of investigation. *Ulothrix zonata* was completely absent in rainy and winter season. *Zygnema sp, Oedogonium patulum* and *Closterium limneticum* were absent in August and September, while *Ankistrodesmus falcatus* was absent in three months of rainy season. The density of Chlorophyceae ranged from 40 to 235 units/Liter. It was maximum in April and minimum in August.

The Cyanophyceae were represented by 5 species. *Oscillatoria chlorine, Anabaena constricta* and *Microcystis aerugenose* were observed throughout the year. *Oscillatoria limnosa* and *Merismopedia punctata* were absent in September and August respectively.

Bacillariophyceae was represented by five species. *Nitzschia subtilis, Synedra affinis* and *Diatoms vuloare* were observed throughout the year. *Navicula viridula* and *Bacillaria paradoxa* were absent in one and two months respectively. The variation in the population density of Bacillariophyceae ranged from 25 to 180 units/Liter and contributed to about 31.73% of the phytoplankton population. The density of *Navicula viridula* ranged from nil to 30 units/Litr, *Nitzschia subtilis* from 15 to 35 units/Liter, *Synedra affinis* from 5 to 40 units/Liter, *Diatmos vuloare* from 5 to 35 units/Liter and *Bacillaria paradoxa* from nil to 35 units/Liter.

Euglenophyceae was represented by a single species i.e., *Euglena pisciformis*. Its density ranged from nil to 20 units/Liter and was absent in September.

During third year of investigation (2013-14), the phytoplankton consisted of 53.20% of chlorophyceae, 23.46% of Bacillariophyceae, 19.41% of Cyanophyceae and 3.93% of Euglenophyceae (Fig. 9.6). It was revealed that the class Chlorophyceae was dominant with annual average of 180 units/ Liter, followed by Bacillariophyceae (80 units/Liter), Cyanophyceae (66 units/ Liter) and Euglenophyceae (13 units/Liter). The total density of phytoplankton was found maximum during February month while it was minimal during September (Table 9.10). In rainy season, the phytoplankton density was low probably due to increased rainfall, increase in water level, high water current, increase in turbidity run off and dilution effect by floods. Similar results had also been observed by Panigrahi and Patra (2013).

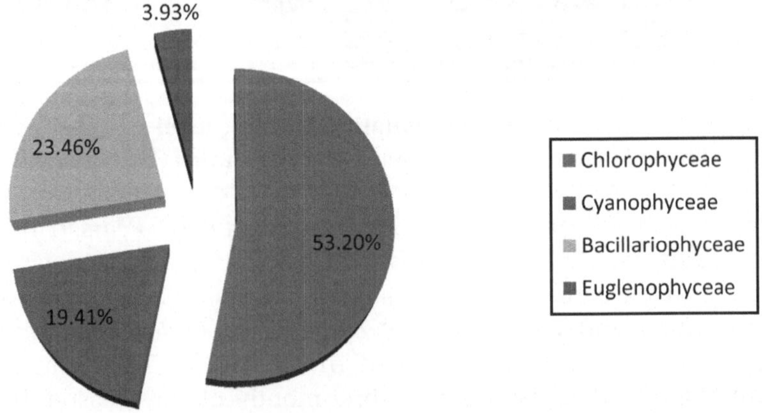

Fig. 9.6: **Quantitative Occurance of Phytoplankton from Bhategaon Reservoir during Year 2013-14**

Table 9.9: Monthly Analysis of Phytoplankton Diversity in Bhategaon Reservoir (Year 2012-13)

Species/Month	June	July	August	September	October	November	December	January	February	March	April	May
Chlorophyceae												
Zygnema sp	15	10	00	00	05	15	15	20	20	20	10	10
Ulotrix zonata	00	00	00	00	00	00	00	00	05	05	10	05
Pediastrum duplex	10	05	05	05	15	15	20	20	20	20	20	15
Pediastrum simplex	10	05	05	05	05	10	15	10	20	15	20	15
Scendesmus armatus	05	15	15	20	20	15	25	25	20	25	35	30
Oedogonium patulum	05	05	00	00	10	15	15	20	20	35	25	25
Ankistrodesmus falcatus	10	00	00	00	10	05	15	15	25	20	25	20
Chlorella vulgaris	05	05	10	10	15	10	15	15	20	15	25	20
Closterium limneticum	15	10	00	00	10	20	25	35	25	25	35	20
Cosmarium contractum	10	05	05	05	05	10	10	15	15	20	30	25
Total	**85**	**60**	**40**	**45**	**95**	**115**	**155**	**175**	**190**	**200**	**235**	**185**
Cyanophyceae												
Oscillatoria limnosoa	10	10	10	00	10	10	10	15	15	20	20	20
Oscillatoria chlorime	05	05	10	10	10	15	10	15	15	20	10	15
Anabaena constricta	15	15	05	10	15	20	20	35	30	30	20	20
Merismopedia punctata	10	05	00	10	15	20	20	20	20	25	20	15
Microcystis aerugenose	10	05	10	15	25	25	30	25	35	45	35	35
Total	**50**	**40**	**35**	**45**	**75**	**90**	**90**	**110**	**115**	**140**	**105**	**105**

(Contd...)

Species/Month	June	July	August	September	October	November	December	January	February	March	April	May
Bacillariophyceae												
Navicula viridula	05	10	05	00	10	15	15	25	20	25	35	30
Nitzschia subtilis	15	20	20	15	35	20	35	30	35	35	35	25
Synedra affinis	10	05	05	05	15	15	25	25	35	45	40	40
Diatoms vuloare	15	10	10	05	10	15	35	25	25	35	35	30
Bacillaria paradoxa	25	10	00	00	15	15	20	25	25	35	35	25
Total	**70**	**55**	**40**	**25**	**85**	**80**	**130**	**130**	**140**	**175**	**180**	**150**
Euglenophyceae												
Euglena pisciformis	05	10	05	00	10	15	05	10	15	15	20	20
Total	**05**	**10**	**05**	**00**	**10**	**15**	**05**	**10**	**15**	**15**	**20**	**20**

Table 9.10: Monthly Analysis of Phytoplankton Diversity in Bhategaon Reservoir (Year 2013-14)

Species/Month	June	July	August	September	October	November	December	January	February	March	April	May
Chlorophyceae												
Zygnema sp	15	05	10	00	15	15	20	20	20	25	20	20
Ulothrix zonata	10	05	05	05	10	15	15	20	25	25	30	25
Pediastrum duplex	10	05	10	00	00	10	15	10	15	15	20	15
Pediastrum simplex	15	10	05	15	15	25	20	25	35	35	25	30
Scendesmus armatus	10	05	10	00	15	15	25	25	20	20	25	15
Oedogonium patulum	20	00	00	10	25	25	20	20	25	25	30	20
Ankistrodesmus falcatus	20	10	10	10	15	15	20	20	25	35	25	25
Chlorella vulgaris	20	10	10	00	25	20	25	35	35	25	35	40
Closterium limneticum	10	10	00	05	20	25	20	30	35	35	35	20
Cosmarium contractum	25	20	10	15	20	20	15	15	35	25	25	25
Total	**155**	**80**	**70**	**60**	**160**	**185**	**195**	**220**	**270**	**265**	**270**	**235**
Cyanophyceae												
Oscillatoria limnosoa	10	05	05	00	05	10	10	15	15	15	15	10
Oscillatoria chlorime	05	05	00	00	05	15	25	25	25	30	25	25
Anabaena constricta	00	00	00	00	10	10	05	10	15	15	10	15
Merismopedia punctata	05	10	05	05	10	10	15	15	25	25	20	20
Microcystis aerugenose	10	10	00	15	15	25	20	20	35	30	30	25
Total	**30**	**30**	**10**	**20**	**45**	**70**	**75**	**85**	**115**	**115**	**100**	**95**

(Contd...)

Species/Month	June	July	August	September	October	November	December	January	February	March	April	May
Bacillariophyceae												
Navicula viridula	10	15	05	05	15	15	20	20	25	20	20	20
Nitzschia subtilis	15	20	05	00	10	20	25	20	25	20	15	15
Synedra affinis	10	15	10	10	10	25	15	15	25	15	25	20
Diatoms vuloare	00	10	15	05	10	10	15	15	20	35	20	20
Bacillaria paradoxa	05	10	15	15	20	10	25	20	35	20	20	10
Total	**40**	**70**	**50**	**35**	**65**	**80**	**100**	**90**	**130**	**110**	**100**	**85**
Euglenophyceae												
Euglena pisciformis	10	05	05	10	10	15	10	15	15	25	20	20
Total	**10**	**05**	**05**	**10**	**10**	**15**	**10**	**15**	**15**	**25**	**20**	**20**

The class Chlorophyceae was represented by maximum species. It was reported by 10 species. The class was represented by *Zygnema sp, Ulothrix zonata, Pediastrum duplex, Pediastrum simplex, Scendesmus armatus, Oedogonium patulum, Ankistrdesmus falcatus, Chlorella vulgaris, Closterium limneticum* and *Cosmarium contractum.*

In case of Chlorohpyceae, *Ulothrix zonata, Pediastrum simplex, Ankistrodesmus falcatus* and *Cosmarium contractum* were recorded throughout the third year of investigation. *Zygnema sp,Scendesmus armatus,Chlorella vulgaris* and *Closterium limneticum* were not observed in one month of rainy season. *Pediastrum duplex* and *Oedogonium patulum* were absent in two months (Table 9.10).

The class Cyanophyceae was represented by five species i.e., *Oscillatoria limnosa, Oscillatoria chlorine, Anabaena constricta, Merismopedia punctata* and *Microcystis aerugenose. Merismopedia punctata* was recorded throughout the year. Its number was high in the month of February and March (25 units/ Liter) and low in rainy season i.e., June, August and September (5 units/ Liter). *Oscillatoria limnosa and Microcystis aerugenose* were absent in one month, and *Oscillatoria chlorine* in two months. *Anabaena constricta* was absent in entire rainy season. The density of this group ranged from 10 to 115 units/Liter with annual average of 66 units/Liter (Table 9.10).

Among Bacillariophyceae, *Navicula viridula, Nitzschia subtilis, Synedra affinis, Diatoms vuloare* and *Bacillaria paradoxa* were recorded. *Navicula viridula, Synedra affinis* and *Bacillaria paradoxa* were observed throughout the third year of investigation with maximum and minimum density in summer and monsoon season respectively. *Nitzschia subtilis* and *Diatoms vuloare* were not seen in one month of rainy season. The variation in the population density of Bacillariphyceae ranged from 35 to 130 units.Liter and contributed to 23.46% of the total phytoplankton population.

In case of Euglenophyceae, *Euglena pisciformis* was recorded throughout the third year of investigation. Its number was high in the month of March (25 units/Liter). This group contributed to about 3.93% of the total phytoplankton population (Fig. 9.6).

CHAPTER - 10

Conclusion and Recommendations

India is one of the mega diversity countries with respect to fresh water species (650+ species) (Molur and Walker, 1998). In freshwater fish diversity India is eighth in the world and third in Asia (Kottelat and Whitten, 1996). There are plenty of culturable species and any further introduction of exotic fish species is unnecessary. For example, with such a variety of culturable carps such as *Catla catla, Labeo rohita* and *Cirrhinus mrigala* why should we go for exotic carps?. The need of the hour is to protect the existing indigenous fish stock and steps for enhancing the quality of the culturable species rather than go in for indiscriminate introduction of exotic species. India has to develop baseline data on the natural population potential of the indigenous species. The waterbodies harbouring endangered fishes must be declared as 'fish sanctuaries' or 'aquatic diversity management areas'. Presently, our freshwater biodiversity is in peril. Checking the entry of exotic species coupled with more awareness on the indigenous species would go a long way in preserving our rich aquatic biodiversity.

Systematic ecology based fisheries investigations on six reservoirs of Marathwada region of Maharashtra were carried out for the period of three years (2011-12 to 2013-14). All the reservoirs are typical example of 'put and take' system of culture-based fisheries. There is a direct relationship between stocking and yield rates. Constant good landings of exotic species suggest that they are well adapted to the lentic condition of the reservoir.

From the account of the study given in the previous chapters, it can be well concluded that all the six reservoirs under present investigation supports a good fishery of exotic species viz., *Oreochromis mossambicus, Cyprinus carpio,Ctenopharyngodon idella* and *Hypophthalmichthys molitrix.*

In Majalgaon reservoir of Beed district exotic species (*Cyprinus carpio* and *Oreochromis mossambicus*) contributed to about 37% of the fish catch in reservoir.

In Wan reservoir, *Cyprinus carpio* and *Oreochromis mossambicus* formed more than 15% of the total catch. The accidental entry of *Oreochromis mossambicus* adversely affected the growth of *Catla catla*.

In Harni (Katgaon) reservoir of Osmanabad district, seed of *Cyprinus carpio* is also stocked with seed of Indian major carps. It is only a single exotic species recorded from this reservoir.Its contribution was 12.02% of the total catch.

In Gharni reservoir of Latur district *Cyprinus carpio* and *Ctenopharyngodon idella* were recorded. Their contribution was about 37% of the total catch. A more important disqualification of *Cyprinus carpio* is its propensities to compete with *Cirrhinus mrigala*. The stocking of *Cyprinus carpio* in Gharni reservoir has nearly eliminated *Cirrhinus mrigala*.

From Siddeshwar reservoir of Hingoli district two exotic species (*Cyprinus carpio* and *Oreochromis mossambicus*) formed 7.16% of the total catch. The catla fishery in reservoir has adversely affected by the accidental entry of *Oreochromis mossambicus*.

Bhategaon is a small sized shallow water reservoir in Hingoli district. Grass carp (*Ctenopharyngodon idella*) formed about 10.17% of the total catch.

From above mentioned account, it can be well concluded that the reservoirs under present investigation on an average supports to about 19.72% of the exotic fish fishery.

Therefore following recommendations are made for conservation of the indigenous fish species and also for developing the fishery of the reservoirs on scientific lines:

1. State Fisheries Department's officials should be given periodic training in identification of exotic fishes as well as existing guidelines which will help them in regulating the illegal culture of exotic fishes in their jurisdiction.
2. State Fisheries Departments shall be vested with adequate legal power (including confiscation and arrest) to enforce the existing guidelines on exotics.
3. Awareness must be created among the public about dangers of unauthorized fish introduction and their potential for causing irreversible damage to environment.Also the need for their careful documentation and study shall be empasised.
4. State and Central governments should invest more in research to develop culture technology for indigenous fishes rather than promoting introduction of exotic fishes.
5. With rapid increase in the human population and the increasing dependence on aquatic resources including water and the continuing introduction of exotic species in natural water bodies,the loss of aquatic

biodiversity is likely to increase further unless proper conservation measures are implemented.Detailed investigations should be initiated to locate the impact of all the introduced species in various water bodies, followed by steps to eradicate the deleterious species.

6. Considering the negative impact of exotic fishes on aquatic biodiversity,stringent regulations should be framed regarding the import of non-native fishes. As per rule,the exotic fish varieties should be cleared by the National Committee on Introduction of Aquatic species in Indian waters,New Delhi before introduction.The committee represented by fisheries development commissioner and experts will study the relevance of import and the potential impact that the new species is likely to produce on Indian aquatic environment.However,illict import and trade of exotic fishes,particularly that of tilapia, continues unabatedly and there are no effective methods nor the political will to enforce the law.The situation warrants a revision of the existing laws and procedure for their implementation.A code of practice,preferably following the guidelines of De Silva (1989) and European Inland Fisheries Advisory Commission (EIFAC) to be adopted to minimize the risk of introduction of species.Proper quarantine standards also be insisted while importing aquatic organisms.

References

Agale, M. C., Patil, J.V. and Patel, N.G. 2013. Study of Seasonal Variations of Phytoplankton and Their Correlation with Physico-chemical Parameters of Budaki Medium Irrigation Tank, Shirpur, Dist. Dhule (M.S.), India. *Euro. J.Zool.Res.* 2(3): 8-16.

Agrawal, A.K. and Rajwar, G.S.2010. Physico-chemical and Microbiological Study of Tehri Dam Reservoir, Garhwal Himalaya, India. *Journal of American Science.* 6 (6): 65-71.

Ahmad, M.S. 1996. Ecological Survey of Some Algal Flora of Polluted Habitats of Dharbhanga. *J. Environ. Pollut.* 3: 147-151.

Ambekar, E.E., Vasudevappa, Chindi and Basavaraju, Y.2008. Impact of Fish Introductions: A Global Perspective, In: Fish Introductions in India: Status, Potential and Challenges (Eds.W.S. Lakra, A.K. Singh and S. Ayyappan), pp. 25-34, Narendra Publishing House, Delhi.

Akbulut, E.N. 2004. The Determination of Relationship Between Zooplankton and Abiotic Factors Using Canonical Correspondence Analysis (CCA) in the Ova Stream (Ankara/Turkey), *Acta Hydrochimica Hydrobiologica,* 32(6): 434-441.

Ang, K.J., Gopinath, R. and Chua, T.E. 1989. The Status of Introduced Fish Species in Malaysia, pp. 71-82. In S.S. De Silva (ed.) Exotic Aquatic Organisms in Asia. Proceedings of the Workshop on Introduction of Exotic Aquatic Organisms in Asia, Asian Fish. Soc. Spec. Publ. 3, 154p. Asian Fisheries Society, Manila, Philippines.

Arthington, A.H. and Mitchell, D.S.1986. Aquatic Invading Species, pp. 34-53. In R.H. Groves and J.J.Burdon (eds). Ecology of Biological Invasions: An Australian Perspective.

Arthington, A.H., Milton, D.A. and McKay, R.J.1983. Effects of Urban Development and Habitat Alterations, on the Distribution and

Abundance of Native and Exotic Freshwater Fish in the Brisbabane Region, Queenland. *Australian Journal of Ecology*, 8: 87-101.

Awasthi, Kirtiman. 2008. Tilapia Fish may have Killed Gharials in Chambal. *Down to Earth*, April 1-5. 2008.

Bais, V.S. and Agarwal, W.L. 1993. Seasonal Variation of Nutrient Content in *Hydrilla verticollata. J. Freshwater Biol.* 3: 259-265.

Baker, R.L.1979. Specific Status of *Keratella Cochlearis* (Goose) and *K. eurlinare ahlao* from (Rotifera and Brachionidae) Morphological and Ecological Consideration. *Canadian Journal of Zoology*, 57: 1719-1722.

Balla, S.A. Liyod, L.N. and Pierce, B.E. 1985. Unwanted Aquarium Fish, *Search*, 16: 300-301.

Barel, CDN, Dorit, R., Greenwodd, P.H., Frayer, G.Huges, H., Jackson, PBN, Kawanabes, H., Lowe, MC Council, TH, Nogoshi, M. 1985. Destruction of Fisheries in Africa's Lakes, *Nature*, 315: 19-20.

Baruah, U.K.; Bhagowati, A.K. and Goswami, U.C. 1999. Culture of Hybrid Magur (*Clarias gariepinus x Clarias macrocepahlus)* in Assam, *Indian J. Fish.* 46(3): 265-272.

Battish, S.K. 1992. Freshwater Zooplankton of India, Oxford Publishing Co. Pvt. Ltd., New Delhi; pp. 233.

Bhat, N.A., Wanganeo Ashwani and Raina Rajni. 2014. The Composition and Diversity of Net Zooplankton Species in a Tropical Water Body (Bhoj Wetland) of Bhopal, India. *International Journal of Biodiversity and Conservation*, 6(5): 373-381.

Bhowmik, M.L.1968. Environmental Factors Affecting Fish Food in Freshwater Fisheries, Kalyani, West Bengal, India, Ph.D. Thesis, University of Kalyani, 238p.

Bijukumar, A. 2000. Exotic Fishes and Freshwater Fish Diversity, *Zoos' Print Journal*, Volume XV (11): 363-367.

Boyd, C.E. and Tucker, C.S. 2009. Pond Aquaculture Water Quality Management. Springer International Edition, pp. 700.

Britton, J.R., Boar, R.R., Grey, J., Foster J., Logonzo, J. and Harper, D.M. 2007. From Introduction to Fishery.

Cambray, J.A. 2003. Impact on Indigenous Species Biodiversity Caused by the Globalization of Alien Recreational Freshwater Fisheries, *Hydrobiologia*. 500: 217-230.

Carlander, H.B. 1954. A History of Fish and Fishing in the Upper Mississipi River, Upper Mississipi River Conservation Commission, 96pp.

CBD. 2005. Invasive Alien Species. Convention on Biological Diversity, http://www.biodiv.org/programmes/cross-cutting/alien/

Chakrabarti, P.K. 1980. Studies on the Hydrobiology of Some Freshwater Fisheries. Ph.D. Thesis, Burdwan University, 251p.

Chakraborty, I. 2004. Limnology and Zooplankton Abundance in Selected Wetlands of Nadia District of West Bengal. *Environ. Ecol.* 22: 576-578.

Chandrakiran, Sharma, K.K. and Sharma, R. 2014. Phytoplankton Community Response to Changing Physico-chemical Environment of Subtropical Lake Mansar, India. *Int. J. Biosci.* 4(11): 95-103. Paper Available on http://www.innspub.net.

Charak, K.S. and Fayaz, F.A. 2006. Ecological Status of Salal Reservoir, Reasi, District Udhampur (J&K). *Fishing Chimes.* 26 (9): 38-40.

Chatterjee, C. and Raziuddin, M. 2002. Determination of Water Quality Index (WQF) of a Degraded River in Asansol Industrial Area (West Bengal). *Nature, Environment and Pollution Technology,* 1(2): 181-189.

Chiba, K., Taki, Y., Saki, K. and Oozeki, Y. 1989. Present Status of Aquatic Organisms Introduced into Japan, pp. 63-70. In: S.S. De Silva (ed.) Exotic Aquatic Organisms in Asia. Proceedings of the Workshop on Introduction of Exotic Organisms in Asia. Asian Fisheries Society, Manila, Philippines.

Courtenay, W.R., JR. 1979. The Introduction of Exotic Organisms, pp. 237-250. In Wildlife and America. H.P. Brokaw (ed.). U.S. Fish and Wildlife Service, Forest Service and National Oceanic and Atomospheric Administration, Government Printing Office,Washington, D.C.

Courtenay, W.R., JR. 1990. Fish Introduction and the Enigma of Introduced Species. Pages 11-20. In Introduced and Traslocated Fishes and Their Ecological Effects, D.A. Pollard (ed.). Australian Bureau of National Resources. Proceeding No. 8, Canberra.

Crossman, E.J. 1991. Introduced Freshwater Fishes: A Review of the North Amercian Perspective with Emphasis on Canada, *Canadian Journal of Fisheries and Aquatic Sciences*, 48: 46-57.

Das, P. 2008. Challenging Experiences of Exotic Fish Introductions: An Overview, In: Fish Introductions in India: Status, Potential and Challenges (Edited by W.S. Lakra, A.K. Singh and S.Ayyappan), Narendra Publishing House, Delhi, pp. 35-44.

Das, R.K. 1996. Monitoring of Water Quality, its Importance in Disease Control. Paper Presented in Nat. Workshop on Fish and Prawn Disease, Epizootics and Quarantine Adoption in India. October 9, 1996. CICFRI. pp. 51-55.

Dehadrai, P.V. 2008. Problems and Prospects of Exotic Fishes in India, In: Fish Introductions in India: Status, Potential and Challenges (Edited By W.S.Lakra, A.K. Singh and S.Ayyappan), Narendra Publishing House, pp. 17-23.

De Silva, Sena S. 1989. Exotics–A Global Perspective with Special Reference to Finfish Introductions to Asia, In: Exotic Aquatic Organisms in Asia (Edited by S.S. De Silva), Asian Fisheries Society, pp. 1-6.

Deniz Innal and Fu¨ sun Erk'akan. 2006. Effects of Exotic and Translocated Fish Species in the Inland Waters of Turkey, *Rev Fish Biol Fisheries.* 16: 39-50.

Department of Wildlife and Fisheries Sciences, Texas A & M University: Aqua Plant: Dissolved Oxygen. http://aquaplant.tamu.edu/contents/dissolved Oxygen.htm. (accessed in August 2005).

De Silva,S.S.1989. Exotics-a Global Perspective with Special Reference to Finfish Introduction to Asia. In: Exotic Organisms in Asia. Proceedings of the Workshop on Introduction of Exotic Organisms in Asia, pp. 1-6, Asian Fisheries Society, Spec. Publ. No. 3, 282p.

Devi, M.J. 1985. Ecological Studies of the Limno-plankton of Three Freshwater Bodies of Hyderabad. Ph.D. Thesis, Osmania University, Hyderabad.

Devi Sarla, B. 1997. Present Status, Potentialities, Management and Economics of Fisheries of Two Minor Reservoirs of Hyderabad, Ph.D. Thesis, Osmania University, Hyderabad.

Dhanapathi, M.V.S.S.S. 2000. Taxonomic Notes on the Rotifers from India (from 1889-2000) IAAB, Hyderabad Publ. 10, 1-178.

Dutta, S.P.S., Khullar, M., and Sharma, J.2010. Limnology of Two Springs Adjacent to Chattha Nullah Jammu. Part III. Zooplankton. *The Ecoscan,* 4: 197-205.

Edmondson, W.T. 1959. Rotifera, pp. 420-497. In: Freshwater Biology (Eds. H.B. Ward and G.C. Whipple) (2nd Edition, W.T. Edmondson) John Wiley and Sons Inc; New York: 1-1248.

Fish Base. 2004. Fish Base Relational Database CD Rom. ICLARM; 2005 Bloomingdak Bldg; Salceds St. legapsi Village, Makati City, Metro Manila 1200, Philippines.

Fletcher, A.R. 1979. Effects of Salmo Trutta on *Galaxias olidus* and Macroinvertebrates in Stream Communities. M.Sc. Thesis, Monash University, Victoria, Australia.

Fokmare, A.K., and Musaddiq, M. 2002. A Study of Physico-chemical Characteristics of Kapsi Lake and Purna River Waters in Akola District of Maharashtra (India). *Nat. Environ. Poll. Tech.* 1: 261-263.

Froese, R. and Pauly, D. 2011. FishBase. World Wide Web Electronic Publication. www.fishbase.org,version (2/2013).

Fuller, P.L., Nico, L.G. and Williams, J.D. 1999. Non Indigenous Fishes Introduced into Inland Waters of the United States, American Fisheries Society, Special Publication 27, Bethesda, Mayland.

Ghatge, S.S., Belsare, S.W., Shelke, S.T. and Bopanna, B. 2014. The Candidature of Pacu, An Exotic Fish Species in Unregulated Aquaculture Systems in the State of Maharashtra. *Fishing Chimes.* 33 (10 &11): 76-78.

Gonzalves, E.A. and Joshi, D.B. 1946. Freshwater Algae Near Bombay.I. The Seasonal Succession of the Algae in a Tank at Bandra. *J. Bomb. Nat. Hist. Soc.* 46: 154-176.

Gracia-Martin, J.L.; Vila, A. ad Pla, C. 1990. Genetic Variation in the Iberian Tooth Carp, Aphanius Iberus, *J. Fish. Biol.* 37(Suppl-A): 233-234.

Gurgel, J.S.S. 1984. Observations on the Stocking of *Saratherodon Niloticus* (Linne, 1766) into DNOCS Public Reservoirs of Northeatsern Brazil. Bamidgeh, 36(2): 53-57.

Howard, G.W. and Maitindi, S.W. 2003. Alien Invasive Species in Africa's Wetlands-some Threats and Solutions. IUCN-the World Conservation Union, the Ramsar Convention on Wetlands, and the Global Invasive Species Programme. IUCN-the World Conservation Union Regional Office for Eastern Africa, Nairobi.

Hussain, M. 1977. Ecobiology of Freshwater Protozoa, Ph.D. Thesis, Osmania University, Hyderabad.

Jain, R. and Sharma, D. 2000. Water Quality of Rampur Reservoir of Guna District (M.P., India). *Environ. Cons. J.* 1(2): 99-102.

Jayabhaye, U.M. 2013. Studies on Physico-chemical Parameters of Wadod Tank of Hingoli District, Maharashtra. Proc. of National Conference on Global Environmental Problems: Impact and Solutions, Netaji Subhashchandra Bose Arts, Commerce and Science College, Nanded 22 & 23 February 2013, pp. 38-40.

Jerome Lazard and Lionel Dabbadie. 2002. Environmental Impact of Introduced Alien Species, 20. In: Encyclopedia of Life Support Systems (EO LSS)-Fisheries and Aquaculture: Towards Sustainable Aquatic Living Resources Management, Paper Available on WWW.eolss.net/sample-chapters/c10/e5-05-04-10.pdf.

Jetithor, S.G. 2010. Studies on Some Aspects of Ecology and Fisheries of Harni (Katgaon) Reservoir in Osmanabad District, Maharashtra, Ph.D. Thesis, Dr. Babasaheb Ambedkar Marathwada University, Aurangabad.

Jhingran, A.G. 1983. Some Observations on the Introduction of Tilapia into Indian Waters. Tech. Report, Bureau of Fish Genetic Resources, CIFRI, Allahabad, 34p.

Jhingran,V.G. and Gopalakrishnan,V. 1974. Catalogue of Cultivated Aquatic Organisms, FAO Technical Paper, 130, 83p.

Johnson, C.R. 1976. Observations on Growth, Breeding and Fry Survival of *Gambusia Affinis Affinis* Under Artificial Rearing Conditions. Proceeding of Conference, California Mosquito Control Association. 44: 48-51.

Joshi, P.S.2011. Studies on Zooplanktons of Rajura Lake of Buldhana District, Maharashtra, India. Science Researcher Reporter, 1(3): 132-137.

Juliano, R.O., R. Guerrero III and Ronquillo, I.1989. The Introduction of Exotic Aquatic Species in the Philippines, pp. 83-90. In S.S. De Silva (ed.) Exotic Aquatic Organisms in Asia. Proceedings of the Workshop on Introduction of Exotic Aquatic Organisms in Asia, Asian Fish. Soc. spec. Publ. 3, 154p. Asian Fisheries Society, Manila, Philippines.

Khabade, S.A. and Mule, M.B. 2010. Studies on Aquatic Insects in Relation to Physic-chemical Parameters of Anjani Reservoir in Sangli District of Maharashtra. In: Advances in Aquatic Ecology (Volume 3), Edited by V.B. Sakhare, pp. 141-147., Daya Publishing House, Delhi.

Khan, A.M., Z. Ali, S.Y. Shelly, Z. Ahmad and M.R. Mirza. 2011.Alien; A Catastrophe for Native Fresh Water Fish Diversity in Pakistan. *The Journal of Animal and Plant Sciences*, 21(2 Suppl.): 435-440.

Khan, R.A. 2003. Faunal Diversity of Zooplankton in Freshwater Wetlands of Southeastern West Bengal, Zoological Survey of India, Kolkata, Occasional Paper No. 204, pp. 107.

Khan, R.A., Barman, R.P. and Mishra, S.S. 2008. Status of Exotic Fishes Introduced in India and Their Impact, pp. 63-78, In: Fish Introductions in India: Status, Potential and Challenges (Edited By W.S. Lakra, A.K. Singh and S.Ayyappan), Narendra Publishing House, pp. 63-78.

Khanna, D.R., Sarkar,P., Ashutosh Gautam and R. Bhutiani. 2007. Fish Scales as Bioindicators of Water Quality of River Ganga. *Environmental Monitoring and Assessment*, 134(1-3): 153-160. DOI. 10.1007/S1066/007-9606-5.

Khatavkar, R.S., Shah, N.V., Rao, K.R. and Navale, R.A. 2004. Variations in Physico-chemical Parameters in Freshwater Tanks in and Around Solapur City, Maharashtra. *J.Aqua.Biol.*19(1): 111-114.

Kiran, B.R. and Puttaiah, E.T. 2010. Water Quality Assessment of Bhadra Reservoir of Karnataka with Reference to Physico-chemical Characteristics. In: Aquatic Ecosystem and its Management (Eds. K.Vijaykumar and B.Vasanthkumar), pp. 71-101, Daya Publishing House, Delhi.

Kodarkar, M.S., D.D. Diwan, N. Murugan, K.M. Kulkarni and Anuradha Ramesh. 1998. Methodology for Water Analysis (Physico-chemical, Biological and Microbiological). Indian Asso. of Aqua. Biologists, Hyderabad. pp. 12-102.

Koliyar, J.G. and Rokade, N.S. 2008.Water Quality in Powai Lake, Mumbai, Maharashtra. In: Proceedings of TAAL-2007: The 12th World Lake Conference (Eds. Sengupta, M. and Dalwani, R.), 1655-1659.

Kottelat, M. and Whitten, T. 1996. Freshwater Biodiversity in Asia with Special Reference to Fish. World Bank Technical Paper No. 343, Washington, 59 pp.

Kumar, A. and Gupta, H.P. 2002. Ecobiodiversity of Aquatic Biota in Certain Freshwater Ecosystems of Santhal Paraganas (Jharkhand), India. In: Ecology and Ethology of Aquatic Biota. Kumar, A. (Ed.), Daya Publishing House, Delhi, India, 1-69.

Kurup, B.M. and Radhakrishnan. 2008. Fish Introduction in Peninsular India with Special Reference to Kerala: Status, Challenges and Potential. In: Fish Introductions in India: Status, Potential and Challenges (Edited By W.S.Lakra, A.K. Singh and S.Ayyappan), Narendra Publishing House, pp. 45-61.

Lagler, K.F. 1978. Freshwater Fishery Biology, W.M.C. Brown Company Publishers, Dubuque, Iowa, pp. 234-259.

Lakra, W.S., Rehana Abidi, Singh, A.K., Neeraj Sood, Gaurav Rathore and T. Raja Swaminathan. 2006. Fish Introductions and Quarantine: Indian Perspective, National Bureau of Fish Genetic Resources, Lucknow, 198pp.

Lakra, W.S. and Singh, A.K. 2007. Exotic Fish Introduction in Indian Waters, *Fishing Chimes,* 27(1): 30-34.

Laskar, H.S. and Gupta, S.2013. Phytoplankton Community and Limnology of Chatla Floodplain Wetland of Barak Valley, Assam, North-East India-Knowledge and Management of Aquatic Ecosystems, 411, 1-14.

Legner, E.F. and Medved, R.A. 1974. The Native Desert Pupfish, *Cyprinodon maculates,* a Substitute for Gambusia in Mosquito Control. Proceedings California Mosquito Vector Control Association, 42: 58-59.

Lendhe, R.S. and Yeragi, S.G. 2004. Physico-chemical Parameters and Zooplankton Diversity of Phirange Kharbav Lake, Dist. Thane, Maharastra. *J. Aqua. Biol.* 19(1): 49-52.

Lloyd, L.N. 1984. Exotic Fish –Useful Additions or 'Animal Weeds'. *Fishes of Sahul.* 1: 39-42.

Lloyd, L.N.1986. An Alternative to Insect Control by Mosquito Fish, *Gambusia Affinis,* p. 156-163. In: T.D. St. George, B.H. Kay and J.Blok (eds.). Arbovirus Research in Australia, Proceedings Fourth Symposium, Brisbone, 1986.

Lloyd, L.N. 1987. Ecology and Distribution of Small Native Fish of the Lower River Murray, South Australia and Their Interactions with Exotic Mosquitofish, *Gambusia affinis holbrooki* (Girard). M.Sc. Thesis, Department of Zoology, University of Adelaide.

Lynne, M.W. 2004. Practical Guide to Identify Freshwater Crustacean Zooplankton, Cooperative Freshwater Ecology Unit, Dept. of Biology, Laurentian University, Sudburg, Ontario, Canada, Available on http://coopunit./aurentian.ca.

Mack, R.N., Simberloff, D.W., Lonsdale, M., Evans, H., Clout, M., and Bazzaz,F. 2000. Biotic Invasions: Causes, Epidemiology, Global Consequences and Control. *Ecol. Appl;* 10: 689-710.

Mahanta, P.C., R. Abidi and D. Kapoor. 2003. Impact of Introduction of Exotic and Genetically Manipulated Fishes in Indian Reservoirs. In: Workshop on Fisheries Management in the Lentic Water System: Stocking of Reservoirs with Fish Seed, CIFRI Publication.

Mark A. Elbag Jr. 2006. Impact of Surrounding Land Uses on Surfacewater Quality. A Thesis Submitted to the Faculty of the Worcester Polytechnique Institute, Worcester, United States in Partial Fulfillment of the Requirements for the Degree of Master of Science in Environmental Engineering.

Mayers, G.S. 1965. Gambusia, the Fish Destroyer. Australian Zoologist. 13: 102.

McKay, R.J. 1978. The Exotic Freshwater Fishes of Queenland, Report to the Australian National Parks and wildlife Sevice,Canberra.

Mckay, R.J. 1989. Exotic and Translocted Freshwater Fishes in Australia. In: Exotic Aquatic Organisms in Asia (Edited by S.S. De Silva), Asian Fisheries Society, pp. 21-34.

McKinney, M.L. and Lockwood, J.L. 1999. Biotic Homogenization: A Few Winners Replacing Many Losers in the Next Mass Extinction. *Trends in Ecol. Evol.*, 14: 450-453.

Mellanby, H. 1963. Animal Life in Freshwater, 6th Edition, Chapman and Hall Ltd; London.

Menon, M.D. and Chacko, P. 1957. Food and Feeding Habits of the Fishes of Madras State. Proc. IPFC Group, 1956.

Menon, M.D. and Krishnamoorthy, B.K. 1956. On the Possible Forage Fish *Tilapia mossambica,* Pt.I. Its Food. Madras State Fisheries Station. Reports and Year Book (1954-55).

Menon, M.D., Krishna Murthi, B.K. and Ramchandran, T.B. 1959. On the Possible Forage Fish, Oreochromis Mossambicus, Pt. II, Growth. Madras State Fisheries Station Reports and Year Book (1955-56).

Meshram, P.U. 2013. Water Quality Evaluation of Elevated Service Reservoirs Located in West Region of Nagpur, India for Their Potability and Risk Management, Proc. of National Conference on Global Environmental Problems: Impact and Solutions, Netaji Subhashchandra Bose Arts, Commerce and Science College, Nanded 22 & 23 February 2013, pp. 42-45.

Michael, R.G. and Sharma, B.K. 1988. Fauna of India and Adjacent Countries, Indian Cladocera (Crustacea: Branchiopoda: Cladocera), Zoological Survey of India, Calcutta, pp. 262.

Minimol, K.C. 2000. Fishery Management in Periyar Lake, Ph.D. Thesis, Mahatma Gandhi Univeristy, pp. 198.

Mishra Arvid, Pandey, A.K., Singh, A.K. and Das, P. 1998, In Fish Genetics and Biodiversity Conservation for Sustainable Production, (Eds.) A.G. Ponniah, P.Das and S.R.Verma), Natcon Publication, Muzaffarnagar, 415-425.

Mishra. Ashutosh, Chakraborty, S.K., Jaiswar, A.K. Sharma, A.P., Deshmukhe Geetanjali and Madan Mohan. 2010. Plankton Diversity in Dhaura and Baigul Reservoirs of Uttarakhand. *Indian J. Fish.* 57(3): 19-27.

Moitra, S.K. and Bhattacharya, B.K. 1965. Some Hydrobiological Factors Affecting Plankton Production in a Fish Pond at Kalyani, West Bengal. *Ichthyologica.* 4(1-2): 8-12.

Molur, S. and Walker (eds.). 1998. Conservation Assessment and Management Plan (CAMP) Workshop Reoprt on Freshwater Fishes of India.Zoo Outreach Organisation,CBSG India,Coimbatore, 156 pp.

Mudgal, L.K., Malakar Babita and Kumar Sushil. 2013. Assessment of Water Quality of Narmada River with Reference to Physico-chemical Parameters at Indirasagar Dam (Punassa), India. *J.Aqua. Biol.* 27(1): 51-55.

Mulani, S.K; Mule, M.B. and Patil, S.U. 2009. Studies on Water Quality and Zooplankton Community of the Panchganga River in Kolhapur City, *J. Environ. Biol;* 30: 455-459.

Murthy, H.S., Gonda, S.S. and Ayyar, V.,1986. Fisheries of Kabini Reservoir in Karnataka, *Fishing Chimes,* 6(7): 36-38.

Murthy, N.S., Gonda, S.S. and Ayyar Murthy,V. 1986. Fishes of Kabini Reservoir in Karnataka, *Fishing Chimes,* 8: 36-38.

Murugan, N., Murugavel, R. and Kodarkar, M.S. 1998. Cladocera: The Biology, Classification, Identification and Ecology, Indian Association of Aquatic Biologists, Hyderabad.

Naik, I.U., 1973. Studies on *Tilapia Mossambicus* (Peters) in Pakistan. *Agric. Pakistan,* 24: 47-76.

Nakamura, M. 1955. Kanto-heiyani Shutsugenshita Ishyokugo (Some Exotic Fishes Appeard at the Kanto Plains). Nihon-Seiboisu-ohiri-gakkaiho 16/ 19:333-337.

Natarajan, A.V. and Menon Ramchandra. 1988. In Exotic Aquatic Species in India. Proceedings of the Workshop on Exotic Species in India, (ed. M. Mohan Joseph), 25-26 April 1988. Special Publication, Asian Fisheries Society, Indian Branch, 63-65.

Needham, J.G. and Needham, R.R. 1962. A Guide to Study of Freshwater Biology. Holden Day Inc; San Francisco, USA.

NEERI. 1979. Water and Wastewater Analysis, National Environmental Engineering Research Institute, Nagpur, pp. 134.

Neil P.Bernstein and John R.Olso. 2001. Ecological Problems with Iowa's Invasive and Introduced Fishes, *Jour. Iowa Acad. Sci.* 108(4): 185-209.

Nico, L.G. and Fuller, P.L. 1999. Spatial and Temporal Patterns of Nonindigenous Fish Introductions in the United States, *Fisheries* 24: 16-27.

Okogwu, I.O., Christopher, D.N. and Florence, A.O. 2010. Seasonal Variation and Diversity of Rotifers in Ehomalake, Nigeria. *J. Environ. Biol.* 31: 533-537.

Pandey, Kamleshwar and Shukla, J.P. 2005.Fish and Fisheries, Rastogi Publications, Meerut.

Panigrahi, Subhashree and Patra, A.K. 2013. Studies on Seasonal Variations in Phytoplankton Diversity of River Mahanadi, Cuttack City, Odisha, India. *Indian J.Sci. Res.* 4(2): 211-217.

Patil, P.V. and Kulkarni, A.N. 2010. Diurnal Changes of Some Physico-chemical Factors in Thodga Reservoir of Latur District in Maharashtra. In: Advances in Aquatic Ecology (Vol. 3), Ed.V.B. Sakhare, pp. 158-162., Daya Publishing House, Delhi.

Pawar, S.B. and Shembekar, V.S. 2012. Studies on the Physico-chemical Parameters of Reservoir at Dhanegaon District Osmanabad (M.S.), India. *Journal of Experimental Sciences*, 3(5): 51-54. Paper available on http://jexpsciences.com

Pejaver, Madhuri, Somani Vaishali and Goldin Quadros. 2004. Physico-chemical Parameters of Two Quarry Lakes Near Thane city, Maharashtra. *J. Aqua. Biol.* 19(1): 107-110.

Pennak, R.W. 1978. Freshwater Invertebrates of the United States, 2nd Ed. John Wiley and Sons, New York, 803 pp.

Pentewar, M.S. 2013. Physico-chemical Analysis of Dhanora Dam Water in Bhokar Tahsil of Nanded District. Proc. of National Conference on Global Environmental Problems: Impact and Solutions, Netaji Subhashchandra Bose Arts, Commerce and Science College, Nanded 22 & 23 February 2013, pp. 51-54.

Phyllis K. Weber-Scannell and Lawrence K. Duffy. 2007. Effects of Total Dissolved Solids on Aquatic Organisms: A Review of Literature and Recommendations for Salmonid Species. *American Journal of Environmental Sciences*, 3(1): 1-6.

Piska Ravi Shankar, Sarla Devi B., and Chary Divakara K.2000. The Present Status of Ibrhimbagh, a Minor Reservoir of Hyderabad. *Fishing Chimes.* 20 (2): 41-43.

Piyakarnchana, T. 1989. Exotic Aquatic Species in Thailand, pp. 119-124. In: S.S. Desilva (Ed.) Exotic Aquatic Organisms in Asia. Proceedings of the Workshop on Introduction of Exotic Aquatic Organisms in Asia, Asian Fish. Soc. Spec. Publ. 3, 154p. Asian Fisheries Society, Manila, Philippines.

Pollard, D.A., Llewellyn D.C. and Tilzey, R.D.J. 1980. Management of Freshwater Fish and Fisheries, pp. 227-270. In Williams, W.D. (Ed.) An Ecological Basis for Water Resource Management, Australian National University Press, Canberra.

Rahel, F. 2002. Homogenization of Freshwater Faunas. *Ann. Rev. Ecol. Syst.*, 33: 291-315.

Rajasekhar, A.V., Sunil Kumar, A., Noothi Sreenu, Krishna Savalla Murali and Piska Ravishankar. 2012. The Studies on Water Quality of Nizamsagar Reservoir, Nizamabad, Andhra Pradesh, India. *Journal of Environmental Research and Development*, 6(4): 991-996.

Rangaswami, G.,1988. Golden Fish Culture in India. NAGA, ICLARM, Manila, 11(1): 24-26.

Rao, I.S. 1982. Ecology of the Manjira Reservoir, Ph.D. Thesis, Osmania University, Hyderabad.

Rao, Ramkrishna,T. 2008. Biotic Invasions: An Overview, In: Fish Introductions in India (Status, Potential and Challenges) (Editors: W.S. Larka, A.K. Singh and S.Ayyapan), pp. 1-9, Narendra Publishing House, Delhi.

Rao, Satyanarayana, G.P. 2008. Introduction of Tilapia in India: Status, Challenges and Potential, pp. 141-146, In: Fish Introductions in India (Status, Potential and Challenges) (Editors: W.S. Larka, A.K. Singh and S. Ayyapan), Narendra Publishing House, Delhi.

Ravindranath, K. 2008. A Note on Aquaculture of Exotic Species in Andhra Pradesh, In: Fish Introductions in India: Status, Potential and Challenges (eds.) W.S. Lakra, A.K. Singh and S.Ayyappan), pp. 105-107, Narendra Publishing House, Delhi.

Rowe, D.K. 2007. Exotic Fish Introductions and the Decline of Water Clarity in Small North Islands, New Zealand Lakes: A multi-species problem. *Hydrobiologia*, 583(1): 345-358, DOI. 10.1007/S 10750-007-646-1.

Roy,T. 1999. Copepoda: Calanoida and Cyclopoida, 2001. Surv. India, State Fauna Series 3: Fauna of West Bengal, Part 10: 287-313.

Sakhare, V.B. 2001. Reservoir Fisheries in Solapur District of Maharashtra. *Fishing Chimes*, 21(5): 29-30.

Sakhare,V.B. 2005. Water Quality of Hingni (Pangaon) Reservoir and its Significance to Fisheries. Advances in Limnology (ed. S.R. Mishra, Dhar), Daya Publishing House, New Delhi, pp. 231-235.

Sakhare, V.B. 2007. Reservoir Fisheries and Limnology, Narendra Publishing House, Delhi.

Sakhare, V.B. and Joshi, P.K. 2002. Ecology and ichthyofauna of Bori Reservoir in Maharashtra. *Fishing Chimes*, 22 (4): 40-41.

Salve, B. and Hiware, C. 2010. Zooplankton Diversity of Wan Reservoir, Nagapur (M.S.) India. The Res. in Sci.and Tech.2(1): 39-48.

Santosh, B. and Singh, N.P. 2007. Guidelines for Water Quality Management for Fish Culture in Tripura, ICAR Research Complex for NEH Region, Tripura Centre, Lembucherra (Tripura West), Publication No. 29.

Sarangi, N.2008. Exotic Fishes and Biodiversity, In: Fish Introductions in India: Status, Potential and Challenges (eds.) W.S. Lakra, A.K. Singh and S.Ayyappan), pp. 123-133, Narendra Publishing House, Delhi.

Sawant, R.S., Desai, P.D. and Desai, J.S. 2011. Physico-chemical Properties of the Uttur Tank in Ajara Tahsil, Maharashtra. *J.Ecobiol*. 29(3): 205-211.

Sawyer, C.H. 1960. Chemistry for Sanitary Engineers, MCGraw Hill Book Co., New York.

Sehgal, K.L. 1983. Planktonic Copepods of Freshwater Ecosystems. Interprint, New Delhi, 169pp.

Shafland, P.L. and Lewis, W.M. 1984. Terminology Associated with Introduced Organisms. *Fisheries*, 9: 17-18.

Shariff, M. 1980. Ocurence and Treatment of Ectoparasitic Disease of Aquarium Fishes in Malaysia, *Malayan Veterinary Journal*, 7: 48-59.

Sharma, A.P. and Pant, M.C. 1979. Certain Physico-chemical Features of Chlorophyll Concentration and Phytoplankton Population in a High Altitude Lake. *Trop. Ecol.* 20: 101-113.

Sharma, B.K. 1999. Freshwater Rotifers (Rotifera: Eurotatoria), 2001. Surv. India, State Fauna Series 3, Fauna of West Bengal, Part II: 341-468.

Sharma, Shailendra, Tali Imtiyaz, Pir Zahoor, Siddique Anis and Mudgal, L.K. 2012. Evaluation of Physico-chemical Parameters of Narmada River, M.P., India. *Researcher,* 4(5): 13-19.

Shastri, Yogesh. 2005. Physico-chemical Characteristics of a Small Percolation Tank. In: Advances in Limnology (Ed. S.R. Mishra), Daya Publishing House, Delhi, pp. 253-257.

Shiel, R.J. 1995. A Guide to Identification of Rotifers, Cladocerans and Copepods from Australian Inland Waters, Cooperative Research Centre for Freshwater Ecology Identification Guide No. 3, Murray Darling Freshwater Research Centre, Ellis Street, Thurgoona, P.O. Box 921, Alburg, NSW 2640.

Shukla, Pallavi, Preeti and Ajay Singh. 2013. A Seasonal Variations of Plankton Population of Maheshara Lake in Gorakhpur, India. *World Journal of Zoology,* 8(1): 91-6.

Siddiqui, S.Z. and Khan, R.A. Comparative Limnology of Few Man-made Lakes in and Around Hyderabad, India. Rec. Zoo. Surv. India. Occ. Paper No. 203: 1-64, Zoological Survey of India, Kolkata.

Singh, A.K. and Lakra, W.S. 2008. Africian Catfish in India, In: Fish Introductions in India: Status, Potential and Challenges (eds. W.S.Lakra, A.K. Singh and S.Ayyappan) pp. 81-91, Narendra Publishing House, Delhi.

Singh, A.K., Pathak, A.K. and Lakra, W.S. 2010. Invasion of an Exotic Fish-common Carp, *Cyprinus carpio* L.(Actinopterygii: Cypriniformes: Cyprinidae) in the Ganga River, India and its Impacts. Acta Ichthyologica et Piscatoria, 40(1): 11-19.

Singh, A.K. and Ponniah, A.G. 2001. In Proceedings of the National Symposium on Fish Health Management and Sustainable Aquaculture, College of Fisheries, G.B. Pant University of Agriculture and Technology,1-2 November 2000, Pantnagar (Eds. U.P. Singh, Chauhan, R.S. and Sharma, A.P.), pp. 93-96.

Simon, K.S. and Townsend, C.R. 2003. Impacts of Freshwater Invaders at Different Levels of Ecological Organization, with Emphasis on Salmonids and Ecosystem Consequences. *Freshwater Biol.* 48: 982-994.

Smith, P.T. 2007. Aquaculture in Papua New Guinea: Status of Freshwater Fish Farming. ACIAR Monograph No. 125, 124p.

Solanki,Venkata Ramanaiah, S.Samba Reddy, Amarjit Kaur and S.Sabita Raja. 2007. Variations in Dissolved Oxygen and Biochemical Oxygen Demand in Two Freshwater Lakes of Bodhan, Andhra Pradesh, India, *Nature, Environment and Pollution Technology*, 6(4): 623-628.

Sreenivasan, A.1967. *Tilapia Mossambica*: Its Ecology and Status in Madras State, India. *Madras J.Fish.*, 3: 33-39.

Sreenivasan, A. 1970. Limnological Studies on Parambikulum Aliyar Project. I. Aliyar Reservoir (Madras State), India. *Schweiz Zeitsh Hydrol.* 32: 405-417.

Sreenivasan, A. 1974. Limnology of a Seepage Type Impoundment, Bhavanisagar Reservoir (Tamil Nadu), India. *Int.Rev. Hydrobiol.* 59(3): 327-342.

Srivastava, Neera; Agarwal Meena and Tyagi, Anupama. 2003. Study of Physico-chemical Characteristics of Water Bodies Around Jaipur. *J.Environ.Biol.* 24(2): 177-180.

Stephanides, T. 1964. The Influence of the Anti-mosquitofish, *Gambusia affinis*, on the Natural Fauna of Corfulakelet. Praktika Hell. Hydrobiologie Institute, 9: 3-5.

Sugunan,V.V. 1995. Reservoir Fisheries of India, FAO Fish.Tech. Pap., 345: 423p.

Sugunan, V.V. 1996. Fisheries Management of Small Water Bodies in Africa, Asia and Latin America, FAO Fisheries Technical Paper (in press).

Sverdrup, H.H., Johonson, M.W. and Fleming R.H. 1942. The Oceans: Their Physics, Chemistry and General Biology. Prentice Hall, New York.

Talwar, P.K. and Jhingran, A.G., 1991. Inland Fishes of India and Adjacent Countries, Vols. 1 and 2. Oxford and IBH Publishing Co. Pvt. Ltd., New Delhi.

Thakur, N.K. 1998. A Biological Profile of African Catfish, *Clarias gariepinus* and Impact of its Introduction in Asia. In Fish Genetics and Biodiversity Conservation (eds.) A.G. Ponniah, P. Das and S.R.Verma; Natcon Publication, Muzzaffarnagar, p. 275-292.

Timms, B.V. and Midgley, S.H. 1970. The Limnology of Borrumba dam: Queenland Proceed. *Royal Soc.South Africa*, 3(2): 37-41.

Tonapi, G.T. 1980. Freshwater Animals of India (An Ecological Approach), Oxford and IBH, New Delhi: 341.

Tripathi, A.K. and Pandey, S.N. 1990. Water Pollution, Ashish Publishing House, New Delhi, 325p.

Tripathi, S.D. 2007. Problems and Prospects of Fisheries Development in India, *Fishing Chimes*, 27(1): 100-106.

Tripathi, S.D. 2008.A Review of Fish Introduction in India, In: Fish Introductions in India (Status, Potential and Challenges) (Edition: W.S. Larka, A.K. Singh and S.Ayyapan), pp. 11-16, Narendra Publishing House, Delhi.

Trivedy, R.K., and Goel, P.K. 1984. Chemical and Biological Methods for Water Pollution Studies. Environmental Publication, Karad (India).

Ude, E.F., Ugwu, L.L.C. and Mgbenka, B.O. 2011. Evaluation of Zooplankton Diversity in Echara River, Nigeria. Conti. *J. Biol. Sci.* 4 (1):1-5.

Unni, K.S. 1985. Comparative Limnology of Several Reservoirs in Central India. *Int. Revue gesamten Hydrobiologia*, 70 (6): 845-856.

Van der Waal,B. 2002. Another Fish on its Way to Extinction? Science in Africa.http://www.scienceinafrica.co/za/2002/January/tilapia.htm.

Van Driesche, J.and Van Driesche, R. 2000. Nature Out of Place: Biological Invasions in the Global Age, Island Press, Washigton, D.C., 363pp.

Vass, K.K. and K. Gopakumar. 2002. Coldwater Fisheries and Research Status in India; pp. 3-29 In K.K. Vass and H.S. Raina (Ed.), Highland Fisheries and Aquatic Resource Management. India. National Research Centre on Coldwater Fisheries (ICAR), Bhimtal.

Vass, K.K. and Sugunan, V.V. 2009. Status of Reservoir Fisheries in India. In: Status of Reservoir Fisheries in Five Asian Countries (Eds. Sena S.De Silva and Upali S. Amarsinghe), NACA Monograph No. 2, Network of Aquaculture Centers in Asia – Pacific, Bangkok, Thailand, pp. 31-54.

Welcome, R.L.1988. International Introductions of Inland Aquatic Species, FAO Fish. Tech. Pap. (294): 318p.

Wetzel, R, G. and Likens, G.E. 2006. Limnological analysis, 3rd Edition, Springer-Verlag, New York, 391.

Wildekamp RH, Valkenburg K.1994. Notizen u¨ ber Zahnkarpfen–Lebensra¨ume in Anatolien. *Die Aquarien und Terrarien Zeitschrift* 47(7): 447-453.

Index

❑❑❑❑❑